Routledge Library Editions

WESTERN ENTERPRISE IN FAR EASTERN ECONOMIC DEVELOPMENT

ECONOMICS

Routledge Library Editions – Economics

DEVELOPMENT ECONOMICS
In 7 Volumes

WESTERN ENTERPRISE IN FAR EASTERN ECONOMIC DEVELOPMENT

China and Japan

G C ALLEN AND
AUDREY G DONNITHORNE

LONDON AND NEW YORK

First published in 1954

Reprinted in 2003 by
Routledge
2 Park Square, Milton Park, Abingdon, Oxfordshire OX14 4RN
711 Third Avenue, New York, NY 10017

Transferred to Digital Printing 2007

First issued in paperback 2014

Routledge is an imprint of the Taylor and Francis Group, an informa business

The publishers have made every effort to contact authors/copyright holders
of the works reprinted in *Routledge Library Editions – Economics*. This has
not been possible in every case, however, and we would welcome
correspondence from those individuals/companies we have been unable to
trace.

These reprints are taken from original copies of each book. In many cases
the condition of these originals is not perfect. The publisher has gone to
great lengths to ensure the quality of these reprints, but wishes to point
out that certain characteristics of the original copies will, of necessity, be
apparent in reprints thereof.

British Library Cataloguing in Publication Data
A CIP catalogue record for this book
is available from the British Library

Western Enterprise in Far Eastern Economic Development

ISBN 978-0-415-31295-0 (hbk)
ISBN 978-1-138-87859-4 (pbk)
ISBN 978-0-415-31294-3 (set)

Miniset: Development Economics

Series: Routledge Library Editions – Economics

WESTERN ENTERPRISE IN FAR EASTERN ECONOMIC DEVELOPMENT

CHINA AND JAPAN

BY

G. C. ALLEN
Professor of Political Economy in the University of London

AND

AUDREY G. DONNITHORNE
Lecturer in Political Economy, University College, London

Routledge
Taylor & Francis Group

LONDON AND NEW YORK

First published in 1954
Second impression 1962

PREFACE

THE genesis of this book demands a brief explanation. The profound changes brought about, or revealed, by the Second World War in the economic position of Western countries and their nationals in the Far East suggested to us, some five years ago, that the time was appropriate for a review of the part that had been played by Western enterprise in the economic development of that region. On the inception of this study, it was obvious that the scope of our research must be restricted, and we therefore decided to confine our attention, in this phase of our work, to four countries, viz. China, Japan, Malaya and Indonesia. This choice was determined largely by a wish to examine the course of Western enterprise in a number of mutually contrasting environments, for in this way we hoped that the diversity of methods and policies pursued by Western firms in 'undeveloped' regions might be brought to light. The present volume, which is concerned with China and Japan, contains the first results of our study.

Our aim has been to describe the beginnings of Western enterprise in the two countries, the local circumstances which determined the character and forms of that enterprise at various times, the relations of Western undertakings with the native economies at different stages in their growth, and finally the effect of the Western impact upon the industrial and commercial life of the countries considered. The review covers the period from about the middle of the last century, when China and Japan were 'opened' to foreign trade, to the present time. We originally intended to end our study with a discussion of the place that Western enterprise might be expected to occupy in these countries during the post-war period; but political events in the Far East since 1949 have suggested the wisdom of deferring this task. *Inter arma*, speculation about long-term economic trends and relationships does well to be silent. The greater part of the book deals with China; but a dominant theme is the contrast presented by China and Japan in their response to the Western intrusion, and, especially in the rôle assigned to Western business enterprise in the two economies. In the final chapter these contrasts are brought into relief. Malaya and Indonesia will be the subject of a subsequent volume upon which we are now engaged.

We consider it important to emphasise the limitations of our purpose. We have not tried to write either an economic history of China and Japan or a comprehensive account of Western contacts with these two countries. Our concern has been with a particular aspect of economic development, and our interpretations and criticisms have validity only within a narrow chamber of reference. Thus we have not sought to pass moral judgments either on the activities of the Westerners or on the policies of the Chinese and Japanese Governments, although at times we may have done so by implication. We have not written as apologists for Western enterprise, nor have we felt called upon to speculate upon whether, or to what extent, the economic developments that resulted from that enterprise contributed towards raising the quality of life of the Chinese and Japanese peoples. Even within the limits which we have set ourselves, we do not claim to have presented more than a preliminary view of this large subject. Much detailed research remains to be done before Western economic activities in the Far East and their consequences can be fully described and understood. In an attempt to break into fresh ground, we have had to content ourselves with a small-scale map and so have not drawn upon many sources of information which would be essential to a detailed study of a particular sector of this territory.[1] Further, the greater part of our data (at any rate in the case of China) has been obtained from Western sources. We recognise that, in spite of our efforts to write objectively, this limitation is likely to have affected both the selection and the interpretation of facts. If our shortcomings provoke Oriental economists to write their version of these events, we shall be well content.

There remains the pleasant task of offering our thanks to all those who have given us advice and help. Some of our most valuable data has come from firms with interests in the Far East, and we gratefully acknowledge their kindness in providing us with information about the history of their operations. In this connection we should like to mention the following: the Arnhold Trading Company Ltd.; the British-American Tobacco Company Ltd.; Cable and Wireless Ltd.; the Chartered Bank of India, Australia and China; the Chinese Engineering and Mining Company Ltd.; Dorman Long and Company Ltd.; the Great Northern Telegraph Company Ltd.; Harrisons, King and Irwin Ltd.; Alfred Holt and Company; the Hongkong and Shanghai Banking Corporation; Imperial Chemical Industries Ltd; Jones, Burton and Company Ltd.; Lever Brothers and Unilever; Mackenzie and Company Ltd.; Matheson and Company Ltd.; Patons and Baldwins Ltd.; the Pekin Syndicate; Pilkington Brothers Ltd.; Platt Brothers (Sales) Ltd.; Charles Schlee and Company; Shell Refining and Marketing Company Ltd.; Standard Vacuum Oil Company; John Swire and Sons Ltd.; Union Cold Storage Company Ltd.; and Wheelock, Marden and Company Ltd.

We are also much indebted to the following persons who have helped us at different stages of the work: Mr. George E. Mitchell, Secretary of the China Association, and his staff who on many occasions enabled us to fill gaps in our material; Mrs. V. S. Robb, formerly of Hankow, and Mr. P. E. Witham, formerly tea adviser to the Chinese Government, to whom we are indebted for information about the tea trade; Mr. J. Leighton-Boyce, who generously put at our disposal data obtained in

[1] e.g. the Jardine Matheson Papers which Mr. Michael Greenberg has used so successfully for his *British Trade and the Opening of China, 1800–1842* (1951).

the course of his researches into the history of the Chartered Bank and whose comments upon our chapters on banking have been most valuable, and Mr. W. C. Cassels of the Hongkong Bank, who gave us the benefit of his advice and experience in the same field. Mr. D. J. Sloss, formerly Vice-Chancellor of the University of Hongkong, Mr. E. Pudney, formerly Commissioner of Chinese Taxation in Hongkong, Mr. G. R. G. Worcester, formerly of the Chinese Maritime Customs, Professor F. E. Hyde of Liverpool University, Mr. J. Caldwell Jones of the Liverpool Chamber of Commerce and Mr. H. Pagel, all gave us the benefit of their knowledge and experience and we are grateful to them. We should like to offer our special thanks to Sir John Masson who from the outset took a keen interest in our work.

Much of the information about Japanese economic development was gathered during a visit to Japan just before the war and it is not possible here to acknowledge the assistance then received. But we should like to thank Mr. K. Asakai of the Japanese Embassy in London for furnishing us with documents concerned with recent economic changes in his country and for enlisting the help of the libraries of the Japanese Foreign Office and of the National Diet to which we are indebted for information about foreign experts in Japan in early times.

It is difficult to express adequately our obligations to the staff of the Royal Institute of International Affairs, especially to Miss M. Cleeve, Research Secretary, and to Mr. and Mrs. A. S. B. Olver of the Far East Department. They went to much trouble in introducing us to firms and persons who were likely to be of service to us and their generous help has been available throughout the period of our researches. We must also express appreciation of the help given by the Librarians at this College, the Foreign Office Research Department and Chatham House. Our colleagues at University College, London have helped us in many ways. The maps included in this volume were drawn for us by members of the Department of Geography. Dr. B. Cheng of the Faculty of Laws kindly commented on our historical introduction. We had the benefit of Mr. J. Lanner's expert criticism of our banking chapters. Mr. A. Kay, Research Assistant in the Department of Political Economy, spent much time in checking references, and in drawing up statistical tables, and we much appreciate the assistance he gave us in preparing the book for publication. We are indebted to Miss Joyce Wood for secretarial assistance and to Mrs. G. C. Allen for typing the manuscript and giving other help in preparing the book for publication. The responsibility for any errors of fact or judgment which the book may contain rests, of course, entirely with us.

Department of Political Economy,   G. C. A.
University College, London.   A. G. D.
May 1953.

CONTENTS

9

PART ONE
CHINA

CHAPTER I

THE COURSE OF WESTERN ENTERPRISE

THE industrial revolution of the West and the expansionist phase that accompanied it coincided with an era of decadence in China. The authority of the Ching dynasty, a Manchurian line which had ruled since the seventeenth century, was waning. The later emperors had fallen far behind their vigorous predecessors in administrative capacity, and by the early nineteenth century the dynasty seemed, in the traditional language of China, to have lost the Mandate of Heaven. Yet the Chinese were still confident of the superiority of their civilisation to all others and they saw no reason to doubt its distinctive excellence even in the industrial arts. For several millenniums their emperor had been the suzerain of a very large part of the human race and the Empire's prestige was still immense. The foundations of its power, however, had been sapped by weakness at the centre during a period when the strength of the West was rapidly increasing. As the Chinese Government became conscious of these trends, its hostility to foreign intruders was sharpened. A deep-seated belief in the superiority of Chinese to aliens was contradicted in every encounter by demonstrations of China's weakness, and the resentment which resulted did not conduce to harmonious relations with foreigners. The West, in accordance with its traditions, claimed that peaceful intercourse and trade between nations were rights which no country should refuse to acknowledge, while China regarded them as favours to be conferred, as far as concerned Chinese territory, under conditions laid down by herself. In Europe—or at least in Great Britain which was in the forefront of economic development—the expansion of trade was considered a praiseworthy purpose to be pursued with vigour. China was proud of her economic self-sufficiency, and her Government never regarded 'the fostering of foreign commerce as an important affair of state'.[1]

In consequence, the first impact of the new types of economic activity came entirely from Western initiative. European commerce was the active agent, while China lay passive. It was not that the Chinese people lacked economic initiative and acumen; these qualities they had long possessed in abundance. But political unrest, arbitrary taxation and the general lack of security of persons and property had inhibited the exercise of Chinese business abilities or had directed them

[1] G. B. Sansom, *The Western World and Japan*, p. 107.

13

into channels which contributed little to the nation's prosperity. Adam Smith observed with justice: 'China seems to have been long stationary and had probably long ago acquired that full complement of riches which is consistent with the nature of its laws and institutions. But this complement may be much inferior to what, with other laws and institutions, the nature of its soil, climate and situation might admit of.'[1] Modern economic life only began in China with the enforced introduction of 'other laws and institutions' through treaties extorted from China by foreign nations.

The experience of China, in respect of westernisation, stands out in contrast with that of other Asian countries. In Japan a strong national government provided the political and institutional foundation needed for economic development. In Malaya and Indonesia this foundation was supplied by the colonial Powers. In China neither the Manchus nor their successors, the Republic, were capable of performing this function (at least until the nineteen-thirties); while the 'open door' policy initiated by the United States and accepted by the other Great Powers prevented the overt colonisation of the country. Instead, the 'unequal treaties' furnished the political and legal basis for the introduction of Western forms of economic life. This basis was variously composed. It included extraterritoriality, by which the nationals of Treaty Powers and their property were placed under the jurisdiction of their own consuls and were exempt from Chinese taxation; Treaty Ports, where foreigners were permitted to reside and trade; foreign settlements and concessions in certain Treaty Ports, that is to say, districts administered by foreign residents and their consuls; a low maximum import duty and freedom from internal levies on imports and on goods bought by foreigners for export; and permission, at first tacit and then explicit, for ships under foreign flags to ply between Chinese ports and along certain major internal waterways. These rights were conceded by China in treaties with eighteen Powers, and the insertion of most-favoured-nation clauses meant that a privilege accorded to one was shared by all. Further, several important public services came to be administered by a foreign staff; they included the customs service, the post office and the salt gabelle. Finally, a leading part in the westernising process was played by Hongkong. This British colony was one of the largest foreign enclaves in China, and its influence on the economic development of the country was profound. The whole elaborate system of foreign rights was built up gradually and modified from time to time. For instance, the number of Treaty Ports grew from five to eighty (including some which China opened voluntarily); the number of foreign concessions increased to over twenty in 1913, but later on declined; and the rate of customs duty was twice revised before China regained tariff autonomy in 1928.

[1] *The Wealth of Nations* (ed. Cannan), vol. I, p. 96.

The history of Western intercourse with China can conveniently be divided into five periods: (1) the early history up to the Treaty of Nanking, 1842; (2) the period from 1842 to the Treaty of Shimonoseki in 1895, years in which privileges were secured by foreigners and enclaves were established; (3) the period from 1895 to the Revolution, 1911, when Western economic penetration began to take the form of investment in industry and transport in China; (4) the period from 1911 to the outbreak of the Sino-Japanese War of 1937, the era of civil war and the retreat from extraterritoriality; (5) the period from 1937 to the present time, during which trade with the West was largely destroyed by war and revolution. The general political and economic character of each of these periods, so far as it has relevence to this study, will be presented in outline.

1. Sino-European Relations before 1842

The nature and genesis of the economic relations which developed between the West and China in the nineteenth century can scarcely be understood without some reference to earlier history. From the time of the Roman Empire until the end of the eighteenth century the out-standing characteristic of trade between China and the West was that, whereas the West provided a ready market for Chinese goods, in China there was little demand for any of the manufactured goods and raw materials that the West could supply. Consequently there was a drain of precious metals to China, and this throughout the centuries gave rise to criticism in Europe of the Eastern trade. Even in the sixteenth century, when the Portuguese secured a foothold at Macao and when other Western countries began to extend their rivalries with one another to the Far Eastern trade, the economic relations between these countries and China did not take the form of the exchange of European for Chinese goods. Part of the exports from China were paid for by the shipping and commercial services which Europeans rendered in carrying to China the natural products of South-east Asia, India and Japan; while the balance continued to be settled by exports of specie to China. Trade with China during the seventeenth century was of the same pattern, which even its great expansion in the eighteenth century left un-disturbed. This was the era of the Old China Trade which must now be described.[1]

The early economic relations between China and England were frigid. Trade was confined to a single port, Canton, and was conducted on the English side by a monopolist, the East India Company, and on the Chinese side by an exclusive association of merchants, the Cohong.

---

[1] cf. M. Greenberg, *British Trade and the Opening of China, 1800–1842*, Chap. I and *passim*. While the nationals of several Western countries participated in this trade, the British were by far the most numerous and important group.

Even if the Chinese Government had been less restrictive in its commercial policy, it is doubtful if, before the beginning of the nineteenth century, the impact of the West would have greatly disturbed the course of commercial and industrial development in China, for at that time Western industries had no technical superiority over the Chinese and the mutual advantages to be obtained from trade between the two regions were limited. The Chinese commodity which was in greatest demand in England and at the end of the eighteenth century accounted for nearly all the purchases of the East India Company in China was tea. In addition, the exports from Canton comprised small quantities of silk, lacquer wares and *chinoiserie*, a trade that was mainly in the hands of the officers of the East Indiamen who were allowed a specified amount of cargo space ('privilege tonnage', so-called) for carrying such goods. Yet while in Great Britain there was an urgent demand for China's tea, China constituted a meagre market for British products. Woollens and hardware were exported to China, but there was, as in the past, a large unfavourable balance which had to be settled by the shipment of silver.

The export of specie provided the chief grounds for the criticism that had long been directed against the East India Company, and it came to an end not through the expansion of the Chinese market for British manufactures, but through the rise in India's trade with China. Early in the nineteenth century a large export of Indian opium and raw cotton to China developed, and although China sent in return some quantity of raw silk, sugar and nutmeg, the balance of trade was strongly in India's favour. Thus it came about in the early decades of the nineteenth century that British purchases of China's tea were paid for by exports of Indian cotton and opium to China and, to complete the triangle, by exports of British goods and services to India, by dues payable by Indians to the East India Company and by the freight earned by British ships engaged in the Eastern trade. The trade between India and China was known as the 'country trade', and was in the hands of private merchants, both Indian and English. This, together with the 'privilege tonnage' of the officers of the East Indiamen, represented a serious breach in the East India Company's China monopoly. By the early thirties more than half the British trade with China was in private hands, and there had also been a development of private trade by the Americans and continental Europeans. The East India Company's monopoly of the tea trade and its command over the machinery for remitting home the proceeds of sales in China were nevertheless bitterly attacked by British merchants and manufacturers who thought that golden opportunities awaited British trade once the monopoly had been destroyed. In 1834 this occurred; but it was not followed by the favourable results that had been expected. Criticism was, therefore, turned

THE COURSE OF WESTERN ENTERPRISE

against the trading arrangements on the Chinese side; namely, the Canton Commercial System and the Cohong.

The Cohong has been described as 'hardly a guild merchant and not quite a Regulated Company. It was a loose association of merchants given the monopoly of foreign trade in order to control it. . . .' The members of the Cohong 'acted together in enforcing control but not in carrying on trade'.[1] It was illegal for a foreigner to deal with any Chinese other than a merchant of the Cohong group. Among the British merchants the view came to be taken that substantial advantages would not accrue from the abolition of John Company's monopoly until the monopoly on the Chinese side was also destroyed and until fresh channels of commercial intercourse between foreigners and Chinese could be opened. As it was, the trade as a whole was very vulnerable, and when, in 1836, the Chinese Government made a real attempt to enforce the prohibition of the import of opium an essential link in Western trade with China was snapped.[2] The abolition of the East India Company's charter, however, meant in practice that the Chinese now had to deal with the British Government in the person of its agent, the Superintendent of Trade, instead of with a trading corporation, and private British merchants who knew that they were regarded as little better than interlopers by the East India Company, could now confidently call upon their Government to protect their lives and fortunes. The Opium War which followed the import prohibition came to an end with the Treaty of Nanking in August 1842. This threw China open to Western trade. The Cohong system was abolished and foreigners could now deal freely with Chinese outside the ranks of the Hong; four new ports (Shanghai, Amoy, Foochow and Ningpo) were opened to foreigners, and British consuls were allowed to reside in them; import duties were limited to 5 per cent *ad valorem*; and Hongkong became a British colony. A supplementary agreement in 1843 granted most-favoured-nation treatment and the extraterritorial jurisdiction of consuls.

The Treaty of Nanking led to a great outburst of optimism among the industrialists and merchants of England. 'The heads of staid manufacturers of Lancashire' were turned by the prospect of 300 million Chinese customers waiting to buy their shirtings.[3] In the 1840's 'an eminent firm at Sheffield' made a large shipment of knives and forks 'and declared themselves prepared to supply all China with cutlery'. The Chinese 'who know not the use of knives and forks (or, as they say, abandoned the use of them when they became civilised)' refused to look at these wares. Consequently the prices they fetched scarcely covered

[1] M. Greenberg, *op. cit.*, p. 53.
[2] Before 1836 a number of edicts prohibiting the import of opium had been promulgated, but no serious attempts were made to enforce them.
[3] *Economist*, 1 September 1849, p. 967.

2   17

their freight and 'the shops in Hongkong were for years afterwards adorned with them, formed into devices, like guns and spears in an armoury'. During the same period 'a London house of famous name' sent out 'a tremendous consignment of pianofortes' in the expectation that the opening of China would mean that at least a million Chinese women would want to learn to play the piano.[1] These hopes soon waned. British business men learned to their cost that Chinese tastes and ways of living differed from those of Victorian England, and that the average purchasing power in the country was extremely low. In later years this optimism often affected Westerners engaged in business with China. Under the influence of such delusions many projects were undertaken which would have been rejected if they had been more rationally appraised.

2. 1842-95

During the fifty years after 1842 the foreigners succeeded in consolidating the position which they had gained by the Treaty of Nanking, and they enlarged the breaches in China's wall of exclusiveness. They firmly established themselves as a privileged group in Chinese society, and from their settlements in the ports and under the shelter of extraterritoriality they embarked on the development of the China trade. The consequences of these early arrangements for regulating the intercourse between foreigners and Chinese were in the end more far-reaching than had been expected by either party. The growth of foreign settlements or concessions, in particular, had an important influence on future economic and political developments. Once the foreigners had been permitted to trade freely in certain ports, they needed residences and places of business. But they shrank from living in the midst of a Chinese population whose standards of hygiene were lower than their own, especially as they would be highly vulnerable in the case of anti-foreign disturbances. The Chinese authorities, for their part, were not anxious to expose the Chinese population to the influence of Western ways of life. It was mutually convenient, therefore, for the foreigners to obtain leases of land at the ports for residential building. Here they could live under the jurisdiction of their own consuls and under the protection of their own police. Once this initial step had been taken, however, the disturbed political conditions in China itself became responsible for a growth in the importance of the settlements far beyond what had been originally contemplated. For these settlements remained oases of peace in a country which was torn from time to time by civil war and where there was little security for person or property. Not merely did the foreigners themselves convert what had been intended

---

[1] *China: Being "The Times" Special Correspondence (by G. Wingrove Cooke) from China in the Years 1857-58*, p. 169.

18

as residential areas into great centres of commercial activity, but many Chinese also sought to escape from the surrounding disorder into the security of the foreign settlements.[1] The influx of Chinese, especially those belonging to the gentry and officialdom, into the International Settlement of Shanghai became very large during the years from 1851 to 1864 when China was devastated by the Taiping Rebellion which gravely impaired the Imperial authority. Few of the Chinese who came to Shanghai at this time had previously been in contact with foreigners. Now they had perforce to observe Western methods in commerce and administration at close quarters, and some of the refugees realised that China might advantageously follow foreign example in certain directions. Impressions gained at this time led to the establishment of Chinese shipping companies and other concerns in the years ahead.

In this period Hongkong developed from being a desolate island into an important commercial centre. The colony, like the foreign settlements and concessions in China, enjoyed peace and quiet even when the rest of the country was disturbed. Although the opening of the Yangtse Valley to foreign trade increased the importance of Shanghai relative to that of Hongkong, yet Hongkong became the entrepôt for much of the trade of South China.

The contrast between the security that could be found under foreign jurisdiction and the insecurity that prevailed elsewhere produced a chain of consequences that left the foreigners in an ever stronger political position *vis-à-vis* the Chinese Government. The incapacity of the Government made it possible for piracy to flourish all along the coast of China. Foreign vessels, sailing craft as well as steamships, were better armed, more seaworthy and swifter than the junks, and they could deal with the pirates more effectively. Owners of junks, therefore, often hired foreign ships to convoy them, and many foreigners made of this a lucrative business. (Some of them, indeed, seem to have rivalled the pirates in their depredations and earned for themselves the sobriquet of 'protecting tigers'.)[2] After a time Chinese merchants realised that it was more economical for them to send their goods in foreign ships rather than to hire these as escorts for junks, especially as goods shipped in foreign vessels could be covered by the new foreign insurance companies in the Treaty Ports and in Hongkong. These companies were not willing to insure junk-borne cargoes.

For some time after the Treaty of Nanking the legal position of the foreign shipping companies engaged in this trade was ambiguous. Until 1863 no formal permission had been given by treaty for ships under foreign flags to take part in the coastal trade. Yet they had not been prohibited from doing so. Consequently, as the benefits to both sides

[1] G. F. Hudson, *The Far East in World Politics*, pp. 19–20.
[2] S. F. Wright, *China's Struggle for Tariff Autonomy*, p. 188.

were clear, no official objection was raised to the growing Chinese practice of chartering or making use of foreign ships between Chinese ports. In 1863 seven-tenths of the British shipping that frequented Shanghai was estimated as being engaged in the coastal trade.[1] These ships included those owned or manned by Singapore Chinese who were British subjects. Sometimes, however, foreign flags were assumed illegally or the right to fly them was granted irregularly by consuls. These practices gave rise to frequent bickerings, and the immediate cause of the second Anglo-Chinese War (1856) was a dispute of this nature.

China's defeat in this war was followed in 1858 by the Treaty of Tientsin, supplemented by the Treaty of Peking two years later. In addition to the treaty with Britain, China also signed new treaties with the United States, Russia and France. These considerably enlarged the privileges of the foreigners. They laid down, among other things, that the foreign Powers should have the right to appoint ministers at the Court of Peking; that three square miles of the Kowloon Peninsula, on the mainland opposite Hongkong, should be ceded to Great Britain; that eleven additional ports, including Newchwang in Manchuria, Tientsin, Chefoo, Hankow, Nanking, Chinkiang, Swatow, and two in Formosa should be opened to foreign trade; that foreigners should be allowed to travel and trade in the interior, and that the navigation of the Yangtse should be open to foreign merchant ships. A further important provision affected the liability of foreigners to inland customs duties. As the maritime customs duty was limited to 5 per cent *ad valorem*, the impoverished Chinese Government could not increase its revenue substantially from that source. During the Taiping Rebellion, therefore, it sought to cover its military expenditure by imposing a tax on goods in transit from one province to another or sometimes even between towns in the same province. By 1858 this tax, known as *likin*, was being collected throughout South China and the Yangtse Valley. The Treaty of Tientsin, however, entitled foreign merchants to commute all inland customs dues by the payment, in addition to the maritime customs tariff, of 2½ per cent *ad valorem* on foreign goods imported or on Chinese produce exported. This clause in the treaty gave foreign merchants an advantage over their Chinese competitors. Although in practice the clause was often ignored by provincial authorities, nevertheless, by permitting foreigners to trade in the interior of China on privileged terms, it laid the foundations for Western economic penetration and made possible many new forms of enterprise.

The political weakness and administrative incompetence of the Chinese Government were directly responsible for the establishment of foreign control over the Chinese maritime customs. In 1853 the Chinese

[1] S. F. Wright, *China's Struggle for Tariff Autonomy*, p. 191.

20

city of Shanghai was occupied by rebels known as the Triad Society. The customs officials were dispersed and the collection of duties fell into arrears. In 1854 the British, French and American consuls met the Governor of the Province to discuss means of improving the collection of duties, and it was then agreed that foreign customs officials should be employed at Shanghai. This created a precedent which was followed with far-reaching results after the second Anglo-Chinese War. The Treaty of Tientsin required the Chinese Government to pay an indemnity to Great Britain and France, and as the Government was already in serious financial difficulties because of the Taiping Rebellion, the Powers sought for a means by which their demands could be met without completely wrecking Chinese finances. It was agreed that the maritime customs should be placed under the control of a foreign inspectorate, and so there arose the famous Chinese Customs Service which under its second Inspector-General, Sir Robert Hart, grew into a highly efficient body, international in composition but faithful in serving the interests of China. Smuggling declined and the Imperial revenues from customs duties rose substantially. This did much to reconcile the Government to the development of foreign trade and to the opening of the new Treaty Ports.

At the same time there were negotiations about the rules governing the import of opium, a subject that had not been mentioned in the Treaty of Nanking. The import of opium was legalised by a declaration which laid down certain conditions, namely, that an import duty of 30 taels a picul should be imposed,[1] that opium should be carried into the interior by Chinese only, that the privilege of commuting *likin* should not apply to opium, and that the Chinese Government should be free to impose whatever *likin* it thought desirable. The main result of legalisation was that henceforth it was possible to control the imports and to substitute a regular duty, paid to the Central Exchequer, for the irregular imposts previously levied for the benefit of conniving officials. Opium was set apart from other imported goods by the fact that the foreign importers had to sell it at the ports and could not market it in the interior. Thus the functions of the Western merchant in respect of opium continued to be curtailed, as in former times, and trade in this commodity is therefore less significant from the standpoint of this study than many other goods which have excited little interest among social reformers or politicians.

In 1858, the year in which China signed the Treaty of Tientsin with Great Britain, a treaty with Russia was also concluded. Sino-Russian relations date back to the mid-seventeenth century when Russian outposts reached the River Amur, and a frontier war broke out. In 1689 the Treaty of Nerchinsk, China's first agreement with a foreign Power,

---

[1] Picul=133⅓ lbs.

defined boundaries and made regulations about trade. It also provided that if either a Chinese or a Russian committed violence on the alien side of the frontier he was to be sent back to his own territory for punishment. From 1693 onwards a number of Russian envoys were sent to China and a Chinese embassy went to St. Petersburg. Meanwhile a flourishing trade developed on the border. In time Russian colonists took over all territory north of the Amur, contrary to the terms of the Treaty of Nerchinsk, which fixed the northern watershed of this river as the boundary. Then, in the middle of the nineteenth century, when the vigorous Muraviev was Governor-General of Eastern Siberia, Russia gained a foothold on the Pacific coast. In 1858, by the Treaty of Aigun, the Amur along its lower reaches was recognised as the boundary and in 1860, by the Treaty of Peking, the Ussuri region, a coastal strip on the Pacific just north of Manchuria and Korea, was ceded to Russia. In 1871, during the Moslem Revolt, Russia occupied Ili, a region of Sinkiang. After protracted negotiations, part of Ili was ceded to Russia by the Treaty of St. Petersburg in 1881; but thanks to the presence of Tso Tsung-Tang's[1] army in the north-west, and to the diplomatic ability of Tseng Ki-Tse,[2] China regained some of the territory which had been occupied.

At about the same time China's southern boundaries were subject to pressure from France. By the Treaty of Saigon in 1874, and the Treaty of Hué in 1883, Annam accepted French protection in place of its former loose allegiance to China. This led to war between France and China in which China was defeated. By the Convention of 1884 (ratified in the next year by the Treaty of Tientsin) the French position in Annam was recognised.

The changes in the legal position of foreigners were accompanied by changes in the character of the foreign trade. It has already been shown that long before the Treaty of Nanking, Western commerce had ceased to depend on an export of specie to China; in fact, the flow of silver had reversed its direction. For some time, however, the trade continued to be highly specialised. Exports consisted mainly of tea and silk, and imports of raw cotton and opium. Gradually the trade became more highly diversified. Cotton piece-goods had been imported from Great Britain in the early decades of the century. This trade grew after the middle of the century and by the middle eighties cotton manufactures

---

[1] A general who showed great skill against the Taiping Rebels and who, during 1867–73, suppressed the Moslem insurrection in North-west China.

[2] Son of Tseng Kuo-Fang, another of the great generals who helped to defeat the Taipings. Tseng Ki-Tse, the son, was appointed Chinese Minister at London and Paris in 1879 and Special Ambassador at St. Petersburg in 1880. He was a distinguished scholar and calligrapher, and in 1881 the Hongkong and Shanghai Banking Corporation asked him to write the Chinese characters that appeared on its banknotes. He was also one of the earliest high Chinese officials to speak English. H. B. Morse, *International Relations of the Chinese Empire*, vol. II, p. 314.

had first place among the imports. In the last quarter of the nineteenth century a demand arose in China for a wide variety of Western manufactures. These included kerosene, which replaced the native vegetable oil for lighting, metal wares, matches, soap, cigarettes and other consumption goods. The growth in the export trade during this period was encouraged by the fall in the sterling value of the tael (i.e. in the value of silver in terms of gold). New lines of exports were also developed. Chinese beans, vegetable oils, bristles and many other products entered world markets. Merchants sought 'some other and more profitable medium than bullion in which to remit the proceeds of their imports, and a trade of greater or less magnitude . . . in consequence . . . developed in articles which a few years before were unknown among our foreign exports [sc. from China], such as sugar, tobacco, hides, camel's wool, straw braid. . . .'[1] At the end of the century, however, silk and tea still accounted for nearly 60 per cent of the total exports.

Such was the broad character of the changes in China's foreign trade which, we must emphasise, still left its size unimpressive even half a century after the Treaty of Nanking—an event which had been expected to open the way to rich and eager markets. Although the estimated volume of exports and imports had grown by 200 per cent and 560 per cent respectively during the period between 1845 and 1890, in 1895 the total foreign trade of this huge country amounted to only about £53 million.[2] Only the fringe of the economy had been affected so far by the commercial activities of the Westerners.

If economic initiative during this period was supplied mainly by foreigners, it must not be supposed that there were not important exceptions. For instance, the difficulties of China during the Taiping Rebellion and in succeeding years convinced the more able among the Chinese officials that the Central Government's power should be strengthened by the adoption of various Western contrivances. Two outstanding men, Tseng Kuo-Fan[3] and Li Hung-Chang,[4] made use of steamships in their campaign against the Taipings. In 1863 Tseng sponsored the establishment in Shanghai of the ironworks which later became the Kiangnan Arsenal. In 1872 Li and other officials were responsible for the formation of the China Merchants' Steam Navigation Company. Another military leader, Tso Tsung-Tang, established a naval yard at Foochow while he was Governor-General of Chekiang

[1] *Chinese Customs Report*, Shanghai, 1876, p. 121.
[2] *See* T. R. Banister, *A History of the External Trade of China, 1834–81*, Chap. III, and p. 170; cf. Appendix A, *infra*.
[3] A Hunanese who won distinction as a commander against the Taipings and who recaptured Nanking from them. In 1860 Marquis Tseng (as he became) was appointed Governor of Nanking.
[4] A native of Anhwei who rose to prominence as Tseng Kuo-Fang's lieutenant in the suppression of the Taiping Rebellion. Li became the most celebrated Chinese statesman of the latter part of the nineteenth century.

23

WESTERN ENTERPRISE IN FAR EASTERN ECONOMIC DEVELOPMENT

and Fukien. Finally, there was Chang Chih-Tung,[1] Governor-General of Hupeh and Hunan, who was among the most progressive officials of his time. He planned to make an industrial centre at Hankow and Wuchang, and in the 1880's he established an ironworks, an arsenal, a cotton mill and mining enterprises in that neighbourhood.

Members of the bureaucracy had special advantages for promoting modern industry and transport, for they could influence Government policy in favour of their projects and their position gave them ample opportunities for amassing the necessary capital. Later in this period other types of Chinese capitalist began to appear. In the Treaty Ports many compradores—an indispensable link between foreign business men and their customers—were becoming wealthy. They formed the first group of Chinese merchants who were not under close Government control, and so were not liable to be mulcted of their gains. Many of the earliest Chinese factories in the ports were financed by compradores.[2]

3. 1895–1911

The next step forward in economic development came after the Treaty of Shimonoseki of 1895. This followed China's defeat by Japan in a war that arose from the rivalry of the two countries in Korea, and it proclaimed the independence of Korea and the cession of Formosa to Japan. China agreed to open additional ports and to allow the subjects of Japan (and consequently of all Treaty Powers) to engage in industrial enterprise at the ports. This led to the establishment of a number of foreign-owned cotton mills and other factories in China, chiefly in Shanghai. The introduction of these foreign industrial undertakings, in turn, inclined the Chinese Government to look with more favour than hitherto on native private industrial enterprise. The Treaty of Shimonoseki imposed on China a heavy indemnity payable in sterling. The Government's financial position was such that, in order to meet this obligation, it had to borrow from abroad and to pledge the customs, salt and *likin* revenues as security. This method of borrowing abroad became usual in later years.

Defeat by Japan revealed the full extent of China's weakness, and there ensued the process which the Chinese call 'the cutting up of the melon'. By this was meant the scramble on the part of foreign nations for naval bases and spheres of influence, a scramble which began in 1896 with the secret concession to Russia of mining and railway rights in Manchuria and of a special position at Port Arthur and Dairen. The next year Germany seized Kiaochow Bay and secured mining and railway rights in Shantung. During 1898 France obtained the lease of

---

[1] Governor, first of Shansi, then of Kwangsi, and later of Hupeh and Hunan. He was interested in railway and industrial development.
[2] H. D. Fong, *Industrial Capital in China*, p. 51.

24

THE COURSE OF WESTERN ENTERPRISE

Kwangchow Bay in South China and a railway concession. In the same year the naval station of Weihaiwei in Shantung, and also some 356 square miles adjoining the colony of Hongkong (the 'New Territories'), were leased to Great Britain. France, Britain and Japan in turn demanded and obtained declarations that the Chinese Government would not alienate to third Powers regions which any of these countries considered to be its own sphere of influence. The American Government tried to put an end to the scramble and to prevent a complete break-up of China by persuading the Powers to declare their adherence to an 'open door' policy which was intended to confer equal trading rights in China on the nationals of all countries.

The Sino-Japanese War had demonstrated the strategic value of railways, and after its conclusion the Chinese Government was disposed to favour the enlargement of its then diminutive railway system. Between 1895 and 1898 it granted to foreigners the right of building railways in Manchuria, Shantung and the provinces adjoining Annam; but it was anxious that in the rest of the country the construction should take place under Chinese control. This work could not be undertaken, however, unless capital could be raised abroad for the purpose, and the result was that railway construction was drawn within the orbit of the fierce diplomatic struggles over China in which the Western Powers were then engaged. Financial groups of various nationalities, backed by their several Governments, competed for the right to build the projected railways, and the earliest loans, which were normally secured on the railway revenues, were accompanied by agreements conferring a considerable measure of control over the lines upon the bondholders. Thus, defeat at the hands of Japan had the effect of enlarging the opportunities for foreign enterprise in China in the measure that it reduced the capacity of the Chinese Government to resist the foreigners' importunities.

By this time the succession of political misfortunes combined with the deepening influence of foreign intrusion upon her economic life had begun to disturb the massive foundations of China's society. Conservatism, for the first time, came under serious attack from within. Many of the younger members of the literati realised that it was impracticable for the Government to continue indefinitely its indiscriminate resistance to Western influences. They saw that if China failed to take over foreign institutions and technical devices on her own initiative, these would be forced upon her from outside. The young Emperor was influenced by these opinions. Under the guidance of Kang Yu-Wei[1] he startled the country by issuing a series of edicts during what came to be known as the 'Hundred Days of Reform'. But the conservative interests which he challenged resisted vigorously, and their champion, the Empress Dowager, regained her commanding position. Both at the Court and

[1] The leader of those who desired reform by constitutional means.

25

throughout North China there was a reaction against everything that savoured of the West. This found expression in the Boxer Movement, which, in 1901, with the connivance and encouragement of the Empress Dowager's Government, launched a campaign of violence against foreigners and Chinese Christians in North China. The foreign Powers intervened, and for a year their military authorities maintained a provisional government in control of the Tientsin-Peking area. The administration was handed back to the Chinese authorities after the signature of the Final Protocol. China agreed to pay an indemnity of 450 million taels (i.e. about £67 million) and to sign new treaties with the Powers.

The ultimate consequence of these attempts by conservative interests to stifle the efforts of the reformers and modernisers was to open new channels through which Western influences were able to penetrate. When, from 1908 onwards, the Western Powers, led by the United States, remitted all or part of their share of the Boxer Indemnity, they did so under arrangements by which the remitted funds were applied for educational purposes and for the purchase of capital equipment from abroad. In the same way the treaties of 1902–3, for which the Protocol had provided, revised China's commercial regulations and, although some of the new agreements were never carried out,[1] the general effect was to destroy many of the remaining barriers to Western enterprise. For instance, the treaties with the United Kingdom and the United States contained a vaguely worded clause which required China to recast her mining regulations, and this clause, as we shall see later, had important consequences for the development of the mining industry.[2]

The humiliations suffered by China discredited the policy of conservatism which the Imperial Government had pursued with such disastrous effects. The reformers were confirmed in their opinions by the victory of Japan over Russia in 1905, for this showed that an Asian country, by adopting Western methods in war and industry, could outmatch even a great European Power. The growth in reformist opinion after this time was closely associated with the rise of a student class trained in Western-style institutions established by the Government, in mission schools and colleges, and in foreign universities. This class was active in fostering a spirit of nationalism, in demanding constitutional reforms, and in advocating a policy of modernisation in political and economic affairs. The influence of the student class on public opinion was demonstrated as early as 1905 when its members led a movement to boycott American imports in protest against immigration restrictions imposed

[1] The treaty with Japan required China to 'establish a system of uniform national coinage and provide for a uniform national currency', and also to unify the system of weights and measures. None of these reforms was carried out. A plan for the abolition of *likin* and a guarantee by the Chinese Government to protect foreign trade-marks likewise came to nothing.

[2] *See* p. 152, *infra*.

26

on Chinese by the United States. Later the students were foremost in the agitation against opium. Foreign Governments could not ignore these manifestations of an incipient nationalism allied to reformist zeal. They gave their help in the campaign to suppress opium smoking, and as a result of international conferences held in 1909 and 1912 and an agreement with the British Government, there was a gradual reduction in China's imports of the drug. In 1917 they ceased altogether.

Even the Imperial Government itself was affected by this reformist temper. Official support was given to Western-type education. The need for extending the railway system was accepted, and in the decade before the First World War several important trunk lines were constructed. By playing off foreign national groups against each other, the Government was able to obtain better terms than formerly for the building of these railways; for the control of the lines was vested in its own hands and not in those of foreign bondholders. Even when the different national groups interested in financing Chinese railways formed a consortium to bargain collectively with the Government, the terms of the new contracts were more favourable to China than those of earlier years. But the Imperial Government was too gravely discredited to be accepted as a leader in China's attempt to come to terms with the modern world. In October 1911 the dynasty was overthrown and a Republic proclaimed under the leadership of Sun Yat-Sen.

4. 1911–37

One of the chief aims of the revolutionary party was to create a political system which would enable China herself to assume the task of modernising her economy instead of leaving this to foreign initiative. The age of economic passivity and official indifference was over, and the Western Powers and Western entrepreneurs alike found themselves obliged to approach China in a new spirit. The creation of modern institutions and the growth of an efficient economy were, however, frustrated by the civil wars which marred the first twenty years of the new Republic's life. In the midst of the turmoil the foreign settlements and concessions stood out as oases of law and order, and industrial development, which was stimulated by the First World War, was almost entirely confined to them. In these circumstances it was natural that China's recovery of rights from the Powers that had exacted them should have been delayed. Nevertheless, the old régime of capitulations was in retreat. During the First World War the Powers agreed to an upward revision of the tariff. After the war, the defeated countries lost their extraterritorial rights, concessions and leases, and their portion of the Boxer Indemnity Fund was cancelled. The Soviet Government renounced the Russian treaty rights with China, and after Chiang Kai-Shek had established his Government at Nanking in 1927 and had

27

broken with his Communist supporters, the United Kingdom's policy became conciliatory. She gave up some of her concessions in China, including the naval base of Weihaiwei, and she remitted her share of the Boxer Indemnity. The outstanding economic event of the period, however, was the restoration in 1928 of China's tariff autonomy. This was followed by a rise in import duties, particularly in those on manufactured goods, and under the shelter of this protection there was an expansion of industry in Shanghai and other centres. Negotiations were begun with a view to ending extraterritoriality; but these were not concluded until 1943.

The Western Powers were now sympathetic towards China's attempts to take control of her own destiny and to put in hand the modernisation of her economy, but her neighbour Japan had her own plans. After the establishment of Manchukuo in 1932, the Japanese proceeded to carry out an ambitious programme of industrial development in that country. This left little scope for the enterprise of other nationals, and many undertakings that had been conducted by Chinese as well as by Westerners had to withdraw. In the middle thirties officially-sponsored Japanese enterprise began to press south of the Great Wall. Nevertheless, the Nanking Government made a successful stand against the calamity of the times and its administration was more stable than that of any Chinese government for many decades. On the eve of the Sino-Japanese War economic prospects were favourable. Outside the areas affected by Japanese penetration there had been a substantial growth of modern industry under Chinese control, while the Government was responsible for several important economic reforms and innovations. In 1935, after a period in which much economic instability had been caused through fluctuations in the price of silver, China abandoned the silver standard and instituted a managed currency. This accorded with a pronounced trend towards the enlargement of the Government's economic activities. For example, a number of officially-sponsored trading companies were formed, and there was a striking increase in the business conducted by the Chinese Government banks in external as well as internal finance. The tide of economic westernisation was in flood and the former official indifference had given place to an active concern by the Government in the ordering of economic affairs. In the spring of 1937 the British Commercial Counsellor at Shanghai stated: 'That Chinese private interests can adapt themselves to modern economic needs is shown by the growth of a number of enterprises, such as Chinese insurance companies, the flour industry, the Chinese cotton industry, the electrical industry and many others ...; the outstanding feature [sc. of China's economic life at that time] ... is the increasing, justified confidence which the Chinese themselves as well as the world at large have in the future of this country, a confidence

28

based on the remarkable growth of stability achieved in recent years and the improved political, financial and economic conduct of affairs —government and private.' Thus the Westerners could no longer claim a monopoly of economic initiative in China. Europeans and Americans now shared the field with the Japanese, the Chinese Government and Chinese private entrepreneurs.

5. 1937–52

The Sino-Japanese War destroyed the hopes of economic development and undermined the new-found stability of the State. Between 1937 and 1945 the east of China, where most of the country's industry was situated, came under Japanese occupation. In that region Japanese business corporations, acting in effect as agents of their Government, became the chief instruments for the administration of economic resources, especially after the outbreak of the Pacific War, when the Japanese confiscated Allied properties. In Free China—the unoccupied part of the country—very little modern industry had existed before the war. The Chinese tried to introduce manufacturing activities into these regions and many small factories were established; but it was not possible to create industrial centres comparable with those on the coast or at Hankow. At the same time, Free China's international trade was narrowly limited by geographical isolation, and most of that trade came to be conducted by Government agencies. In this respect as in most others the war stimulated the growth of State participation in economic affairs. Yet, at a time when the Government was trying to extend the scope of its activities, its efficiency was declining and it was ceasing to discharge adequately even the ordinary functions of government. During the later years of the war and in the early post-war period there was a runaway inflation which completed the administrative collapse.

The war occasioned the final stages of the Westerners' abandonment of their privileged legal status in China. To support Chinese morale and to demonstrate their goodwill, the United States and the United Kingdom in 1943 signed new treaties with the Chungking Government by which they relinquished their extraterritorial rights and their remaining concessions and settlements. Between 1943 and 1947 the other Treaty Powers followed this example. After the war the Kuomintang Government's National Resources Commission took over the former Japanese industrial assets in China.[1] This meant that a very large part of China's modern economy passed under State control. In commerce, too, there was a further extension of Government activity. Thus, vast new responsibilities, legal, political and economic, were assumed by the Government at a moment when its administrative competence was most rapidly

[1] Apart from such industrial equipment in Manchuria as was removed by the Soviet forces in 1945.

deteriorating. When in 1949 the Communists displaced the Kuomintang they inherited this economic policy, but they brought to its execution a ruthless efficiency which they also displayed in ending the inflation.

The dominance of the State in the economic affairs of post-war China meant that the Westerners could entertain no expectation of recovering their former importance in the country's economy. To this there was one qualification. Between 1937 and 1941, when Shanghai was in decline, Hongkong had advanced both commercially and industrially. After the war the disturbed conditions on the mainland increased the economic attractions of the colony and a considerable industrial expansion took place. In China itself the Western entrepreneurs' attempts to reach a prudent accommodation with the new order continued until the establishment of Communist rule put an end to most of their economic activities on the mainland, though not to their hopes.

CHAPTER II

THE WESTERN MERCHANT IN CHINA

WESTERN enterprise penetrated into many different sectors of the Chinese economy. In the course of time it concerned itself with internal and external trade, banking, insurance, shipping and its ancillary services, land transport, manufacturing, mining and public utilities. These various branches of economic activity will be considered in turn. At the outset, however, it is well to note that most of them grew directly and inevitably out of the original interest of the Westerners in fostering a profitable Chinese foreign trade. The merchant firm thus became, and remained, the typical representative of Western enterprise in China. At the same time, the leading merchants did not normally confine themselves to strictly mercantile business. Although foreign trade remained their chief preoccupation, the scope of their activities was usually very wide, and throughout the modern era (i.e. from 1842) a large proportion of the dealings between Chinese and Westerners was in the hands of firms with an extensive range of interests, commercial, financial and industrial.

The reasons for this diversity in the interests of the typical, large merchant firms are not far to seek. Foreign merchants who established themselves in the Treaty Ports after 1842 were obliged, in the absence of a Chinese financial and commercial system of a modern type, to provide many of the auxiliary services which in the great trading centres were usually left to specialists. They therefore undertook various kinds of banking and foreign exchange business; they entered the shipping trade; and they promoted insurance companies. They were drawn into these activities mainly because it was only by broadening the basis of their businesses that they could foster or preserve their mercantile interests. The functions which a Western trading firm had to assume were determined primarily by the backwardness of the Chinese in everything that appertained to a modern commercial society. Once these subsidiary enterprises had been set up, they began a career of their own, and in time they had effects on the Chinese economy and on the business practices of the Chinese that were not contemplated when they were first established.

Important as these other activities ultimately became, it was mercantile enterprise which from the earliest period of Sino-European relationships until the present has predominated. To this enterprise China owed the inception and development of her modern overseas trade. It was the Western merchants who first saw the commercial possibilities of various Chinese products and introduced them into world markets. Some of these goods had long been important articles in China's internal economy. Others had little value in China until the Western merchants created a foreign demand for them. These pioneering activities were hazardous, and many ventures failed to yield the results that had been expected. The Western merchants also brought into being new demands on the part of the Chinese. This in itself was disruptive of the traditional social and economic system. As Sir George Sansom has said, in another context, the influence of Europeans upon Asian life 'was exercised mainly by the introduction of new commodities rather than by the communication of ideas'. In bringing about social change in China, 'objects of trade, which are silent but convincing', have certainly been very persuasive.[1]

The Western merchants were not content to rely upon the response of Chinese dealers and producers to the new demands which they brought to bear on the Chinese economy. They had to interest themselves intimately in the organisation of the supply of goods required for the export markets. This sometimes meant that they became directly responsible for the establishment of new industries or for the reorganisation of existing ones. Directly or indirectly they had a profound effect on the methods of conducting the internal trade of the country. Their functions included the setting up of standards of quality, the collection of goods from multitudes of small and widely scattered producers, and the preliminary processing of materials for export. One of the merchants' major difficulties was to obtain supplies of a consistent quality, and they had to wage a continual battle against adulteration. Further, they had to organise the sale of imported products up country, to educate consumers in their use, and sometimes to provide post-sales services.

In some lines of trade and at certain periods the Western merchant was called upon to provide extensive credit to the native dealers, although the practice varied from trade to trade and from time to time. For instance, at Wenchow in Chekiang the local dealers were reported in 1892 to be too poor to undertake more than a peddling trade. So, the foreign merchant was obliged to send his agents from farm to farm to buy produce and 'in any and every case a money advance [had to] be made before any quantity, however small, [could] be obtained'.[2] On the other hand, in some regions and trades the Chinese dealers might sell on credit to the foreigner. In the import trade, the provision of long credit by the Western merchant was more general. On ordinary

---

[1] G. B. Sansom, *op. cit.*, pp. 152, 158.
[2] *British Diplomatic and Consular Reports on Trade*, No. 1212, Wenchow, 1892, p. 2.

merchandise, over a large part of our period, he was accustomed to give thirty or ninety days' credit, and he sometimes provided most of the Chinese dealer's working capital in this way. Much longer credits were given on machinery and other capital goods. The merchant was often involved in these also, although during the present century his risks in this type of trade were shared with others—foreign industrialists, bankers and Government agencies.

It would, of course, be misleading to give the impression that the whole of China's foreign trade began with and entirely depended upon the Western merchant. There was, indeed, a commerce that owed nothing to him, and this must not be overlooked. For instance, China and South-east Asia had traded with one another for centuries past, and some of this trade remained in Asian hands. A report from Chefoo in 1864 stated: '. . . a fleet of about 35 Siamese ships visits the port every year, arriving with the South-west monsoon and returning with that from the North-east. This annual trip they have been in the habit of making for many years.'[1] Old-established commercial relations between the southern ports of China and South-east Asia were naturally even closer. Nor must the ancient caravan routes be forgotten. For centuries a tenuous commercial contact between China and the Near East had been maintained by land. Further, in the eighteenth and early nineteenth centuries Russian expansion across Central Asia and Siberia stimulated overland trade. Russian merchants traded with North China long before the Treaty of Nanking allowed other foreigners to do business in that region. Nevertheless, the great bulk of China's international trade during the past century has taken the form of the exchange of sea-borne goods with Western Europe, America and India, and in the inception of this trade European and American merchants took the initiative and its conduct remained predominantly in their hands. We shall now review their methods of trading in general and the forms of commercial organisation which they created and used at different periods during the last century. This will be followed by an examination in some detail of the part played by the Western merchants in fostering the trade in particular commodities.

The methods by which the China trade was conducted underwent considerable changes in the century after 1842. These changes affected the structure of the foreign firms themselves, the relations of these firms with the Chinese, and the geographical field of the firms' activities. Political and economic developments in China, the introduction of new types of goods into the import and export trade and various advances in technique all had a powerful impact on methods of doing business. Yet these changes cannot be described by any simple general statement. From time to time strong trends could be observed, but these were

---

[1] *Chinese Customs Report*, Chefoo, 1864.

liable to change their direction—so much so that there was, towards the end of the period, a return in some degree to methods of trade employed at the beginning.

Before the Treaty of Nanking, private trade with China was conducted mainly by 'agency' businesses.[1] These firms, which were commonly partnerships, had for the most part evolved from the 'supercargoes' who had been employed by Calcutta or Bombay merchants to travel with their ships from India to Canton and to dispose of the cargoes on arrival. Some of these 'supercargoes' settled in Canton as resident agents. Their principals, or 'correspondents' as they were called, consigned the goods to these resident agents who earned an income in the form of commissions for the various services which they rendered. Manufacturers and merchants in Great Britain (for example, in the cotton piece-goods trade) used agency firms in the same way as the Indian firms that consigned raw cotton and opium. These agents usually had numerous correspondents in different countries; but most of them had especially close ties with one or two firms in India or Great Britain. Sometimes the relationship between the agent and the correspondent was so intimate as to mean that they could be regarded almost as branches of the same undertaking. Few of these agency houses confined themselves to commission business. Most of them also took part in speculative ventures, buying and selling on their own account. The extent of this speculative business depended on the temperament of the proprietor and the resources at his command.

For its commission business an agency house needed little capital; but in the thirties the leading houses operated with large resources which they employed not merely in speculative ventures but also in banking, insurance and shipping activities. The absence of modern banks in China meant that the financial operations required for international trade had to be undertaken by those who bought and sold the goods. The wide differences between rates of interest in the Western world and China, moreover, gave remunerative opportunities to those who, by their foothold in China and by their links with the West, could control the channels of capital supply. So, apart from carrying on foreign exchange business, the agency houses conducted other forms of commercial banking. They accepted deposits placed with them by merchants in India and the West and by the officers of the East Indiamen, and they made loans to the Hong merchants. Further, they engaged in insurance business, either in their capacity as agents for foreign principals, or jointly as in the Canton Insurance Society which was controlled by several managing agency houses and was capitalised partly by them and partly by Indian correspondents.[2] The agents also owned ships.

Some of these agency houses were very large. For instance, the

---

[1] cf. M. Greenberg, *op. cit.*, Chap. VI.   [2] *ibid.*, p. 171.

greatest of them, Jardine Matheson, was said to have been responsible for one-third of Canton's foreign trade during the thirties, and at the outbreak of the Opium War it owned twelve ocean-going vessels.[1] The history of this firm, which spans the whole of our period, affords a useful illustration of the general development of Western mercantile activity. One of the founders, William Jardine, was a surgeon on an East India Company vessel plying between Calcutta and Canton. In this capacity he was allowed seven tons of 'privilege tonnage', and the profits earned from this cargo gave him the taste and opportunity for larger ventures. So in 1819 he left the Company's service and established himself in business at Canton. The other founder, James Matheson, after leaving Edinburgh University, worked in his uncle's firm at Calcutta and then went on to try his fortune at Canton. There he and Jardine went into partnership with two other British merchants, Magniac and Beale. In 1832, after Magniac and Beale had retired, Jardine Matheson and Company was founded; it was then and has since remained a private firm. Jardine Matheson was quick to take advantage of the opportunities afforded by the destruction of the East India Company's monopoly; for in 1834 it sent a ship laden with tea to London, and in the next year it built the first merchant steamer to run in the China seas. From the beginning its interests were diverse and in the course of time they were extended. Its various shipping interests, which were merged in 1881 into the Indo-China Steam Navigation Company (a public company managed by the parent concern), led it into many ancillary businesses, such as the ownership of wharves and warehouses in Shanghai and Hongkong. It participated largely in railway development, and, in very recent times, in the provision of technical services at Hongkong for air transport companies. From the beginning it was prominent in the insurance business, and in later years it embarked upon many manufacturing undertakings at Shanghai, including a dried-egg factory, a press-packing plant, cotton mills and a brewery.

Until 1860 Jardine Matheson's chief rival was Dent and Company, a British concern which also dated from the pre-Treaty period. Dent's, however, was one of the many firms which failed in the Overend and Gurney crisis of 1866. Thenceforward Butterfield and Swire became Jardine Matheson's chief rival. This concern had its origin in the Liverpool merchant firm, John Swire and Sons, which traded with New York and Australia. During the interruption of cotton imports caused by the American Civil War, John Swire, the head of the firm, looked about for alternative lines of business, and ultimately he decided to open an office in Shanghai. In 1873 this firm, which had an early and continuous connection with Alfred Holt and Company (the Blue Funnel Line), formed the China Navigation Company to take over its shipping

[1] *ibid.*, p. 185.

interests in China waters. Shipping later became its paramount concern, and after 1902 Butterfield and Swire's trading activities were discontinued. Like Jardine Matheson, this firm was among the pioneers in manufacturing industry; and it operated a shipbuilding and ship-repairing yard and a sugar refinery at Hongkong.

Firms in the China trade that could boast of such long and prosperous careers as these have always been exceptional. It is true that the abolition of the East India Company's monopoly in 1834 and the opening of the country to foreign trade a decade later attracted new merchant firms to China; but many of these enterprises were short-lived. There was an easy optimism about trading prospects for which many Western merchants paid very dearly in these early days. Indeed, it would seem that while a few firms enjoyed for a long period a dominating position in the China trade and emerged from every crisis stronger than before, in general the rate of mortality among Western firms has been very high.

The elimination of many of the new firms that established themselves in the later thirties and the forties left those that remained in a powerful position for seizing the opportunities that offered after the Treaty of Nanking. Certainly, the next twenty years came to be regarded in retrospect as a halcyon time. Although foreign commerce was still restricted to a very few ports, in those the position of the Western merchant was unchallenged. Chinese traders were content to deal through him and had no thought of engaging in foreign trade themselves. This, so it seemed to future generations of China merchants, was the era of the 'princely Hongs'. These great merchant houses possessed ample resources for trading on their own account and for keeping large stocks of imported goods on hand. Business then seemed less exacting than it became in the more highly competitive days ahead. In 1867 the *China Mail*, in its review of the period before the Treaty of Tientsin, commented: '. . . in those days a few commercial houses of gigantic wealth, and, as it was thought, unassailable stability, controlled the few markets which were accessible to the foreigner. The interior was unknown. The coast was traversed at rare intervals by a few steamers freighted almost exclusively on foreign account. The princely expenditure of the leading Europeans was easily supported by their almost fabulous profits. Few Chinese had devoted themselves to the study of English or to the transaction of business with foreigners, and competition in trade was as yet undreamt of.'[1] Even though we must allow for the exaggerations of a journalist intent upon pointing the contrast to conditions in his own day the impression which the article conveys is probably accurate enough.

[1] Article on 'The Revision of the British Treaty with China' in the *China Mail*, 5 March 1867.

The Treaties of Tientsin and Peking, which gave the foreigners the right of travelling and doing business in the interior, altered the conditions of trade with China and gave fresh opportunities to the enterprising. In the course of the next fifteen years China became linked with Europe by telegraph, and this too opened the way to new methods of trading. The activities of the Western merchants, moreover, had by this time brought about economic developments within China which reacted on the structure of Sino-Western commercial relationships. Chinese merchants themselves were now sufficiently experienced to invade certain areas of trade which had hitherto been occupied exclusively by the foreigners, and by the eighties their competition had led to modifications in the rôle assigned to the Western commercial community in China. In the next decade the British merchant, who had up to that time set the pace in the commercial expansion of China, found his position menaced by the Germans, who pressed home their attack with new competitive weapons. In the twentieth century they were joined by the Japanese whose place in the economic development of the country became increasingly important down to the end of the Second World War. Throughout the whole period the constituents of the import and export trade were changing, and new commodities meant innovations in methods of doing business. All these changes must now be traced in some detail.

In the days when the activities of the Western merchants had been confined to the ports their connections with the sources of supply of goods for export were necessarily tenuous. Their purchases were limited to those commodities of which the supply to the ports was effectively organised by the Chinese merchants. They were precluded from surveying the interior resources of China with a view to the development of new types of export commodities, or from participating in the internal transactions needed to open fresh channels of trade. The Chinese for their part were not qualified to estimate which products of the interior might be acceptable to Western markets. It was partly for these reasons that in the early days of commercial intercourse the range of goods exported from China was so extremely narrow.

Once the foreigners had gained the right of travelling and trading in the interior they soon took advantage of the opportunities for fresh enterprise and they sought even in the most distant regions for goods suited to the export markets. The first ventures were, of course, usually tentative and experimental, and many years often elapsed before a substantial trade was worked up. The development of the wool trade from North China provides an example of what was attempted and achieved. As early as 1860 foreign merchants had sent their agents to Mongolia to buy camel's wool,[1] but it was not until two decades later

---

[1] *British Consular Trade Report*, Tientsin, 1864, p. 3.

that the trade became important. In 1882, however, a foreign agent was sent to Kweihwacheng on the Mongolian frontier, to foster the wool trade in that neighbourhood. The venture was successful and in subsequent years this agency moved still farther west so that it migh† draw on additional supplies. The result was that the export of sheep's wool from Tientsin increased from 142 piculs in 1879 to 207,574 piculs in 1894.[1]

This experience found its parallel in other parts of China, and the career and activities of Archibald Little, a British merchant who was responsible for developing the wool trade of Szechwan, are illuminating. In 1859 Little arrived in China as a tea-taster to a German firm. Before long he went into business on his own and in the 1880's he turned his attention to the upper Yangtse region, especially to the rich province of Szechwan.[2] Although Little is perhaps best remembered for his part in the introduction of steamships to West China, the enterprise which he displayed as a merchant is also noteworthy. He believed that if exports were increased, imports would take care of themselves. 'It is with the desire of helping to prove this axiom', he wrote, 'that I myself established agencies in the Far West of China for the collection of varied produce which at the time of my first visit to that region, fifteen years before, were looked upon by the natives as almost worthless.'[3] In 1885 Little opened wool-purchasing agencies in the towns of Tachienlu and Sungpan, two important marts near the Tibetan border.[4] He had many difficulties to overcome. The trade was hampered by disturbances among the tribespeople and by the attempts of local Chinese dealers to corner the produce. Little's costs were increased by the heavy *likin* and octroi duties, thefts during transport, and the high proportion of dirt in the wool. Nevertheless he succeeded in developing the export of Szechwanese wool to the United States where it was in demand for the manufacture of carpets. In the 1890's the annual wool exports from Chungking ranged between 7,000 and 22,000 piculs.[5]

French traders, also, were pioneers in the Far West. During the nineties, for instance, a French merchant brought musk and rhubarb from Tachienlu to Chungking for subsequent export to Europe.[6] Yunnan, on the borders of Indo-China, became an important field for French enterprise. In 1900 the Compagnie Lyonnaise l'Indo-Chinoise

[1] *British Diplomatic and Consular Reports on Trade*, No. 2487, Tientsin, 1899, p. 12.
[2] A. Little, *Gleanings from Fifty Years in China*. For biographical details, *see* the Foreword by R. S. Gundry.
[3] *ibid.*, p. 48.
[4] *The China Association Report*, 1900, Appendix F.
[5] *Chinese Customs Decennial Report*, 1892–1901, Chungking, p. 146; *The China Association Report*, 1900, Appendix F; *British Diplomatic and Consular Reports on Trade*, No. 2059, Chungking, 1897, p. 10, and No. 2249, Chungking, 1898, p. 8.
[6] *British Diplomatic and Consular Reports on Trade*, No. 2059, Chungking, 1897, p. 12.

opened a branch at Mengtsz in the south of the province,[1] and in 1914 a Parisian house was engaged in the musk trade of Tengyueh, a Yunnan-Burma frontier town. 'On behalf of this firm a French merchant [made] arduous journeys at considerable intervals to Atuntsu in the extreme north of this district, on the borders of Tibet' to collect musk.[2]

In addition to these pioneering ventures by individual traders, the foreign Chambers of Commerce sponsored missions to investigate commercial opportunities of inland regions. As early as 1869 Mr. Michie and Mr. Francis, delegates of the Shanghai Chamber of Commerce, travelled up the Yangtse as far as Chungking and wrote a report which described the products of Szechwan and the foreign goods which they found on sale in Chungking.[3] In 1896 the Mission Lyonnaise d'Exploration Commerciale en Chine toured Yunnan and Szechwan. This mission included delegates from five French Chambers of Commerce—experts in silk, a mining engineer, and representatives of various other interests. About the same time a Japanese commercial mission visited Chungking and made exhaustive inquiries into economic institutions and affairs.[4] These are but a few examples of the numerous merchant explorers who penetrated far into China, either on their own initiative or under the sponsorship of Chambers of Commerce.

The majority of the new foreign ventures after 1860 naturally occurred in the less distant provinces and quite often the foreign merchant was able to build up his business on the foundations of an already well-established internal trade. Examples are to be found in the braid trade of Chefoo and the hide trade of the north-east provinces. Even in cases of this sort, however, the foreign merchant's functions were seldom limited to buying in bulk from local dealers the goods which he afterwards exported. Frequently he had to set up an elaborate collecting organisation which could obtain supplies from small producers scattered over a wide area. This task could seldom at the outset be left to Chinese merchants because, as a rule, these lacked the working capital necessary to undertake it as well as technical knowledge of the qualities required. Besides the collecting organisation the foreigner frequently had to introduce arrangements for grading, sorting and cleaning the material, or in other ways for preparing it for export. Chinese goods lacked uniformity in quality—a consequence of the small scale of production and the absence of large native factoring organisations—and when the demands of the foreigners brought about an increase in supplies the average quality usually fell because the producers resorted to adulteration. The foreign merchants were, therefore, obliged to concern themselves with the supervision of the producers, or local dealers, as

[1] *Chinese Customs Decennial Report*, 1892–1901, Mengtsz, p. 451.
[2] *British Diplomatic and Consular Reports on Trade*, No. 5470, Tengyueh, 1914, p. 4.
[3] *British Consular Trade Report*, Hankow, 1869, p. 185.
[4] *Chinese Customs Decennial Report*, 1892–1901, Chungking, p. 167.

well as with various processes preparatory to export. Sometimes, when it was found to be more profitable to export the material in a semi-manufactured form instead of in its raw state, the foreign merchant had to organise the necessary manufacturing processes in the absence of a Chinese industry capable of undertaking them. As trades grew in size and supplies had to be obtained from wider areas, the merchant was often driven to process the materials in the local centres so as to avoid deterioration. Thus, a merchant often found himself obliged, if he were to build up a trade at all, to undertake functions which, in more highly developed economies, would have been performed by specialists.

Some examples may help to throw light on the tasks which confronted the Westerners.[1] In the bristle trade the merchants soon found that they could not rely on the quality of the treated bristles supplied to them by the Chinese. They, therefore, adopted the practice of buying raw bristles and treating them in their own establishments. Again, in the hide export trade, as the merchants extended the area from which they drew supplies, they had to undertake in each locality the curing and compressing of the hides before dispatch to the commercial centre for export. Some of them found it profitable to set up tanneries and to export the leather instead of the hides. Merchants were often induced to undertake these preparatory manufacturing processes by the cheapness of Chinese labour. Indeed, some of the new export trades had their basis, not in an already existing Chinese industry nor even in the presence of local supplies of materials, but rather in the resources of cheap labour. For instance, the braid trade, which at first drew on local supplies of rushes, later came to depend on imports of better quality material from Japan which was worked up by the skilful Chinese workers. Some of the trades which the foreigners created or expanded had a complex organisation. For instance, in the hairnet trade, the hair was bought by the foreign merchants from local Chinese dealers, shipped to Europe for bleaching and dyeing and then sent back to China for manufacture into hairnets for subsequent export. This industry thus depended on the performance in foreign countries of key processes which could not be undertaken efficiently in China, even though the raw material was Chinese in origin and the main manufacturing operation took place in China.

Although as time went on some of the functions originally performed by the foreign merchants passed to the Chinese, in the actual conduct of the export trade itself this happened only to a limited extent. The foreign merchant not merely had a more detailed knowledge than his Chinese counterpart of the requirements of Western markets, but he

---

[1] Detailed information about the trades referred to in this paragraph is given in subsequent chapters.

was also in a better position for supplying working capital, for maintaining standards of quality, and for undertaking various specialised subsidiary services. Even when the foreign merchant did not himself undertake the subsidiary services, he had easy access to other foreign firms which provided them. For instance, the substantial growth in the export of groundnuts from China became possible only because, at the instance of the foreign merchants, the shipping companies installed special ventilators in the holds of their ships.

In the import trade the Chinese dealer could obtain a footing more easily than he could in the export trade, and so the functions of the Western import merchant in some lines of business were diminished as the trades became well established. Even in the sixties a writer in the *China Mail* had lamented that 'a new race of competitors, both Chinese and foreign, [had] arisen to struggle with the great capitalistic firms of former days, whose fortunes they [had] shaken without advantage to themselves'.[1] This lament may well have been inspired by the troubles attendant upon the financial crisis of 1866 rather than by a secular decline in the fortunes of the 'princely Hongs'. By the middle of the next decade, however, there is evidence that foreign merchants were contracting certain of their activities in the smaller ports in the face of competition from the local Chinese dealers. These were now beginning to buy their supplies of imported goods, especially textiles, from foreign houses in the great centres, particularly Shanghai and Hongkong, and the foreign merchants who had established themselves in the other 'open' ports after 1842 found themselves by-passed. 'Foreigners have little left to them than the export trade', wrote the British consul in Canton in 1875,[2] and the same complaint was heard in other places during the seventies and eighties, notably Tientsin, Chefoo and Ningpo.[3]

The fact that these laments were heard in subsequent decades shows that while the Chinese were encroaching on the foreigner's preserves they did not succeed in ousting him entirely from the smaller ports. It may be presumed that in the first flush of optimism foreigners established businesses at most of the ports to which they were given access, and that they assumed functions which they could not maintain once the Chinese merchants had interested themselves in the trade and had acquired experience of it. Thus, the foreigner's share of Foochow's trade fell by half during the course of the eighties, and by 1891 the import of opium and piece-goods and the storekeeping trade in that port had passed almost completely into Chinese hands. Wenchow had

---

[1] Article on 'The Revision of the British Treaty with China' in the *China Mail*, 5 March 1867.

[2] *British Consular Trade Report*, Canton, 1875, p. 10.

[3] *Chinese Customs Decennial Report*, 1882–91, Chefoo, p. 46; 1882–91, Ningpo, p. 369, and 1870–2, Tientsin, p. 45.

been opened to foreign ships in 1877, but during the eighties these withdrew because of the unprofitable character of the business.

It is clear that these developments led during the last decades of the century to an increasing concentration of the Western merchants' import activities in the larger ports. The introduction of a steamer service on the Yangtse had similar effects on the character and methods of the China trade. As the steamers that made the passage to Hankow became more numerous and as freights fell, it became easier for foreigners to operate from that centre. At the same time, however, Chinese dealers found an advantage in buying direct from the foreign importers in Shanghai instead of leaving the local trade in the hands of the foreign merchants. Thus, while the commerce of Hankow as a whole grew as time went on, an increasing proportion of it passed into Chinese hands.

The growth in the capacity of the Chinese dealers to undertake functions in connection with foreign trade created opportunities for new types of business. Some of these dealers were able to display more initiative than formerly in ordering goods from the foreigners and they began even to specify the ultimate supplier. As this happened the merchant proper, who bought and sold on his own account and carried large stocks of goods in his warehouse, became less essential to the conduct of trade between China and the West. In many lines of business he was no longer required to assume all the risks of the trade, for an increasing amount of business, both import and export, was done after orders had been received by the merchant at prices settled in advance. In some cases the functions of the Western merchant were reduced to those of a commission house. The development of this commission business made it possible for small Western firms to operate successfully, since large resources were not required for such business. The small merchant firms, which increased in numbers very considerably during the nineties, were undoubtedly assisted by the appearance of foreign-style banks and of other concerns with specialised commercial or financial functions. In all these changes the rise of the cable services had an important part to play. During the early seventies China was linked with the line that ran across the Russian Empire from Europe to Vladivostock and by others that came by India.[1] This enabled orders for goods to be telegraphed to Western merchant firms in China who bought goods on commission for dispatch to their customers. In the established trades, therefore, it was no longer necessary for a merchant to buy goods outright and to ship them abroad at his own risk.

The increase in the amount of commission business in both the import and the export trade was emphasised in a report of the Shanghai

---

[1] J. H. Clapham, *An Economic History of Modern Britain, 1850–86*, p. 217.

Commissioner of Customs in his review of the decade 1882–91. 'Now', he wrote, 'a very large and increasing amount of foreign produce is bought on commission, orders being conveyed abroad by telegram, and the tael price and rate of exchange being settled before the order is despatched. Similarly the silk trade is largely done now on orders from Europe, and purchases from the Chinese merchant are not completed until the finance of the transaction is definitely arranged and the laying down cost calculated to the fraction of a penny.'[1] The continual fluctuations of the exchange encouraged this practice. Where the exchange and the market risks were shifted from the merchant to either the supplier in Europe or the Chinese dealer, then the foreign merchant became little more than an agent who required only small capital. The actual process of importing and exporting, however, still remained firmly in the hands of the Western merchant throughout the nineteenth century and the early decades of the present century. It was not until after 1930 that the Chinese firms themselves began to undertake that business on any scale. At that time also the Chinese Government started to purchase direct from Western producers. Yet before the outbreak of the Second World War these developments were significant chiefly because of the new trend which they disclosed in China's foreign economic relations, for the great bulk of China's imports and exports still passed through Western firms.

If during and after the last quarter of the nineteenth century there was a tendency for the functions of the foreign merchant to contract in some lines of business, it must not be thought that this was present universally. We have already shown that after 1860 it had become legally possible for Westerners to operate in the interior. Just as in the export trade there was an attempt to find new sources of supply by pioneering ventures in distant provinces, so in the import trade an opportunity was given for Western firms to push sales by 'merchandising' methods throughout the country. These tendencies became pronounced during and after the nineties of last century, and they were to be observed especially in connection with types of goods previously unfamiliar to the Chinese, including many proprietary articles. There is evidence that rather earlier than this the more vigorous members of the foreign communities in China, as well as Western manufacturers on the lookout for new markets, were dissatisfied with the conventional methods of trading and regarded with impatience what they considered to be the lethargy of the older merchant houses. These critics believed that if foreign traders were to open agencies in the interior and to circumvent the middlemen, instead of merely waiting for the Chinese dealers to buy from them at the ports, a great expansion of business would result. An exponent of this view, A. R. Colquhoun, wrote a series of letters to

[1] *Chinese Customs Decennial Report*, 1882–91, Shanghai, p. 323.

The Times in this vein in 1884. He stressed the need 'to push our manufactures into the country and pay the producer direct for his tea and silk, with the cottons, manufactures and broadcloths, which we send to China'.[1] Colquhoun complained that foreign merchants in China took too short a view of trading possibilities and neglected schemes which would come to fruition only in the long run.

Even at that time not all the Western firms deserved this censure. We have already shown that long before Colquhoun wrote many firms had begun operations in the interior and individual pioneers had explored the resources of distant provinces. But during the last decade of the nineteenth century the operations of importing firms in the interior were greatly enlarged. In one sense this extension of activity may be regarded as the response of Western enterprise to the competition of the Chinese as already described. In the early years of the present century the adoption of these methods of trading was rapid. C. F. Remer, writing of European commerce in China between 1899 and 1913, remarked upon the great increase of 'salesmanship'.[2] He pointed out that in that part of the import trade which had not been taken over by Chinese, foreign merchants now followed their goods inland, while some Western manufacturers had built up great distributive networks that covered almost the whole of China.

The Germans appear to have taken the initiative in these new developments, both in introducing new articles into the import and export trade and in employing more direct methods of trading. This was, to some extent, the result of their late appearance on the scene. They found themselves faced by well-entrenched British merchants, and in order to force themselves into the market they had to adopt new methods and to find new articles of trade. Their success was considerable. From the 1890's onwards British merchants frequently lamented that the Germans were ousting them from their former supremacy. This was the dominant theme of the report, published in 1896, of the official committee set up to inquire into British trade in Hongkong. The testimony of one of the witnesses before this committee is worth quoting: 'Nearly the whole growth in exports from the East, so far as regards new articles, is owing practically to the German. He has been the first to see the value of any new article, the first to experiment, the first to send home, the first to find out what it was worth. . . . He will take up an article that is entirely unknown to the Chinese and begin to make a market for it. It may be infinitesimal at first, but he pushes and pushes it until it is quite a respectable article to handle. He will take up articles that British merchants would cast aside as too small to trouble with. . . . [The

[1] A. R. Colquhoun, *The Opening of China* (six letters reprinted from *The Times*), p. 37.
[2] C. F. Remer, *Foreign Trade of China*, pp. 128 *et seq.*

Germans] were the first here to start the system of employing time sales-men or brokers. I mean salesmen attached to their own houses. This man is paid a salary and gets commission. He goes about to find an opening for any new article.'[1]

The German commercial organisation of the time was distinguished by the close collaboration between manufacturers and merchants whose fortunes in the development of foreign markets were from the beginning of Germany's commercial expansion intimately linked. So, although the German penetration of the China market was normally undertaken by merchant houses with headquarters in the ports, the methods of sale were largely determined by their suppliers who gave financial and technical assistance in the introduction of new articles of trade. For instance, in the sale of arms and ammunition and of dyestuffs—trades which were largely in the hands of Germans in the early years of the present century—'the manufacturers insisted upon the elaboration of an extensive up-country organisation, defrayed the bulk of the expense, sent out experts to assist in the work and allowed a generous commission of not less than 5 per cent to their agents for the services rendered. These agencies had a dual advantage. In the first place they provided the German merchant in China with a handsome annual profit; and, secondly, they furnished him with an organisation free of expense which he was able to utilise for the sale of those other lines of imports in which he was interested.'[2] Close links between manufacturers and merchants also characterised the Japanese whose trade began to grow rapidly in the early years of the twentieth century. They too adopted these direct methods of sale. The typical British commercial organisa-tion was different. As Great Britain had had a great foreign trade long before the rise of large-scale industry, her merchants early acquired a dominating position, and at first the manufacturers rarely intervened in distribution. If in later times they became dissatisfied with the mer-chants' ways, they frequently set up their own sales organisation.[3]

These distributive networks, whether established by general merchants or by manufacturers, were composed of Chinese agents under the supervision of itinerant European inspectors. These in turn were normally controlled by regional or district managers. The Chinese

[1] *Report on British Trade in Hongkong*, 1896, Witness I, pp. 8 *et seq.*
[2] Speech by T. M. Ainscough, Special Commissioner of the Board of Trade in China, to members of the Far Eastern Section of the London Chamber of Commerce and the China Association on 24 November 1915. Printed with the *China Association Report*, 1915.
[3] According to the Shanghai Customs Report of 1923, the total number of foreign firms in Shanghai in 1914 was 628. Of these, 202 were British, 117 Japanese, 102 German and 71 American. In 1923 the total had risen to 1,695, of which 1,047 were Japanese, 228 British, 165 American and 70 German. The amount of business conducted by these various national groups was not, of course, in proportion to the number of firms in each of them; but the trend shown by the figures is nevertheless significant.

agents were in some cases placed in all cities and even in villages. They were required to provide guarantees of good faith before appointment; sometimes in addition to or instead of this guarantee they made a deposit with the company. It was the practice for goods to the value of the guarantee or deposit to be consigned to these agents for sale at prices fixed by the suppliers. The agents worked on a commission basis and made frequent returns of sales and unsold stock. Cigarettes, kerosene, alkalis, soap, dyes, medicines, Japanese and Russian textiles and other types of standardised or proprietary goods were marketed in this way with great success. In the engineering trade Western manufacturers, either through specially appointed agents in China or through association with Western merchants, tried to maintain direct contact with their customers. In 1915 it was estimated that at least 11 per cent of the imports into China were distributed by these direct methods.[1]

Although these distributive practices were employed mainly for the newer types of proprietary goods produced by very large concerns, it was not confined to them. The Japanese, for example, employed these methods for a considerable part of their trade. But the methods were not always successful. For instance, about 1900 many Lancashire mills began to send out their own men and to set up offices in Shanghai. Experience showed, however, that this method of selling cotton textiles was very costly, and the large merchant houses again came into favour as the distributing media for this class of goods. This tendency was confirmed after the financial crisis of 1921–2 when it was seen that the Chinese dealers were much less likely to default on their obligations to an important merchant house, whose connection was very valuable to them, than to some small firm or to the representative of a single foreign manufacturer. A later experiment in the direct selling of cotton textiles was also unsuccessful. In 1927 a number of Lancashire cotton firms formed the Eastern Textile Association to undertake the marketing of standardised cloth in China; but the venture failed chiefly through the losses incurred by the fall in silver during the early years of the world depression. These experiences threw some doubt on the wisdom of the policy of 'eliminating the merchant', and during the thirties a compromise solution of the problem was widely adopted. Manufacturers became accustomed to giving their agencies to general merchants but sent out members of their own staffs to work in the market. This was especially the case with engineering concerns.

The changes in methods of trading that have been described were common to many other countries during this period, and the fact that they appeared in the China trade also is an indication that both commercial and social intercourse between Westerner and Chinese was

[1] T. M. Ainscough's estimate, in *China Association Report*, 1915.

becoming easier than in the past and that China was being drawn within the orbit of the modern world. This may explain the contemporaneous decline of that famous institutional figure, the compradore, who had been called into being by the impact of Western trade upon Chinese society. It will be remembered that in the early years of the nineteenth century the foreign traders of Canton were allowed to deal with the Chinese only through the Hong merchants. When this restriction was abolished in 1842, the Western merchants were able to enter into direct relationships with Chinese dealers of all kinds, and it might have been expected that the type of intermediary represented by the Hong would at once have disappeared. The Hong merchant had, however, played an essential part in the trade relationships between men from such different civilisations as those of China and Europe, and so, when he disappeared from the scene, a substitute had to be found. It may be said that he was transmuted into the compradore who, for three-quarters of a century, occupied a key position in China's foreign trade. The explanation of his importance is not far to seek.

At the beginning of the modern period the number of Chinese who could speak English was small. The Western traders could not speak Chinese; until recent years few of them even tried to learn the language. Moreover, they understood only dimly the exceedingly complex social and commercial structure of China. Financial and commercial dealings in that country have always been closely bound up with personal relationships, and this has made it very difficult for outsiders to move easily in Chinese business circles. It was, therefore, necessary for Western firms to employ an official who understood Chinese commercial practices and had intimate relationships with Chinese business houses. Through him, the compradore, the Western merchant firm made contacts with its Chinese customers and suppliers, and all its transactions with the Chinese passed through his hands.

The compradore was (at least nominally) an employee of the Western firm, although he was paid by commission rather than by a fixed salary. He was responsible for recruiting and supervising all members of the Chinese staff and for guaranteeing their integrity. He attended to the purchases from and the sales to Chinese dealers and he had charge of the credit arrangements with them. Before he was engaged by a foreign firm, he was required to give substantial guarantees in the form of cash or of titles to real estate in the Treaty Ports. Thus he had to possess considerable means. Indeed, he was often as wealthy as his Western employer, and he sometimes engaged in trade on his own account. 'Although nominally servants,' wrote a British consul in 1878, '[compradores] are in reality traders and often partners in large native Hongs, dealing in the same commodities as their masters.'[1] A foreign newspaper in China once described the compradores as being not only the axle on which the whole wheel of the Westerner's business with the Chinese turns, but very often also the hub, spokes and rim, 'in fact, the whole wheel, save the paint, which may be taken to represent the firm which gives it the colour of its name'.[2] This statement was a gross exaggeration so far as the larger Western merchant houses were concerned, but it may well have been true for some of the smaller firms.

The compradore and the foreigner usually enjoyed harmonious relations. Yet the system lent itself to abuse, especially when, as in Hankow during the 1860's, men were taken on as compradores who had neither the necessary personal standing nor adequate resources. A consular report from that city in 1865 refers to 'the dangerous facilities afforded to the Chinese compradores and servants for trading on their employer's credit and capital'.[3] Foreign merchants often sold goods on credit against Chinese bankers' orders which matured in periods that varied from three weeks to three months. The bankers' orders were left until they matured at the disposal of the compradores, who used them to finance transactions on their own account. 'At this moment', the report continued, 'there is not a compradore in the place who is not more or less involved with his employers and amongst the native traders generally.'[4]

Soon complaints were made, not only of abuses, but of the whole compradore system itself. In 1875 the Customs Commissioner at Chefoo spoke of compradores as being antiquated, having 'survived the state of things which brought them into existence'.[5] He recognised that changes would have to be slow, but he urged European merchants to learn at least a smattering of Chinese, for their ignorance of the language remained a leading cause of the survival of what he considered to be an outmoded institution. Three years later the British consul at Kiungchow, Hainan Island, upbraided foreigners for the 'serious want of activity, not to say carelessness', which was clearly demonstrated when 'a leading firm in Hongkong admitted in the Chamber of Commerce that they [were] entirely dependent on the information supplied to them by their Chinese employees'.[6] This consul believed that compradores were superfluous middlemen who extracted a commission whether their employers gained or lost; 'while the foreigner goes into bankruptcy', he said, 'the compradore emerges wealthy and respected'. At

---

[1] *British Consular Trade Report*, Kiungchow, 1878, p. 110.
[2] Quoted in Kuang Yung-Pao's article, 'The Compradore: His Position in the Foreign Trade of China', in the *Economic Journal*, December 1911.
[3] *British Consular Trade Report*, Hankow, 1865, p. 135.
[4] *ibid.*
[5] *Chinese Customs Report*, Chefoo, 1875, p. 78.
[6] *British Consular Trade Report*, Kiungchow, 1878, p. 110.

the end of the century, the Hon. Ho Kai, a Chinese member of the Hongkong Legislative Council, gave his opinion that the compradore certainly made as much profit as the foreign merchant in the import trade.[1] Intermediaries are always unpopular; but it is difficult to believe that the compradore would have survived so long and would have enjoyed such high rewards for his services if he had not performed a valuable function in Sino-European trade. No doubt if the Western firms had been able, from the early days of that trade, to recruit a sufficiently large staff of Europeans well versed in the intricacies of Chinese commercial society, the compradore would not have been necessary; but this condition was not fulfilled during the nineteenth century.

After 1900 the system began to decay. The assumption by foreign manufacturers of direct control over the distributive channels of certain classes of imports excluded the compradore from a growing area of trade, or at least greatly reduced his responsibilities. In the general merchant houses the necessity for his services was lessened through the increase in the number of Chinese who spoke English. Further, from the beginning of the First World War, British firms began to encourage their staff to learn Chinese. Continental Europeans, especially the Germans, had previously shown more energy in the pursuit of linguistic competence than had the British. In 1915, however, the British Chamber of Commerce in Shanghai opened a Chinese language school, and in the following year a similar school was started by the Hongkong General Chamber of Commerce. Attendance at the courses in these schools was not confined to British subjects, and business men of other nationalities took advantage of them. During the inter-war period some Western firms required young members of their staff to attend classes in Chinese and paid bonuses to those who passed examinations. It became customary at that time for foreign firms to employ a few Europeans with a sound knowledge of Chinese to deal directly with their Chinese agents in the interior.[2]

Another factor which helped to reduce the part of the compradore in foreign trade was the growth of the importance of Japanese firms in China. Many of the Japanese were acquainted with the Chinese language, and for this and other reasons were able to establish direct contacts with the Chinese more easily than the Europeans. Consequently they seldom employed compradores. After the First World War the decline in the system was accelerated, and it had almost vanished by the 1930's, except in Hongkong.[3] The compradores who

[1] *British Diplomatic and Consular Reports*, Miscellaneous Series, No. 458. Report of Consul Bourne on the Trade of Central and South China, 1898, p. 94.
[2] We are indebted for this information to Mr. G. Mitchell, Secretary of the China Association, and to Mrs. V. S. Robb, formerly of Hankow.
[3] H. D. Fong, *Cotton Industry and Trade in China*, vol. I, p. 261.

were still employed by Western firms in China Proper had duties more narrowly limited than in the past. Their work was largely confined to giving advice in dealings with Chinese officials and to guaranteeing Chinese employees. They no longer bought and sold on behalf of their employers as in former times.

The result of these changes was that between 1919 and 1937 the organisation of foreign business in China and the relations between the Western merchants and their Chinese customers and suppliers assumed a form which corresponded much more closely than in earlier times to those regarded as normal in the West. As was to be expected, moreover, Chinese firms with an organisation modelled on that of the West came into being, and their methods of doing business followed the Western pattern. Some of them built up their own connections with foreign countries and carried on the whole business of importing and exporting. For instance, in 1929 there were in Canton four Chinese firms which conducted a direct trade with Europe and America, and, between them, were responsible for from 15 to 20 per cent of the exports from that city.[1] Nevertheless, the bulk of China's foreign trade was still conducted through British, American, Japanese and other foreign firms in the chief ports, with the British well in the van.[2] Five years later this still remained true, although the share handled by Chinese firms was steadily increasing.[3] By this time, however, the distinction between Chinese and Western concerns was less sharply drawn than formerly. During the twenties and thirties it became increasingly common for Chinese to be taken into partnership, or to be appointed directors in foreign firms; while Chinese shareholding in companies technically alien also increased. All this was additional evidence of the extent to which China was being drawn into the Western economic system.

During the decade before the outbreak of the Second World War the most significant innovation was the establishment of trading corporations by the Chinese Government. Some of these enjoyed monopolistic privileges. Concerns such as the China Vegetable Oil Corporation and the China Silk Corporation were just becoming important trading bodies when the Sino-Japanese War broke out in July 1937. Western merchants in China naturally regarded the activities of these Government corporations with misgivings. They were threatened, too, by the growing tendency of the Chinese Government to deal directly with overseas manufacturers; this practice was followed, for instance, in the purchase of goods from the funds of the remitted Boxer Indemnity.

---

[1] United Kingdom, Department of Overseas Trade, *Report on Economic Conditions in China*, to September 1929, p. 41.
[2] *ibid.*, to August 1930, p. 6.
[3] *ibid.*, 1933–5, p. vi.

Inter-governmental barter trade between China and Germany also made its appearance, and encroached upon business formerly conducted by merchant houses. Thus, even before the war let loose calamity on the China trade, the Western merchants were facing a contraction in their spheres of opportunity.

CHAPTER III

THE ORGANISATION OF THE
EXPORT TRADE: TEA AND SILK

FOR a full realisation of the part played by foreign merchants in the initiation and conduct of China's foreign trade, the generalised account given in the previous chapter needs to be supplemented by particular description. No attempt will be made, however, to provide a detailed history of the several trades, for the intention is merely to bring to light the diversity of methods employed while at the same time establishing the broad similarity of the problems that confronted the foreign merchant engaged in various lines of business. We shall concern ourselves, first, with a number of representative export commodities, and second, with a few of the leading imports. It is natural to begin with tea, the commodity which made up the bulk of China's exports to Europe before the modern era and continued to occupy an important place among them until recent times. The trade fell into two distinct sections, the leaf-tea trade which was mainly with Europe and the United States, and the brick-tea trade, which was almost exclusively with Russia. These sections will be treated separately since they were differently organised.

1. The Tea Trade with Western Europe and America

The export trade in leaf tea was built upon a great internal trade of ancient origin, and tea culture in China continued, even after a large export had been created, to be directed primarily towards supplying the home market. Furthermore, the establishment by foreigners of tea plantations was ruled out by the prohibition on the foreign ownership of land outside the Treaty Ports. These two conditions largely determine the rôle of the foreigners in this trade. They were precluded from organising the production of tea on a large scale (as they were able to do in India and Ceylon), and since the exports formed only a small part of the total supply, the foreigners could not exert as strong an influence upon the methods of production, treatment and sale of tea as in the case of goods produced primarily for export. The great distance that separated the tea-growing regions from the Treaty Ports was an additional reason why foreign influence over the organisation of tea production was comparatively weak. Yet the effect of these conditions must not be exaggerated, for, as we shall see, the foreign merchant was able at least to modify Chinese trade practices and certain methods of production and treatment. His inability to re-mould the trade, however, left him with a more narrowly limited rôle than in many other lines of business, and the ultimate decline in China's tea export, in the face of competition from elsewhere, can be attributed in part to this fact.

The foreigners did not, of course, willingly accept this limitation of their functions. The prohibition of the foreign ownership of land was circumvented in a few localities and a certain number of tea plantations were established by foreigners, as at Tamsui in Formosa in 1877, at Foochow by the Sino-British Foochow Tea Company at the end of the century, and at Amoy a few years later.[1] None of these ventures survived for long, however, and the attempts by foreigners to undertake the processes of treatment preparatory to sale were equally unsuccessful. This was true even of North Formosa, where the cultivation of tea began as a direct result of the opening of a Treaty Port at Tamsui. There the firing and packing of tea were, at the inception of the trade, undertaken by British firms; but about 1872 the Chinese took up these processes and gradually ousted the British firms.[2] This was in contrast with the practice in Japan where the leaf was usually sold to the foreign merchants before the preparatory processes had been completed.

The normal practice was for the foreign merchant to buy the tea from Chinese dealers at the ports and, except for the Russians, it was rare for the foreigners to go into the country districts to make their purchases. Between the export merchant and the Chinese peasant cultivator there was usually a long chain of intermediaries, though the number of these probably varied in different times and in different regions. B. P. Torgasheff, an authority on the tea trade, stated in 1926 that the tea often passed through ten middlemen between the grower and the exporter, and that a picul of tea bought in Anhwei for $1.50 (Mex.) sold for $14 (Mex.) at Shanghai.[3] This statement was borne out by a British observer in the late 1930's. The small cultivator usually undertook the preliminary drying of the tea and then sold it to a Chinese dealer, who manufactured it before disposing of it to a Chinese Hong for ultimate sale to a foreigner at the ports.

It does not appear that the foreigners normally played an important part in financing the trade before the tea actually came into their possession; but the practice varied from time to time and according to the type of foreign merchant engaged in the trade. Thus, consignments of tea were sometimes financed either by foreign merchants or by foreign and Chinese banks before their arrival at the ports. At Foochow, for instance, it seems to have been the custom during the eighties for

[1] *British Consular Trade Report*, Tamsui and Keelung, 1877, p. 146; *British Diplomatic and Consular Reports on Trade*, No. 1907, Foochow, 1896, p. 9; Foochow, No. 2072, 1897, p. 16; Foochow, No. 2243, 1898, p. 12; Amoy, No. 3066, 1902, p. 5.
[2] *Chinese Customs Report*, Tamsui, 1875, p. 209; 1876, p. 91.
[3] B. P. Torgasheff, *China as a Tea Producer*, p. 80.

foreigners to make advances to their compradores and tea brokers for up-country purchases,[1] and there is evidence that in 1869 foreign banks at the port gave credit for this purpose.[2] But in some centres Western firms were accustomed to settling their accounts with the sellers only once a year,[3] and in the opinion of a British merchant with a long experience in the trade, the amount of credit given by Chinese tea dealers to foreign exporters exceeded the amount given by the latter to the former. This was in sharp contrast to the practice in other commodities, especially those in which the export trade did not rest on the foundation of a large and long-established home trade.

Although the influence of the foreign merchants on the organisation of the trade was restricted, they were impelled to do what they could to remove its worst defects. They tried to instruct the Chinese cultivators and dealers in improved methods of preparation. For example, in 1890 Russian and British merchants in Hankow sent skilled agents to the Chinese tea firms in the country districts to teach them how to select leaves, and fire them so as to produce tea suitable for the Russian market.[4] But the influence was usually indirect. It was exercised chiefly by insistence upon standards of quality and by vigorous complaints whenever adulteration was found. For instance, the United States Customs Regulations about quality were made known to the Chinese dealers through the foreign buyers at the ports. Improved methods of packing were also introduced at the instance of the foreigners; in the 1930's Jardine Matheson made a formal request to the Government Bureau of Testing and Examining that effective means should be taken to improve tea packing-cases, and this had a considerable effect.[5]

While foreign enterprise did not penetrate very deeply into the internal organisation of the tea trade, it long remained without serious challenge in the actual business of exports. This was true both in the period when the trade was in the hands of the 'princely hongs' which, as successors to the East India Company, bought and sold on their own account and assumed all the risks of the market, and also in the later years of the nineteenth century when a share of the business passed into the hands of the smaller commission houses which bought on behalf of merchants in Europe and America and borrowed their working capital from the foreign banks in China. Until the 1930's foreign enterprise remained almost entirely responsible for the finance, organisation and transport of the tea from the time of its purchase at the ports until it was sold on the London tea market or elsewhere. The work of sales promotion was exclusively in foreign hands, and for many

[1] *Chinese Customs Report*, Foochow, 1865.
[2] *British Consular Trade Report*, Foochow, 1869, p. 76.
[3] *ibid.*, Shanghai, 1878, p. 18.
[4] *British Diplomatic and Consular Reports on Trade*, No. 888, Hankow, 1890, p. 11.
[5] T. H. Chu, *Tea Trade in Central China*, p. 26 and pp. 241–2.

years representatives of the leading exporting houses made annual tours in the United Kingdom, the continent of Europe and North America to solicit orders.

Efforts of the Chinese to obtain a share of this export business, either in partnership with foreigners or independently, were not lacking even in the early years of the modern period. Thus, about 1853 tea exports from Foochow began through 'the enterprise of an American merchant in alliance with Chinese'.[1] In 1864 large shipments from Foochow and elsewhere by Chinese firms were sent on consignment to Britain, and these Chinese were said to have made a profit at a time when the foreign merchants were losing money.[2] Again, in 1880 there is evidence of tea being shipped from Foochow 'entirely on Chinese account'.[3] These instances were, however, exceptional during the nineteenth century in spite of the predictions that Chinese would soon supersede Westerners in the tea trade; and this was to be expected for the Chinese were seriously handicapped in their efforts to gain control of a substantial share of the exports. Whereas the Chinese had to pay very high rates of interest to the native banks in order to finance export shipments, the foreigners had access to credit at low rates. Moreover, the latter were naturally more familiar than the Chinese with the taste and the market technique of Western countries, and this was an important advantage in a business which depended for its success upon skilful mixing and blending.

Even in the twentieth century, Chinese attempts to enter the export trade had little more success than in earlier times. Two examples may be quoted. The China Tea Company Ltd. was established in 1914, and twenty years later it claimed to be 'the oldest Chinese firm engaged in the production and marketing of tea which deals directly with foreign countries'.[4] Though it survived, its business was never very large. Again, at Ningpo some Chinese merchants embarked upon the export of green tea to the United States, but they lost heavily as their product failed to conform to the standards of quality demanded by the American Customs Regulations, and in 1926, after the failure of this venture, the whole of the tea exporting business of Ningpo reverted to foreign merchants.[5] During the 1930's the Chinese Government began to participate in the tea trade as in several others. It sponsored the establishment of the National Tea Corporation in the hope of ousting both the Chinese and foreign exporters. Soon after the outbreak of the war with Japan in 1937 this corporation made large contracts with the Russian Government for the sale of tea. Nevertheless, such tea as could

[1] A. Michie, *The Englishman in China*, vol. I, p. 121.
[2] *British Consular Trade Report*, Foochow, 1864, p. 82.
[3] *Chinese Customs Report*, Foochow, 1880, p. 179.
[4] Advertisement in the *China Press Special Supplement*, 10 October 1936.
[5] B. P. Torgasheff, *China as a Tea Producer*, p. 40.

subsequently be procured for the markets of Europe and America continued to be supplied mainly by Western firms.

From about 1870 the export of tea entered upon a long period of decline which has persisted until today, and a discussion of the causes of this decline may throw further light on the organisation of the trade. The Chinese nationalists naturally found a scapegoat in the foreign merchant, who was accused both of abusing his key position in the export trade and also of a lack of enterprise in introducing efficient modern methods of organisation. Thus, a student of the tea trade wrote: 'Being aware of the commanding influence they hold over the tea exportation of Hankow, the foreign firms lose no chance to devalue the tea leaf internationally. The former price of the Lao Ch'a leaf was 600 cash per catty, but it was reduced to half that price. . . . The devaluation has been intensified since the establishment of the Centro-sojus, for the Soviet agency purchases directly from the planter on a large scale. The market price of the leaf is thus entirely controlled without any redress.'[1] This criticism does not make sense. It is apparently argued that the foreign merchants had a monopsonistic control over the Hankow market whereas, in fact, the foreigners competed fiercely among themselves, and the tea which they bought for export formed only a small proportion of the total supply. If the charge of 'devaluing the tea leaf internationally' means that the foreign merchants deliberately set out to reduce the world market price of China tea, then the answer is that such a policy would be of no advantage to them unless the price elasticity of demand were high, and in that case the tea producers themselves would benefit from the larger sales. Since, however, the exporters of China tea were competitive not only among themselves but also with the tea companies of India, Ceylon and Java, they certainly lacked the power to control the world price.

The charge that the trade was conducted inefficiently and that this was the main cause of its decline deserves more serious attention. It was based on the supposition that the number of middlemen was excessive, and it was argued that the foreigners had made few efforts to eliminate the superfluous dealers even though this would have meant a reduction in the cost of the tea at the ports. This charge is not confined to Chinese critics. For instance, the British consul at Foochow in 1889 argued that foreigners could bring down costs by learning Chinese, buying tea direct from the farmers and bringing it down to the ports under transit passes.[2] It was observed that the Russians for their part conducted much of their business in this way.

It is doubtful whether the criticism amounts to more than saying that

[1] T. H. Chu, *op. cit.*, p. 232.
[2] *British Consular Trade Report*, Foochow, 1889, p. 9. A reference to the commercial importance of learning Chinese appears on p. 49, *supra*.

the British merchants accepted the organisation of this trade as they found it, for within the framework of Chinese trading methods and conventions there is no convincing evidence of a superfluity of middlemen. Even if the foreigners had been prepared to offend Chinese public opinion against the 'breaking of rice bowls', it is debatable whether, for reasons already given, they had the power to effect a thorough reorganisation of the industry. To have bought direct from the growers or from local Chinese merchants would have meant the large-scale use of transit passes, and this was apt to arouse the opposition of provincial Chinese authorities. The example of the Russians is pertinent; but the Russian trade was smaller and did not involve long-distance transport to the nearest Treaty Port. Direct trade, moreover, would have been far more expensive for the British than the Russians because of the higher salaries of British employees. If one accepts the charge that, judged from the standards of the West, the organisation of the tea trade was inefficient, the explanation must be sought chiefly in the political and legal obstacles placed in the path of Western enterprise in its efforts to overcome the deficiencies in Chinese business organisation. These obstacles were surmounted in some trades, but in the tea trade the conditions were relatively unfavourable.

Enterprising Chinese achieved no more success than foreigners in this respect. Thus, in 1915, the Chinese Government made an attempt to develop a plantation industry, a type of undertaking from which, as we have seen, foreigners were excluded. Model tea plantations were organised in the Kimun district of Anhwei. The experiment depended, however, on the initiative and energy of the Minister of Agriculture, Chow Tze-Chin. On his fall from office this enterprise collapsed.[1] Privately owned Chinese plantations were discouraged by the insecurity that attached to conspicuous possessions in China, while the high rate of interest obtainable for commercial loans meant that little capital was available for agricultural or industrial investment. About 1919 the Ningchow Tea Plantation Company was established and produced some good quality tea, but it remained small and had no imitators.[2]

For China tea to have retained its hold on world markets, in the absence of a plantation system organised on a large scale, some central directing authority charged with the maintenance of standards of quality would probably have been essential. In Japan this authority was supplied by the Government and the larger exporting firms, and for this reason Japanese tea displaced Chinese tea in the American market where they were once rivals.[3] Over the greater part of this period, however, the Chinese Government was unprepared to accept responsibility even for maintaining law and order, and was far from competent to impose

---

[1] B. P. Torgasheff, *China as a Tea Producer*, p. 85.   [2] *ibid.*, pp. 86–7.
[3] *See* pp. 200–1, 226–7, *infra*.

regulations of this sort even if it had considered their enactment a proper function of government.

It may well be that even if institutional influences had been favourable, China would have lost ground to India and other countries in world markets. The tea-growing districts of China had insufficient rainfall to yield as high an output per acre as those in the competing countries, and the growing season was too short to justify investment in modern machinery and the employment of a permanent labour force. Without these it would have been difficult for China to have produced very large supplies of tea of a uniform quality such as were needed if the competition of other suppliers was to be met. Furthermore, there was a change of taste, especially in the all-important British market. So China tea maintained its position only in countries where standardised quality was less essential than in Great Britain, and where green tea was still preferred, as in North Africa. It would be fruitless to speculate on what might have happened if the China tea trade had been faced only with these technical difficulties; but it cannot be doubted that the institutional causes made an important contribution to its decline.

2. The Tea Trade with Russia and Central Asia

Tea compressed into brick-like slabs had been sent from China to Russian Central Asia by the overland route long before the modern era. This trade was entirely in the hands of Chinese merchants until 1863 when Russian tea merchants settled in Hankow.[1] The Russians soon came to control the trade in leaf tea to Russia and also learned how to prepare the bricks which were made from the dust and residue of the leaf and were in demand in Central Asia. Within a few years they surpassed the Chinese in the art, and by 1866 all the brick tea that passed through Tientsin on its way to Siberia was being made by the Russians or under their supervision.[2] This included even the considerable quantities of tea still sent on Chinese account.[3]

While the Western European merchants left the internal organisation of the tea trade largely as they found it, the Russians, far from accommodating themselves to the Chinese methods of manufacturing and handling, entirely transformed the structure of the tea trade in which they were engaged and assumed control even of its early stages. In the first place, they adopted the practice of buying their leaf directly from the peasant grower, and for this they were sometimes held up as an example to the British traders.[4] Russian firms frequently made contracts for the produce while the tea was still on the bush.[5] In the second place

[1] *Chinese Customs Decennial Report*, 1882–91, Hankow, p. 172.
[2] *British Consular Trade Report*, Tientsin, 1868, p. 165.
[3] Baron Richthofen, *Letters 1870–1872*, p. 122.
[4] *British Consular Trade Report*, Shanghai, 1875, p. 25.
[5] B. P. Torgasheff, *China as a Tea Producer*, p. 11.

the Russians not merely undertook the manufacturing process but were also able to devise a new technique for producing the brick. At the outset they had modelled themselves on the Chinese tea merchants and had set up hand presses in the tea-growing districts. Early in the seventies, however, they introduced steam-driven apparatus and built factories in Hankow to house it. This enabled them to close their country establishments and to centralise the process of manufacture.[1] In 1875 two brick-tea factories were being operated at Hankow. A contemporary report states that one of the factories, 'the machinery of which was devised by Mr. Cherepanoff himself, has been a perfect success, and great things are expected of the more elaborate machinery of the other, designed and sent out from England, when it has got properly into working order'.[2] These were substantial ventures. Each factory required an investment of between one and two million silver dollars[3] and workers had to be attracted from a distance by the offer of high wages.[4] The greater efficiency of the mechanised process, however, more than compensated for the additional expense. While a hand press could turn out sixty 'baskets' (each containing a set number of bricks) with a wastage rate of 25 per cent, a steam press could make eighty similar 'baskets' a day with a wastage of only 5 per cent. The saving brought about by the use of the mechanical method was said to be one tael a 'basket'.[5] There is a reference to the employment of a Scottish engineer at one of these factories.[6] Other brick-tea factories were opened by the Russians at Foochow and Kiukiang, but they were not as large as those at Hankow.

The striking contrast between the Russians and the Western Europeans in their methods of conducting the tea trade can be variously explained. During the seventies a British consul attributed the success of the Russians to their adaptability to Chinese ways and to the vigorous protection afforded to them by their Government.[7] A more important cause was that whereas the leaf-tea exports represented only a small proportion of the total output, the brick tea was produced almost entirely for export, and so the trade was more susceptible to foreign methods of organising it. The process of manufacturing brick tea also lent itself more easily to mechanisation than that required for preparing leaf tea for the market. It has already been suggested that so far as direct contact with the growers was concerned the lower salary scale of the Russians compared with that of Western Europeans was doubtless

---

[1] *Chinese Customs Report*, Hankow, 1876, p. 22.
[2] *British Consular Trade Report*, Hankow, 1875, p. 46.
[3] T. H. Chu, *op. cit.*, p. 210.
[4] *Chinese Customs Report*, Hankow, 1877, p. 15.
[5] *ibid.*, Hankow, 1878, p. 43.
[6] J. Walton, *China and the Present Crisis*, p. 125; and S. Townley, *My Chinese Notebook*, p. 208.
[7] *British Consular Trade Report*, Shanghai, 1875, p. 28.

an important factor; but the possibility that the Russians were more enterprising than the Western merchants cannot be dismissed.

The Russian success gave rise to imitators among the Chinese. In 1906 some Chinese business men from Kwangtung and Fukien set up a brick-tea factory at Hankow on the Russian model.[1] This concern, the Hsin Sang Brick Tea Manufacturing Company, originally had a capital of 250,000 taels and was evidently smaller than its foreign counterparts.[2]

The introduction of mechanised methods, together with improvements in transport, led to a marked increase in the volume of brick-tea exports to Russia during a period in which sales of China's leaf tea to the West were falling. No figures are available to show the amount of tea which the Chinese merchants used to send by the ancient caravan routes before the factories were opened. It is, however, safe to say that it cannot have been nearly as much as the 255,000 piculs dispatched to the Russian Empire from Hankow alone in 1891. In 1915 the export of brick tea exceeded 600,000 piculs.[3]

This flourishing trade was disrupted by the Russian Revolution. At that time there were four brick-tea factories at Hankow, three Russian and one Chinese, and in good years each of them produced at least 100,000 'baskets' of bricks.[4] The Revolution cut off the main market and practically destroyed the industry. One of the Russian factories adapted itself to the press packing of miscellaneous goods, and another passed for some years into the hands of a British tea merchant firm.[5] This factory and the Hsin Sang factory operated intermittently until 1930 when it again became possible to make regular shipments to Russia. All these, however, had to be made through the Hankow branch of Centrosojus, the Soviet buying agency established at Shanghai.

3. Raw Silk

The export of silk provides another example of an ancient trade which was greatly expanded during the nineteenth century as a result of the initiative of foreigners, but later stagnated in the face of competition from elsewhere. The Western merchants succeeded up to a point in improving the quality of the Chinese product so as to render it acceptable in Western markets, and for a time they and the Chinese silk merchants and producers were rewarded by a large increase in the volume of trade. But the Westerners lacked the power to insist upon

[1] T. H. Chu, *op. cit.*, p. 205.
[2] *ibid.*, p. 211.
[3] B. P. Torgasheff, *China as a Tea Producer*, p. 14.
[4] T. H. Chu, *op. cit.*, p. 221.
[5] Contrary to statements by T. H. Chu, Harrisons, King and Irwin really did control this factory for some years and did not merely give it the protection of their name.

the drastic changes in methods and organisation that later became necessary if Chinese silk were to hold its own in competition with the well-organised Japanese trade, and there was no Chinese authority which could do what was required.

The raw silk exported from China to the West during the past century was of two distinct types. The first was the traditional type of silk produced from worms fed on mulberry leaves, and this came from Central and South China. The second type, tussore or pongee silk, came from North China and was produced from silkworms fed on oak leaves. In addition, an export trade in waste silk was built up. Throughout our period the bulk of the export trade in all these products was in the hands of foreign traders, and the references to occasional Chinese participation serve only to emphasise the predominance of the former. For example, it was recorded in 1870 that certain Chinese merchants were then shipping silk on their own account; but the commodity was inferior silk which the foreign merchants had rejected. This provoked a wry consular comment on Chinese activities in the trade: '. . . the goods being wholly unadapted to the foreign markets, great losses inevitably ensue; whereupon the Chinese exporter jumps to the conclusion that he has been cheated by his foreign agents, and . . . forthwith repudiates the whole transaction'.[1] It is true that certain Chinese filature owners had some success in operating an export trade through agents at the Treaty Ports. Thus, producers of pongee in Shantung managed to build up an export trade in their product by appointing special exporting agents at Hongkong and other ports, and according to a Chinese authority direct exportation through Chefoo and Tsingtao became the rule in the nineties.[2] Yet, as late as 1934, it seems that the export of Cantonese raw silk was entirely controlled by foreign firms,[3] and at most periods these predominated even in the pongee trade.

The foreign firms were of various types. Some were general merchants, such as Jardine Matheson; others were specialists in silk. Many of the latter were branches of silk houses in Europe or the United States; for the manufacturers of Lyons found advantage in setting up purchasing establishments in China so as to ensure the quality of their supplies. One of the most striking examples of the close contacts established by the foreigners with the Chinese sources of supply was provided by Debenham and Company, the London retail store. This company opened a buying branch for silk fabrics at Chefoo in 1915 and immediately afterwards pongee exports from that centre nearly trebled.[4]

In the early years of the modern era the foreign merchant usually bought the silk for export from Chinese dealers in the ports. Later the

[1] *British Consular Trade Report*, Shanghai, 1870, p. 13.
[2] D. K. Lieu, *China's Industry and Finance*, p. 227.
[3] *Chinese Economic Journal*, October 1934, p. 381.
[4] *Chinese Customs Report*, Chefoo, 1915, p. 360.

scope of their activities was extended in two directions, first, through their search for new geographical sources of supply, and, second, through their efforts to overcome the defects in the Chinese product. Originally the main source of supply was Canton, but in the sixties pongee silk from Shantung was introduced into foreign markets through the enterprise of the foreigners. It was not only foreign merchants who were active in discovering new sources of supply, for the initiative often proceeded from customs officials and consuls. For instance, it was a British consul at Newchwang who first drew attention to the possibilities of trade in the tussore silk of that district, and 'through his instrumentality worms and cocoons were sent to Shanghai to the Chamber of Commerce and subsequently to Lyons'.[1] Again, a British consul at Ichang was responsible for introducing in 1893 samples of Ichang silk to a British firm at Shanghai.[2]

Foreign merchants soon found that if the silk exports were to increase, it was necessary not merely to extend the geographical scope of their purchasing operations but also to concern themselves with the organisation and technique of silk production. Even in the days of the Canton Cohong, the foreigners had complained of the quality of Chinese raw silk. These complaints became more vociferous as the silk manufacturing trade in Europe and America became increasingly mechanised, for the mechanised processes could only be successful if silk of a uniform quality were provided. Even the careful application of the results of scientific research and skilful organisation have been only partially successful in satisfying this condition in the Japanese silk trade of the twentieth century. The Chinese were never noted for a capacity to produce large supplies of any commodity to a uniform quality, and in silk production, which necessarily takes place in small units, the problem was especially troublesome. If improvements were to be effected the foreigners had to interest themselves in the two main stages of the industry, cocoon production and reeling. Cocoon production was naturally difficult to organise, for it occurs in peasant households widely dispersed over areas where supplies of mulberry leaves are available. In Japan, where the problem was firmly and efficiently tackled, improvements in the quality of the cocoons was brought about through the institution of a system of controls over silkworm eggs. Suppliers of eggs were licensed and had to satisfy official standards of quality, and silk raisers were obliged to obtain their eggs from these licensed producers. This system, however, depended on the existence of a government alert in economic affairs and administratively competent. It could not be contemplated in China. So, in the absence of any system in the selecting

[1] *British Consular Trade Report*, Newchwang, 1872, p. 82, and *Chinese Customs Special Series*, No. 3: Silk, 1881. Report from Newchwang, p. 11.
[2] *British Consular Trade Report*, Ichang, 1883, p. 282.

and grading of eggs, the cocoons lacked uniformity and were often diseased.

The foreigners made attempts to eliminate these troubles and until very recent times it was only they who concerned themselves with the problem. Customs officials were among the first to be active in this field. For instance, in 1880 the customs officials of Ningpo, after inquiries into the local silk industry, drew up a scheme to eradicate the prevailing silkworm disease.[1] The Inspector General of Customs presented this scheme to the *Tsungli Yamen*[2] and, according to the British consular report of 1895, was '. . . instrumental in introducing into China the Pasteur system of treating diseased silkworms'.[3] In the middle nineties the Chekiang provincial authorities opened a school of sericulture and employed Japanese teachers. This institution produced good cocoons, and eggs supplied by it were widely distributed.[4] Yet these and similar efforts touched only the fringe of the problem, and little permanent improvement was achieved.

The extent of China's failure to deal with this problem was brought out in the findings of the International Committee for the Improvement of Sericulture in China. This body, which was set up in 1917 and given a grant from the Government, consisted both of Chinese official and private members and also of foreigners, among whom were representatives of the French, British, American and Japanese Chambers of Commerce in Shanghai.[5] In the course of its work the committee tried to spread the use of Pasteur methods and distributed eggs from France and Italy.[6] According to its judgment the proportion of diseased silkworm eggs need not be more than 8 to 12 per cent, and yet in 1930 the actual proportion was put at 75 to 80 per cent. During the 1930's governmental activity in this field became more systematic. Experimental stations for the improvement of cocoon production were set up by the Kiangsu Provincial Government,[7] and in 1934 the National Economic Council established the Sericulture Improvement Commission to deal with the problem on a national scale. This was to be regarded as a striking innovation, for, as Dr. Mari (a sericulture expert sent to China by the League of Nations) declared, in the past 'no systematic attempt [had] been made either to select or to improve the best varieties of silkworms'.[8] But the attempt came too late. In 1930 the world

[1] *Chinese Customs Decennial Report*, 1882–91, Ningpo, p. 382.
[2] Ministry of Foreign Affairs.
[3] *British Diplomatic and Consular Reports on Trade*, No. 1803, China, 1895, p. 26.
[4] *ibid.*, No. 2449, Hangchow, 1899, p. 15.
[5] H. M. Vinacke, 'Obstacles to Industrial Development in China', *Annals of the American Academy of Political and Social Science*, November 1930.
[6] *Chinese Economic Monthly*, October 1924. The introduction of foreign eggs was sharply criticised in 1935 by Dr. Mari, a sericulture expert sent to China by the League of Nations. He held that the introduction of Japanese eggs had lowered the quality of the Chinese silkworm.
[7] *North China Herald*, 3 February 1931.   [8] *ibid.*, 17 July 1935.

market for raw silk had entered upon a long period of depression, and before the end of the decade production was reduced further, first through the outbreak of war, and later through the successful competition of synthetic fibres, especially nylon.

The importance to the export trade of a high-quality standardised product obliged the foreign merchant to interest himself not merely in the methods of cocoon production but also in the reeling process and in the conditioning of the raw silk itself. Attempts by foreigners to improve reeling methods began very early in the history of the trade. A historian of the American silk industry makes the following reference to these: 'By 1840 the situation had become so unbearable that an important effort was made to secure the better preparation of the Chinese silk for the market. It had been wound by hand from stationary bamboo sticks up to that time, a most primitive and unhappy method. Improved reels, comprising a winding frame moved by a crank and one or two other improvements, were sent to China. Samuel W. Goodridge of Hartford, Connecticut, sent ten of these reels and A. A. Low of New York sent sixteen of them. Instructions were also forwarded as to re-reeling the fibre and assorting the sizes.'[1] The Chinese refused to make use of this equipment, although, as may be inferred from a reference to the next attempt at improvement, it had some influence on their own technique. In 1853 John T. Walker, a prominent New York silk importer, went to China for the purpose of improving methods. He noticed that the reeled silks from Canton were better than those from Shanghai and sent some Shanghai bales to Canton to be re-reeled. 'As the Canton reels were built on the American idea, Mr. Walker sent both reels and reelers to Shanghai to introduce the new style. The first re-reeled silk reached New York in 1854. The lesson was not well learned, however, for the silk soon deteriorated and the importation soon ceased.'[2] These efforts on the part of foreigners continued throughout the century, and not all of them failed. For example, the improvement in the quality of Manchurian tussore silk and the consequent rise in its export during the eighties were attributed 'to the greater care given to the rearing of the worm and to the instruction given by foreign experts on the proper methods of reeling cocoons'.[3] Again, it was reported in 1898 that a foreign firm at Chungking was trying to persuade the local producers to alter their style of reeling and of making up skeins so as to render the product more suitable for the French market.[4]

The most effective way of getting the silk properly reeled was for the

[1] F. R. Mason, *The American Silk Industry and the Tariff*, p. 15.
[2] *ibid.*, p. 16.
[3] *British Consular Trade Report*, Shanghai, 1887, p. 8.
[4] *British Diplomatic and Consular Reports on Trade*, No. 2249, Chungking, 1898, p. 8.

foreigners to assume control of the reeling process, and there are numerous references in consular reports and elsewhere during the sixties, seventies and early eighties to the establishment of foreign filatures. Although the evidence about them is conflicting in many particulars, what emerges very clearly is that they all encountered serious difficulties. Chinese who were likely to be adversely affected by more efficient reeling methods were hostile to the foreign filatures, and they placed obstacles in the way of an adequate supply of cocoons. Very few skilled workers were available, and there were marketing problems attending the sale on the European market of what was virtually a new product, namely Chinese steam filature silk. So formidable were these difficulties that most of the early filatures had only a short life. One of the earliest of these ventures was that of Ezra R. Goodridge and Company, an American firm of silk and ribbon manufacturers, which opened a branch in China in 1867 and later set up a filature.[1] If we may identify this filature with that mentioned by the British consul in Shanghai in 1872 as having been established a few years previously, we can conclude that its experience was typical of that of foreign enterprise in this industry during that period. 'The innovation', wrote the consul, 'met with so much opposition from the Chinese middlemen and people who would, through its adoption, be thrown out of work, that the enterprising foreigners who have set up the machinery were unable to obtain a supply of cocoons at anything like reasonable rates.'[2] The result was that this filature went out of production for some time. According to a Chinese customs publication of 1881, two filatures had been opened by foreigners in Shanghai during the sixties. One of these operated for five years, from 1861 to 1866. The other, set up in 1866, survived for only a few months after which its machinery was sent to Japan. The British consul in Shanghai in 1876 regarded these attempts to introduce foreign reeling methods as having had such negligible effects as to lead him to say that 'no steps whatever' had been taken to introduce European style filatures into China in striking contrast with what had been done in Japan.[3]

During the next few years several new filatures were set up, and these had a more successful existence. One was started by an American firm in 1878 and two others in 1882 by British firms, including the Ewo filature of Jardine Matheson.[4] Together these employed several hundred Chinese workers; they used the same processes as those found in France and Italy; and their managers declared them to be 'in competition with similar establishments in those countries and not with the

[1] F. R. Mason, op. cit., p. 16.
[2] British Consular Trade Report, Shanghai, 1872, p. 145.
[3] ibid., Shanghai, 1876, p. 16.
[4] H. D. Fong, 'China's Silk Reeling Industry', Monthly Bulletin on Economic China, December 1934, p. 492. 'Ewo' is Jardine Matheson's Chinese name.

native industry'.[1] Their product was much more uniform than ordinary Chinese silk, but they had the usual difficulties in getting supplies of cocoons, and it was not long before one of them had to close and the others had to reduce their output.[2]

During this period a few filatures were established by Chinese and by Anglo-Chinese concerns. It was the practice to employ European managers in all of them, and skilled workmen from the Rhône Valley were brought out to provide the nucleus of the labour force.[3] Yet, in the eighties, this industry continued to meet with serious difficulties and its output remained very small. Thus in 1891 foreign-owned filatures were responsible for only 1,500 bales of raw silk out of the total of 61,000 bales of raw silk exported from Shanghai.[4] Four years later it was reported that filature silk represented only a quarter of Chinese silk exports; the remainder was hand-reeled silk. From that time onwards, however, the filature industry expanded rapidly. By 1901 there were twenty-eight filatures in Shanghai[5] and three at Foochow. Most of them were owned by Chinese, although some of them still employed European (usually Italian) managers. In 1911, of the twenty-five filatures in Shanghai, only five were owned by Europeans,[6] and the majority of the new mills established during the great expansion of the industry that took place during the First World War were Chinese-owned. Most of these Chinese filatures were financed by syndicates and were quite small with an average capital of about $50,000 (Mex.). Their owners sold the silk through brokers, who often had a financial interest in them, to the foreign exporters, and they depended heavily on advances from the Chinese native banks which were also interested in the marketing of the cocoons. By the early thirties most of the silk exports from China consisted of filature silk, although hand-reeled silk still predominated in the domestic market.

The spread of filatures meant an improvement in the average quality of the silk. In 1901 a Customs Report stated: 'The quality of the silk of the best marks produced by filatures under European supervision is said to compare favourably with anything produced in France or Italy, although it is apt to be more mixed and consequently will not wind so well. The product of the Japan filatures, which are the chief competitors of China, has not quite the same strength of thread.'[7] Whether or not this is a correct judgment of the relative qualities of Chinese and Japanese silk, there is no doubt that by this time the latter had secured

[1] *British Consular Trade Report*, Shanghai, 1878, p. 24.
[2] *ibid.*, Shanghai, 1884, p. 227.
[3] A. R. Colquhoun, *op. cit.*, p. 28.
[4] *British Diplomatic and Consular Reports on Trade*, No. 1101, Shanghai, 1891, p. 13.
[5] *Chinese Customs Decennial Report*, Shanghai, 1892–1901, p. 511.
[6] J. Dautremer, *La Grande Artère de la Chine: Le Yangtseu*, p. 66.
[7] *Chinese Customs Decennial Report*, Shanghai, 1892–1901, p. 511.

an ascendancy in the world markets. This was confirmed after the First World War, and in 1930 while China's exports of silk amounted to £13·5 million[1] Japan's were £42·5 million.[2] For a time it seemed as if the Japanese might play a considerable part in the Chinese silk trade. For instance, in 1917 they established a large filature in Shantung, where there was then only one other filature in existence. This Japanese filature, however, did not depend on local supplies of cocoons, but imported cocoons from Japan. It was the cheapness of Chinese labour that attracted this enterprise; but its subsequent development was thwarted by political troubles.

During the early years of the present century machinery was not only applied to the production of filament but was also used in spinning waste silk. This product had previously been used for caulking vessels for it was difficult to turn it into a satisfactory yarn by manual methods. Machine spinning, however, enabled the waste silk to be put to good use, and a substantial export trade in the commodity grew up.[3] This is another example of how commercial intercourse with communities with superior technical equipment raised the value of China's products. The foreigners also took the initiative in arranging for the testing of silk. One venture of this kind was started in the eighties. At that time foreign demand for Canton silk was adversely affected by its high moisture content and by its consequent liability to mildew. Some of the chief exporters, therefore, opened a conditioning house modelled on that in use in Lyons.[4] 'The principle of conditioning', wrote the Commissioner of Customs, 'is to dry silk so completely that not a trace of moisture remains in it, and to add to this weight of silk absolutely dry an allowance of 11 per cent . . . the quantity of water that silk in its normal state ought to contain.'[5] This conditioning house was reported to be successful. A later undertaking for testing the quality of raw silk was established jointly by Chinese and Americans. In 1921 the General Guild of Silk and Cocoon Merchants of Kiangsu, Chekiang and Anhwei sent a delegation to the International Silk Exhibition in New York where an agreement was signed with the Raw Silk Testing Company for the opening of a testing depot at Shanghai. The Chinese and American partners each agreed to contribute half the initial cost; the management was in the hands of the Raw Silk Testing Company, which was responsible for meeting any financial deficiency. The depot was opened in 1924 and the silk which it passed and graded escaped the obligation of test on entering into the United States.[6]

[1] T. R. Banister, *op. cit.*, p. 191.
[2] Oriental Economist, *The Foreign Trade of Japan*, p. 55.
[3] *British Consular Trade Report*, Canton, 1879, p. 16; Ichang, 1883, Appendix I, p. 294.
[4] *Chinese Customs Report*, Canton, 1880, p. 260.   [5] *ibid.*, Canton, 1881, p. 7.
[6] *Chinese Economic Journal*, November 1928, 'The Silk Export Trade of China.'

Despite the achievements of the foreigners in developing markets for Chinese silk and in modernising the organisation of methods of silk production, the trade, as we have seen, failed in competition with the Japanese. Some reasons for this failure have already been given; but as the explanation goes to the root of Chinese commercial backwardness it may usefully be elaborated. The silk trade, for its successful organisation, needed a high degree of centralisation at some points and a wide dispersion at others. The production of cocoons is necessarily a manual process and is highly suited to small-scale peasant agriculture. If, however, large quantities of uniform silk are to be provided—and uniformity is necessary for the subsequent manipulation of the silk on knitting frames or power looms—then there must be centralised supervision over certain processes. In Japan this supervision was provided in two ways: by the licensing of egg-producers as already described, and by the establishment of close relations between groups of silk raisers and particular filatures. If a filature is established in a silk raising area, then it becomes a source of supply of egg-cards as well as the customer for the cocoons. It is thus well placed to exercise supervision over the whole process. But this means that the filatures must be widely dispersed just as the cocoon raisers are. Centralised control is again necessary at the port through which the silk passes for sale abroad, for at that point reliable testing and conditioning arrangements must be set up. These conditions for the successful conduct of the silk trade could not be satisfied in China. First, there was no central authority capable of or interested in establishing a licensing system for egg-production. Secondly, the insecure conditions in the interior and the obstacles in the way of setting up foreign enterprise there meant that the filatures were mainly concentrated at the Treaty Ports, and so were not in close touch with the actual producers of the cocoons. It is true that some of the managers of the larger filatures used to go up-country to buy supplies of cocoons,[1] but this was not equivalent to a continuous supervision over the process of silk-raising. Thirdly, it was comparatively late in the history of the trade that satisfactory conditioning arrangements were established—again, the Government's lack of interest in economic organisation was mainly responsible for the delay. The conclusion must be that this trade which in most branches is necessarily a small-scale industry depends for its success on central supervision and government intervention at a few key points. China lacked a government competent to exercise the supervision and it was largely because of this that she lost so much of the silk trade.

[1] J. Walton, *op. cit.*, p. 103.

CHAPTER IV

THE ORGANISATION OF THE EXPORT TRADE: MISCELLANEOUS GOODS

1. VEGETABLE OIL AND OIL PRODUCTS

THE exports of vegetable oil and of other products of seeds and nuts did not become substantial until the early years of the twentieth century, although the origins of the trade can be traced back for many decades. The products fell into two main groups, first, edible oils such as bean, groundnut, cotton-seed and sesamum oils, together with their by-products, and, second, wood oil used in the manufacture of paint and varnish. In the world as a whol fats were becoming scarce at the beginning of the present century because of the fall in the supplies of whale oil and the rise in consumption in Europe and America. The foreign merchants in China, who constituted the link between the resources of that country and the demands of the outside world, were able to tap those resources and eventually to build up a large business. The decline in the older staple exports, tea and silk, was thus partly offset by the expansion of this new trade.

The development of vegetable oil exports did not depend solely upon the commercial contacts with the West, nor even upon the capacity of Western firms to introduce modern methods of expressing the oil. It required the simultaneous infusion of new techniques into several different branches of China's economy, especially into transport. Thus, new methods of storage and carriage by sea had to be introduced, and scientific methods ensuring the purity of the product (e.g. examination by spectroscope) had to be adapted to this purpose. Some of the chief sources of the supply of the materials, moreover, were made accessible only by the activities of Western shipping in Chinese waters and by the construction of railways in China itself. Indeed, in some branches of the trade, the original function performed by the Westerners was the provision of efficient transport for oil and oil products between different parts of the country. Foreign enterprise thus started by helping to expand an internal trade, and then, when overseas market conditions became favourable, it was well placed for taking advantage of them. The foreigners were confronted with many of the problems that they met with in other branches of Chinese trade. As with other products in a period of growing demand, adulteration was common and the difficulty of maintaining a regular flow of materials was formidable. These were indeed the main obstacles to the enlargement of exports, except in Manchuria, where in later years the trade was in Japanese hands. These general statements will now be illustrated by reference to a few of the main classes of product.

(a) Soya Beans and Bean Products

As soon as the northern ports were opened to foreign residents, the crude manual methods of expressing the oil from the beans and of making the bean cake attracted attention. In 1866, five years after the opening of Newchwang, Thomas Platt and Company, which was already established there, ordered from the United Kingdom machinery for processing oil and cake by steam power. The mill in which this plant was installed began operations in 1868. A European supervisor and two European engineers were employed.[1] The venture, however, was unsuccessful. The machinery proved to be unsuitable and there was opposition from those Chinese who followed the older methods of production. In 1872, therefore, the mill was closed, and it was not until 1896 that another power-driven bean mill was opened in Newchwang. This enterprise was controlled entirely by the Chinese, although to avoid official interference, it was nominally a foreign concern.[2] The machinery used in the mill was manufactured in Hongkong and was worked by Chinese without any foreign help.[3] Within a few years, three more mills were established. The daily production of these four mills was declared to be 15,600 bean cakes, each of about 48 catties. These cakes were much better than those made by the older methods, being stronger and drier, and their cost of production was lower. For instance, the cost of five machine-made cakes was 25 taels and the yield of oil 22 catties, compared with 30 taels and 20 catties for the same number of hand-made cakes.[4] Thus, by the end of the century machinery was making headway in this industry in spite of its unfortunate start.

Meanwhile, there had been a development of trade in bean products between Manchuria and the rest of China. Before the foreigners intervened, bean oil, used for food, and bean cake, used as a fertiliser, had been sent by junk to South China. The coming of foreign-owned steamships, however, brought profound changes to this trade. The immediate effects are well brought out in the report of the British consul at Chefoo in 1870; bean cake and oil were being shipped to South China 'to an extent undreamed of in the days when a few unwieldy junks formed the sole and uncertain means of transportation between North and

[1] *British Consular Trade Report*, Newchwang, 1866, p. 265; 1868, p. 89.
[2] *Chinese Customs Decennial Report*, Newchwang, 1882–91, pp. 22 and 24.
[3] *British Diplomatic and Consular Reports on Trade*, No. 1967, Newchwang, 1896, p. 9; *Chinese Customs Decennial Report*, Newchwang, 1892–1901, p. 22.
[4] *ibid.*

South'.[1] Five years later the Chefoo consul took up this theme and declared that the trade in bean cakes 'affords a capital illustration of the way in which the opening of Chefoo has benefited all classes of Chinese alike. It gives employment to a large number of junks in collecting the beans from the small ports around the gulf; it has made the fortunes of a number of merchants in Chefoo who buy the beans and manufacture the bean cake; it enables the southern sugar growers to obtain an article which they imperatively want for their sugar crops at a cheaper rate;[2] and lastly it affords the bean farmers in the north a ready market for their produce and so enables them to purchase in return many of the luxuries of life which would otherwise be beyond their reach.'[3] It was some years, however, before steamships completely ousted the junks from this trade. Some of the shippers of bean oil preferred to send it by junk because the frail paper-lined baskets in which it was stored suffered less damage than when dispatched by steamer;[4] but this disadvantage did not apply to bean cake, and steamers were both quicker and cheaper than junks. The difficulty of carriage, which was common to all classes of oil, was removed by the provision of vessels with specially fitted tanks for bulk shipment, although these did not become usual until after the First World War.

At first this coastal trade by steamer was entirely in the hands of foreigners. Later their functions were reduced to those of carriers, for the Chinese merchants were said to have better knowledge of the needs of small consumers and they could enforce claims more easily.[5] In the foreign trade in bean products, however, the initiative was taken entirely by Western merchants. Having noted the popularity of the North China bean cake as a fertiliser in the South China sugar districts, they decided to explore the possibilities of marketing it elsewhere. In 1876 a cargo was sent from Newchwang to Ceylon for use on the coffee plantations, and there was a similar venture three years later.[6] It does not appear that regular shipments to Ceylon followed; but a new market was found in Japan, and in the last decade of the nineteenth century exports of Chinese bean products to that country steadily increased.[7]

The next stage in the expansion of the bean trade was reached when the Japanese, after the Russian war of 1904–5, established their sphere of influence in Manchuria. It was thus Eastern and not Western merchants that turned this trade into one of the major branches of world commerce. The starting-point was when Mitsui Bussan in 1908

[1] *British Consular Trade Report*, Chefoo, 1870, p. 52.
[2] Bean cakes were used as fertiliser.
[3] *British Consular Trade Report*, Chefoo, 1875, p. 27.
[4] *Chinese Customs Decennial Report*, Newchwang, 1882–91, p. 1.
[5] *British Consular Trade Report*, Amoy, 1878, p. 6.
[6] *Chinese Customs Report*, Newchwang, 1880, p. 10.
[7] *Chinese Customs Decennial Report*, Chefoo, 1892–1901, p. 51.

made a trial shipment of soya beans to England and followed it up soon afterwards with a large cargo.[1] This began the career of the soya bean in international trade, for the European as well as the Japanese demand proved to be very large. The Western firms which operated in Manchuria could not hold their own in the face of Japanese competition. By 1912 most of the British merchants that had entered the Manchurian bean trade at the beginning had withdrawn or had greatly curtailed their activities. From then on it was the Japanese who supplied the drive and initiative in Manchurian economic development.

The export of beans was not, of course, confined to Manchuria. Central China also developed a foreign trade, chiefly in horse beans, during the early years of the present century, although this trade never reached the size of that of Manchuria. Foreign-owned bean mills were set up and some bean cake was exported from this region to Japan for use as a fertiliser. In 1909 the export of beans themselves came into prominence; but it soon declined because the Hankow bean was inferior to the Manchurian and the admixture of imitation beans destroyed the reliability of the shipments.[2] Nevertheless, on the eve of the First World War a number of foreign merchant firms in Hankow were interested in the bean trade, and at Shanghai a flourishing export had been worked up by a German firm.[3] The subsequent development of the great Manchurian trade, however, left little opportunities for the rest of China.

(b) Groundnuts

Groundnuts are said to have been first introduced into Shantung by an American missionary in the middle of the nineteenth century,[4] but cultivation on a large scale did not begin until the nineties.[5] The rise of this trade owed much to the construction of the Tientsin-Shanhaikwan Railway 'which runs through much land which is covered with sand, well suited for the growth of nuts but of which little use could be made until carriage by rail was possible'.[6]

The Germans took the lead in developing the export of groundnuts to Europe. In 1908 a German merchant made the first shipment from Tsingtao,[7] and from then on the trade grew steadily. Shantung

[1] *Far Eastern Products Manual*, No. 212.
[2] *Chinese Customs Report*, 1909, Part II, p. 35. At Chungking the farmers were reported to employ children to make mud beans which were added to their consignments.
[3] *British Diplomatic and Consular Reports on Trade*, No. 5119, Changsha, 1912, p. 14.
[4] *The Economic Development of Shantung, 1912-21*. U.S. Dept. of Commerce, Trade Information Bulletin, No. 70, p. 7.
[5] *Far Eastern Products Manual*, No. 88.
[6] *British Diplomatic and Consular Reports on Trade*, No. 2487, Tientsin, 1899, p. 14.
[7] *The Economic Development of Shantung, 1912-21*, p. 7.

groundnuts were liked in Europe because of the excellence of the oil expressed from them. The channels of trade were various. The normal practice, at any rate during the twenties, was for the foreign exporter to buy either from Chinese dealers at the ports or from the Tsingtao Ground Nut Exchange. This Exchange had been organised by Japanese, Chinese and European merchants,[1] and it set up standards of quality as well as providing a centre for spot and forward dealings.[2] Some foreign firms, however, preferred to send their agents into the producing regions to buy direct from the farmers and this practice was continuing as late as 1936.[3] They undertook the shelling, sorting, grading and drying of the nuts before exporting them.[4]

One of the chief obstacles to the growth of the export trade lay in the liability of the nut to deteriorate during the voyage. This greatly troubled the pioneers in this industry. In 1910 it was reported from Kiaochow that, because of bad stowage and the absence of proper ventilation 'most shipments of the last crop arrived in a heated and mouldy condition which led to heavy claims and allowances'. The foreign merchants of Kiaochow, through their Chamber of Commerce, took the matter up with the shipping companies, with the result that all the large liners installed special ventilators for the cargo.[5] This illustrates the close dependence of certain Chinese export trades upon the specialised shipping facilities that only the foreigners could provide. Indeed, without this foreign transport many valuable Chinese resources for long remained untapped. For example, the export of groundnuts from Chefoo was very small until 1923 when two shipping companies, one American and the other German, began to call at the port to take cargoes direct to foreign countries.[6]

In addition to exporting the nuts themselves the foreign merchants also developed a trade in groundnut cake and oil. The first shipment of cake occurred in 1924 when a Japanese millowner at Tsingtao sent a consignment to the United States for use as cattle fodder.[7] Oil for export was bought from Chinese-run oil mills in Hankow, Shanghai, Tientsin, and Tsingtao. Other types of oil seeds and oil products in which a foreign trade was worked up by Western merchants during the early years of this century were cotton-seed oil and sesamum seed. In 1902 foreign merchants introduced machinery to clean sesamum seed, and they were then able to sell it in competition with the Indian product.[8]

---

[1] *Chinese Economic Journal*, October 1932, 'Peanut Oil Trade.'
[2] *ibid.*, November 1927, 'The Export Peanut Trade of China.'
[3] *ibid.*, October 1936, 'Production and Export of Ground-nuts.'
[4] *British Diplomatic and Consular Reports on Trade*, No. 4438, Chefoo, 1909, p. 7.
[5] *ibid.*, No. 4682, Kiaochow, 1910, p. 7.
[6] *Chinese Customs Report*, Chefoo, 1923, p. 2.
[7] *ibid.*, Kiaochow, 1924, p. 5.
[8] *British Diplomatic and Consular Reports on Trade*, No. 2969, Hankow, 1902, p. 14.

By 1920 the extraction of cotton-seed oil had become an important industry in Shanghai where it engaged three foreign and six Chinese mills. The foreign mills turned out oil for export, but they were, as in so many other trades, handicapped by the difficulty of obtaining a regular supply of materials.[1]

(c) Wood Oil

Wood oil, or tung oil, had long been used by the Chinese in making paint and varnish, and the export of this oil, like that of bean products, thus arose out of an internal trade of wide extent and ancient history. Even the foreigners were concerned in the domestic trade as carriers long before they began exporting the oil abroad on their own account. Thus, it was said in 1877 that although over 240,000 piculs of wood oil were shipped from Hankow by steamer alone, this product 'only interested such foreigners as were engaged in the local carrying trade'.[2]

The first shipments of wood oil to Europe were made in 1897-8. It found favour with the varnish makers because of its rapid drying qualities,[3] and after the turn of the century the trade throve. West China was the chief region of production and Hankow the leading port for refining and shipment. Through the enterprise of a German firm Changsha also became an important centre.[4] Although foreign merchant firms initiated the export trade, they did not retain their dominance in it for very long. After the First World War an increasing share of it was taken by the Chinese, either as independent merchants, or as agents of overseas importers. By 1929 much of the Hankow trade was in the hands of the Chinese agents of American importers, and a year later the Department of Overseas Trade stated that the wood oil export trade, which was growing steadily, was 'controlled largely by American speculative distributors, working in close conjunction with Chinese merchants'.[5]

The chief perplexities of the pioneers in the wood oil export trade were caused by adulteration and the difficulties of carriage. Chinese suppliers were inclined to mix cheaper and inferior oils with wood oil. As the Commissioner of Customs in Hankow wrote in 1923: 'As in so many other instances in China a decline in quality upon an increased demand being apparent has already set in, and adulteration with oils of lesser value, such as sesamum, is already the rule and not the

[1] British Diplomatic and Consular Reports on Trade, No. 4747, Shanghai, 1910, p. 12.
[2] British Consular Trade Report, Hankow, 1877, p. 64.
[3] British Diplomatic and Consular Reports on Trade, No. 2601, Hankow, 1900, p. 11.
[4] ibid., No. 4897, Changsha, 1911, p. 14; and No. 5119, Changsha, 1912, p. 15.
[5] United Kingdom Department of Overseas Trade, Report on Economic Conditions in China, to August 1930, p. 63.

exception.'[1] This meant that the oil had to be clarified before it could be exported, and sediment equivalent to 20 per cent of the total weight of the oil was sometimes extracted.[2] Scientific testing of quality by spectroscope was also introduced.

As with other oils, it was essential to devise a suitable container before the success of the export trade could be assured. Originally the native dealer had used bamboo boxes. These were later replaced by wooden casks which were coopered at Hongkong or Hankow from staves imported from Britain.[3] Even these were unsatisfactory as the oil penetrated into the wood. Steel casks were too expensive, but after various experiments the problem was solved by the consignment of the oil in bulk.[4] By 1923 a large fleet of bulk oil lighters owned by the foreign firms existed at Hankow and pipe-lines from the go-downs to the Bund were laid down.[5] Later, other technical improvements were brought about in the effort to reduce costs in this highly competitive business. Foreign merchants, including the American distributing firms and their Chinese agents, introduced important changes in the treatment and handling of the oil. 'Up-to-date installations were erected at Wanhsien, Chungking and Changteh, having for their object the shipment of refined oil in bulk to Hankow and thence direct to the consuming countries without passing through installations at Hankow.'[6] This tended to eliminate the old-fashioned native dealer.

During the 1920's the steady growth of the trade was impeded by the civil war. The flow of supplies was liable to frequent interruption, and there were in consequence wide fluctuations in prices. In these circumstances paint and varnish manufacturers abroad were naturally induced to seek for alternative sources of supply. The production of wood oil in the United States was encouraged, and during the thirties the increasing use of synthetic substitutes dimmed the prospects of the Chinese trade.[7] Nevertheless, the export of wood oil continued to rise, and in the years immediately before the outbreak of the Sino-Japanese War about half of China's output was still sold abroad.[8] By this time the foreign merchants were being exposed to serious competition as a result of the Government's new interventionist policy, and from 1936

[1] *Chinese Customs Report*, Hankow, 1923, p. 3; *Chinese Customs Decennial Report*, Hankow, 1902–11, p. 347; *British Diplomatic and Consular Reports on Trade*, No. 4897, Changsha, 1911, p. 14; United Kingdom Department of Overseas Trade, *Report on Economic Conditions in China*, to August 1930, p. 63.
[2] *Chinese Customs Report*, Shasi, 1919, p. 450.
[3] *British Diplomatic and Consular Reports on Trade*, No. 1945, Hankow, 1896, p. 13; No. 2795, Hankow, 1901, p. 11.
[4] *ibid.*, No. 3280, Trade of China, 1903, p. 48.
[5] *Chinese Customs Report*, Hankow, 1923, p. 4.
[6] United Kingdom Department of Overseas Trade, *Report on Economic Conditions in China*, to August 1930, p. 63.
[7] *North China Herald*, 21 August 1935. Speech by the U.S. Commercial Attaché.
[8] *Far Eastern Survey*, 6 November 1935, p. 180.

the officially-sponsored China Vegetable Oil Corporation began to dominate the trade.

2. EGG PRODUCTS AND FROZEN MEAT

The peasantry of China produced a number of farm products for which the enterprise of foreign merchants found markets abroad. Supplies, at any rate at first, were available at very low prices and labour for preparing the goods for export could be obtained very cheaply in the country districts. In their turn, the merchants furnished the working capital and the commercial and technical knowledge needed for processing the goods and for preserving them in their long journey to the market. As in some other classes of goods, however, the development of the trade was handicapped by the primitive condition of the Chinese economy and by the consequent difficulty of maintaining satisfactory quality not only in the raw products themselves but also in the materials needed for processing them. Some of the trades, therefore, met with unforeseen obstacles and, even when they were established, there was never an assurance of regular supplies.

One of the first products in this class to be exported in substantial quantities was albumen. Eggs were collected from the peasants, and the albumen was then separated from the yolks and made into slabs. These were used in Europe and America for photographic purposes and in the manufacture of confectionery. The earliest foreign ventures in this trade, like so many other pioneer enterprises in China, were unsuccessful. Thus, in 1872, an American firm started in this trade, but soon had to abandon it.[1] The same fate overtook a French firm which opened factories at Hoihow and Pakhoi in 1896.[2] About the same time, however, a number of albumen factories were set up in Central China, most of them by Germans, and these met with better fortune. Three firms, two German and one Austrian, began to manufacture albumen in Hankow in 1897. Their factories opened only during the clutch season for eggs, about four months in the year. The scale of the undertakings was large; one of the firms used between 30,000 and 40,000 eggs a day during the season.[3] In the same year two albumen factories in Wuhu were started also by Germans, and the records of these ventures throw light on the impact of this type of enterprise upon the local labour supply. The competition for employment was so strong that when the first factory began operation, 'the premises were actually invaded by country lasses anxious for the job of breaking eggs and separating the white from the yolk at the modest wage of about 1s. 3d.

[1] *British Consular Trade Report*, Chefoo, 1872, p. 32.

[2] *British Diplomatic and Consular Reports on Trade*, No. 1983, Pakhoi, 1896, p. 5; No. 2012, Kiungchow, 1896, p. 5; No. 2150, Kiungchow, 1897, p. 5.

[3] *ibid.*, No. 2126, Hankow, 1897, p. 9.

a week. Only about 20 were wanted and about 200 applied.'[1] At about the same time an albumen factory under Chinese ownership was opened near Wuhu and was said to have done well.[2] German albumen factories are known to have been operating at Chinkiang at the end of the nineteenth century.[3]

The prosperity enjoyed by these firms was short-lived. By 1901 there remained only one albumen producer at Hankow, where shortly before there had been five.[4] The industry at Wuhu also contracted. One of the German firms went out of business at the turn of the century, and the factory of another passed into British hands. The two Chinese albumen factories which had been established there also ceased to produce albumen. The causes of this decline are to be found both on the marketing and on the supply side. As with so many Chinese products, supplies proved to be very inelastic, with the result that the increased demand led to a steep rise in the price of eggs. For instance, the cost of duck eggs at Hankow doubled within a few years of the opening of the factories. The market could not stand the consequent rise in the price of albumen, since at this time the natural product was meeting with competition in Europe from synthetic substitutes. The firms that had entered this trade, moreover, found it impossible to maintain a satisfactory quality. This applied not only to the Chinese concerns, whose demise was ascribed directly to their careless methods of processing,[5] but also to the foreign firms which were handicapped by their inability to obtain supplies of good quality salt, an essential ingredient in processing albumen. They could not import salt, as this was prohibited by the Government in order to protect its own monopoly, and the quality of Chinese salt was deplorably low. For a time the firms were able to import 'boracic mixture' (i.e. a mixture of salt and boracic acid) which, being unsuitable to domestic use, did not affect the Government's monopoly. But in 1897 this also was banned with disastrous consequences for the trade. In 1899 the British consul at Wuhu described Chinese salt as 'an exceedingly dirty product' which even after two washings, in the course of which some 40 per cent was lost, was found to retain sufficient dirt to make a thick deposit. The price, too, was about four times that of foreign salt. The consul concluded that unless the ban on imports of salt was modified, it was probable that the preparation of egg products would cease.[6]

This foreboding was realised so far as albumen was concerned, but

---

[1] *British Diplomatic and Consular Reports on Trade*, No. 2182, Wuhu, 1897, p. 7.
[2] *ibid.*, No. 2340, Wuhu, 1898, p. 12.
[3] *Chinese Customs Decennial Report*, Chinkiang, 1892–1901, p. 444; I. L. Bishop, *The Yangtse Valley and Beyond*, p. 57.
[4] *Chinese Customs Decennial Report*, Hankow, 1892–1901, p. 303.
[5] *British Diplomatic and Consular Reports on Trade*, No. 2667, Wuhu, 1900, p. 8.
[6] *ibid.*, No. 2457, Wuhu, 1899, p. 8.

a technical advance at the beginning of the present century not merely saved the egg-products trade but enabled it to expand enormously. This was the introduction of refrigeration which completely transformed the nature of the trade. Henceforth the product exported consisted of frozen eggs—whole eggs or in liquid form. This export was first developed by the Japanese, who sent the eggs to Japan for re-export to Europe. The trade did not, however, become substantial until large firms built refrigerating plants and made arrangements with the shipping companies for the satisfactory carriage of the eggs.

The chief concern in this trade was the International Export Company, a subsidiary of Union Cold Storage Limited. It opened its first factory in China in 1908 at Hankow at a cost of about £30,000. Pigs and poultry were frozen as well as eggs, and it made its first shipment of frozen products in May 1909.[1] The P. and O. and the Blue Funnel Line provided specially equipped ships.[2] A few years later the International Export Company opened a branch at Nanking and the export of frozen eggs from that city grew rapidly.[3] The company also established a plant at Tientsin. It devised an elaborate organisation for collecting supplies. and employed more than 150 purchasing officers who were located in the various cities and bought eggs from local collectors.[4] The concern had many competitors. Before the First World War the Germans had a share of the trade. Then, after 1914, their place was taken by Japanese merchants, who developed a substantial export to their own homeland.[5] The Chinese also participated. The first Chinese owned egg-product factory, apart from the former concerns in the albumen industry, was established in 1909, and ten years later there were over a hundred of them. Most of these were very small, and it was not until 1923 that the first large egg factory under Chinese ownership began production. This was the China Egg Produce Company at Shanghai. After five years it greatly enlarged its plant and in 1929 opened a branch at Tsingtao.[6]

The inter-war period saw a steep rise in the export of eggs in various forms, dried, frozen whole eggs and frozen liquid eggs. Indeed, during those years China became the leading supplier of egg products in world markets. The foreigners, who had been responsible for starting the trade, had the chief part in maintaining it. This was mainly because, after the coming of refrigeration, substantial economies could be secured by operating on a large scale and only foreign firms could afford the capital outlay required. Thus in the early thirties the International

[1] *Chinese Customs Report*, Hankow, 1908, p. 213.
[2] *ibid.*, Hankow, 1909, p. 260.
[3] *ibid.*, Nanking, 1914, p. 624; and *British Diplomatic and Consular Reports on Trade*, No. 5124, Nanking, 1912, p. 8.
[4] *Chinese Economic Journal*, February 1934, p. 158.
[5] *Chinese Customs Report*, Kiaochow, 1922, p. 16.
[6] *Chinese Economic Journal*, February 1934, p. 161.

Export Company's purchases of eggs at Hankow were at the rate of about 200,000 crates (of 850 eggs each) every year, and in the period immediately before the Sino-Japanese War it was accustomed to buy 100,000 eggs a day from the single market town of Tinghsien, in addition to large numbers at other places.[1] Jardine Matheson also took part in this trade and in 1920 established a subsidiary, the Ewo Cold Storage Company, for the manufacture and export of dried eggs. A factory was built at Shanghai and later extensions enabled it to undertake the processing of liquid and shell eggs also. French and American firms also participated.[2]

Most of the eggs passed through three ports, Shanghai, Hankow and Tientsin. The Chinese Government, which in the early days had by its regulations thwarted the growth of the egg-products trade, tried during the thirties to foster it. In 1936 it required that all eggs for export should be subject to inspection by the Government Bureau of Inspection and Testing, established at that time.[3] This indicates that the Chinese had at last realised that the maintenance of standards of quality was essential to a flourishing export and that, in the circumstances existing in China, the Government had to accept responsibility for ensuring adherence to those standards.

The export of frozen products was not limited to eggs. The International Export Company, which had taken the lead in building up the trade in frozen eggs, used its plants for freezing meat and poultry. The first factory, situated at Hankow, began these operations in 1908 by freezing 'many thousands of chickens and ducks, pheasant, snipe and wildfowl from geese to teal' as well as 'some hog deer' and about 4,500 pigs. These were exported in P. and O. and Blue Funnel ships along with the frozen eggs.[4] The company obtained its supplies of pig, fowl and game through agents sent into the country districts.[5] As usual, the growth in demand sent up prices very steeply, and both Chinese and foreign consumers in Hankow complained of this result of the company's activity, although, no doubt, the producers had other views.[6] The Chinese Government also objected on the ground that this trade was outside the provisions of the treaties.[7] Nevertheless, the company was able to extend its business substantially in the years before the First World War. It even took part in the actual production of the

[1] *Chinese Social and Political Science Review*, October 1937, 'A Study of the Egg Trade in the Peiping Area'; *Chinese Economic Journal*, September 1932, 'Wuhan Commerce.'
[2] *Chinese Economic Journal*, February 1934, p. 161; and September 1932, 'Wuhan Commerce.'
[3] *Chinese Customs Report*, 1936, 'Trade of China', p. 79.
[4] *ibid.*, Hankow, 1908, p. 213.
[5] *ibid.*, Hankow, 1909, p. 292.
[6] *ibid.*
[7] *British Diplomatic and Consular Reports on Trade*, No. 4529, Hankow, 1909, p. 23.

livestock, not always with happy results. Thus, when a foreign expert in stuffing was brought to China 'to convert the scraggy Hupeh fowl into the semblance of the succulent Surrey fowl . . . the chickens accepted the stuffing but marked their protest by dying in thousands', as they were not accustomed to such rich fare.[1]

When the company tried to find a market for Chinese pork, it met with its most serious difficulties, not in China but in Europe, where there was a strong prejudice against it. The type of pig frozen by the company was not the 'scrawny scavenger of the streets' as seen by the tourist in China, but the Hunan variety which was 'more like the chubby pig of the story-books and [was] probably the pig which was taken to England and America to improve the home stock'.[2] These Hunan pigs were kept on farms and had adequate food. Before shipment the carcasses were medically inspected. Yet, in spite of assurances by the Chinese Customs Service and by the British consul at Hankow, an outcry arose in Britain against the import of Chinese pork. The Local Government Board sent an official to investigate the conditions under which the pigs exported by the International Export Company were reared and fed. He visited many farms in different districts and commented upon 'the excellent manner in which these pigs were reared', 'Model farms in England', he added, 'would not suffer by following the method of the Hunan pig rearer.'[3] The International Export Company also exported lard, intestines and feathers from Hankow, but the poor quality of the local salt prevented the curing of bacon fit for overseas markets. Although the company still had technical problems to solve in connection with the cold storage of poultry, the prospect for many of these trades seemed very favourable on the eve of the First World War. The war itself, however, put an end to the business which did not revive after 1918. Thus, here again was a Chinese export which enjoyed a short-lived prosperity, only to fall away to insignificance.

3. HIDES AND SKINS

Just as the rise of the egg export trade was made possible by the introduction of refrigeration, so the development of a large export of hides and skins depended on Western technical innovations, such as press-packing and scientific methods of curing. In these and other cases, the impact of modern technique upon a primitive economy permitted certain commodities, hitherto almost worthless, to enter into international trade on a large scale.

[1] *Chinese Customs Report*, Hankow, 1909, p. 292.
[2] *ibid.*, Hankow, 1908, p. 213.
[3] *ibid.*, Hankow, 1909, p. 292.

In 1876 a British firm in Hankow began to press hides mechanically. This resulted in a large saving in freight to Europe and in consequence the export of cow hides from Hankow rose steeply, from 5,000 piculs in 1875 to 20,000 in 1876 and to 50,000 piculs in 1877, when demand was being stimulated by the Russo-Turkish War.[1] In China, however, as we have already seen, a rapid increase in the output of any commodity was almost invariably accompanied by a deterioration in quality. In the skin trade customers soon began to complain of bad curing, and the demand declined. The foreign merchants sought for a remedy in two directions. First, they introduced new methods of chemical preparation which were more reliable than the traditional methods followed by their Chinese suppliers,[2] and secondly, one of the foreign firms decided to tan the hides in China instead of exporting the skins. It established a tannery in Shanghai, where a European manager and engineer and 200 Chinese labourers were employed and where the machinery was of the newest pattern. This enterprise prospered. Besides exporting its products, the tannery carried out a contract for leather with a Chinese provincial government.[3] During the eighties demand from abroad increased, and every year the area from which the merchants in Hankow drew their supplies was extended. The centralisation of the trade in Hankow was chiefly due to the fact that the hydraulic pressing carried out there saved freight on exports and enabled the buyers to offer good prices.[4] The difficulty of preserving hides as the area was further extended was overcome by sending preparations with which the products were given a preliminary treatment before they left the place of origin.[5]

With growth of the trade the price of hides increased. 'Till lately', wrote the British consul in Ichang in 1883, 'hides were wasted or sold for a trifle. Recently the demand for them in Hankow for the home market has caused them to be looked after.'[6] In 1896 the consul at Chungking remarked that the demand for hides for export had meant that they were no longer available for many of their former domestic uses, such as for the soles of shoes, shields and buckles.[7] Among the pioneers in this trade the Germans were even more prominent than the British, and during the early years of the present century they had the largest share of the exports. After the First World War their place was taken by the Japanese.[8]

[1] *British Consular Trade Report*, Hankow, 1876, p. 27; 1878, p. 19; *Chinese Customs Report*, Hankow, 1877, p. 13.
[2] *Chinese Customs Report*, Hankow, 1878, p. 44.
[3] *British Consular Trade Report*, Shanghai, 1878, p. 25; 1879, p. 156.
[4] *British Diplomatic and Consular Reports on Trade*, No. 888, Hankow, 1890, p. 2.
[5] *British Consular Trade Report*, Shanghai, 1885, p. 5.
[6] *ibid.*, Ichang, 1883, p. 294.
[7] *British Diplomatic and Consular Reports on Trade*, No. 1945, Chungking, 1896, p. 12.
[8] Ho Ping-Yin, *The Foreign Trade of China*, p. 324.

Most of China's hide exports came from the Yangtse Valley, but the goatskin and dogskin trades as well as the fur trade were centred in Tientsin and other North China ports, at least in the earlier years. Foreign merchants sent their Chinese agents to distant parts to buy these skins as well as wool and other natural produce,[1] and they organised the manufacture of skin rugs. In 1881 over 200,000 goatskin rugs were exported from Tientsin; most of them went to the United States, where they were used on the floors of railway carriages.[2] Messrs. Baudinel, a firm which were pioneers in the Manchurian bristle and wool trade, were also responsible for beginning the export of skins and furs from Newchwang. In 1884 this company sent specimens to London and San Francisco, and in subsequent years shipped large quantities of them.[3]

A large export of untanned skins from North China was also started at this time. The impetus was given by the war between Chile and Peru which had disturbed the skin market in New York. Agents were sent abroad to find new sources of supply, and some of them came to North China. As the local practice of drying skins in the sun was found to have been the cause of the failure of the previous experimental shipments of untanned skins, better methods of preparation were introduced. In consequence, the export from Tientsin of untanned goatskins rose from about 14,000 in 1883 to nearly 2,700,000 in 1899.[4] During the twentieth century the increase in the goatskin exports continued, and by 1922 American tanneries were giving orders to Hankow direct.[5] It was estimated in 1936 that China produced about one-tenth of the world's supply of goatskins. The best skins came from the Yangtse Valley; those exported from Tientsin were used mainly for lining purposes. China's goatskins enjoyed a good reputation for quality, and this was attributed in part to 'an excellent system of grading'.[6] An export of sheepskins also developed.

4. BRISTLES

Pig bristles were an article of internal trade long before the enterprise of foreign merchants turned them into one of China's chief export commodities. The bristles came from several sources of supply, but it was those from North China which first attracted foreign attention. In 1873 there is mention of shipments of bristles from Tientsin to South

[1] *British Consular Trade Report*, Tientsin, 1885, p. 2.
[2] *ibid.*, Tientsin, 1881, p. 127.
[3] *ibid.*, Newchwang, 1884, p. 132; *Chinese Customs Decennial Report*, Newchwang, 1882–91, p. 4.
[4] *British Diplomatic and Consular Reports on Trade*, No. 2847, Tientsin, 1899, p. 13.
[5] *Chinese Customs Report*, Hankow, 1922, p. 21.
[6] *Far Eastern Survey*, 22 April 1936, p. 91.

China,[1] and when ten years later consignments were sent to Europe they at once aroused keen demand.[2] Messrs. Baudinel were responsible for developing the trade in Newchwang,[3] while Tsingtao also became an important centre. As in other branches of trade in North China, the Western exporters seldom sent their own agents into the producing areas to collect the goods, for they preferred to buy from Chinese in the ports, who undertook the collection of the produce from the local suppliers.[4] The growth of the trade, however, depended on the willingness of the foreign exporters to advance the working capital necessary to finance these transactions. As the British consul in Tientsin wrote in 1908: 'The business is in the hands of native dealers who have little or no capital, and foreign firms are asked to advance funds sometimes for months before the cargo arrives in its raw state.'[5] The dressing of the bristles by the Chinese dealers was often unsatisfactory, and in the early years of the present century foreign merchants began to undertake this process themselves.[6]

Another source of supply was West China. Chungking bristles, which eventually became a well-known article of international commerce, were unknown in the West until 1891 when a British merchant recruited skilled workers in Tientsin and went to Szechwan to try to build up the bristle trade there.[7] At first the raw bristles were sent to the ports for treatment. Later (in 1896) Archibald Little's firm, the Chungking Trading Company, established a factory in Chungking for cleaning and sorting the bristles.[8] This venture was very successful, and numerous competitors, both Chinese and foreign, entered the business. The organisation of the trade was complicated and dealings were attended with considerable risk, for, as in North China, the collection of the bristles presented difficulties. At first, no regular bristle market existed in Chungking, and 'merchants had to entrust their money to more or less honest brokers who went up-country and collected goods parcel by parcel. If the broker were a rascal, or if the country were disturbed by bandits, the merchant had to put up with delay and loss.'[9] As the trade began to expand the usual problem of adulteration was encountered, and because of this the leading exporters in the early days, instead of buying the bristles ready treated, usually preferred to take them in a raw state and process them in their own establishments.

[1] Chinese Customs, *Catalogue of Exhibits at Vienna*, 1873, p. 26.
[2] *ibid.*, 1878, p. 51; *British Consular Trade Report*, Tientsin, 1883, p. 273.
[3] *British Consular Trade Report*, Newchwang, 1884, p. 133.
[4] *Far Eastern Products Manual*, No. 23.
[5] *British Diplomatic and Consular Reports on Trade*, No. 4275, Tientsin, 1907–8, p. 9.
[6] *ibid.*, No. 5344, Tientsin, 1913, p. 5.
[7] *Chinese Economic Journal*, April 1934, article on Bristle Trade.
[8] *Chinese Customs Decennial Report*, Chunking, 1892–1901, p. 145.
[9] *British Diplomatic and Consular Reports on Trade*, No. 2249, Chungking, 1898, p. 8.

By the end of the first decade of the present century the Chinese were beginning to undertake the business of sorting which had previously been done under foreign supervision, and as time went on they took over an increasing share of the trading functions in this commodity.[1] The actual business of exporting Szechwan bristles, however, remained almost entirely in the hands of foreign firms until 1912 when some local Chinese organised a company for this purpose.[2] This challenge was of little consequence, and fifteen years later the export of bristles from Hankow, which had become a centre for the trade, was still concentrated entirely in foreign hands. This was largely because the Chinese intermediaries, even during the twenties and thirties, had few resources of their own and therefore depended on Western exporters to finance their operations. In the Hankow trade at that time the bristles were normally collected by jobbers who sold them through local middlemen to Chinese wholesale dealers. The latter cleaned and sorted the bristles before selling them, usually through a compradore, to a foreign exporting house at Hankow. It was customary for the foreign exporters to advance 90 per cent of the purchase price to the Chinese dealers before the delivery of the bristles.[3]

5. STRAW BRAID

The development of an export trade in some kinds of manufactured or semi-manufactured goods was dependent upon the willingness and capacity of the foreign merchants to initiate and organise the actual production of the commodities, and the presence of cheap raw materials and labour often encouraged them to do this. Sometimes, however, an export developed out of an industry already established in China. In such cases the foreign merchant's part was to persuade the producers to modify their goods to suit foreign taste and to see that standards of quality were raised or maintained. This was so in the straw braid manufacture. When Chefoo was opened to foreign trade in 1862 the plaiting of straw and the making of straw hats were already well-established local industries. Foreign merchants soon saw that a market for the braid might be created abroad, and export shipments began.[4] The trade prospered; and in 1891 straw plaiting was described as 'the chief industry of parts of the Province'.[5] Its expansion brought great benefits to the people, for, as it was a by-employment of the peasantry, it gave them opportunities of supplementing their incomes during the slack seasons of agriculture.

[1] *Chinese Customs Report*, Chungking, 1909, p. 196.
[2] *Chinese Economic Journal*, April 1934.
[3] *Chinese Economic Monthly*, May 1926, article on Hankow Bristles.
[4] *Far Eastern Products Manual*, No. 213.
[5] *Chinese Customs Decennial Report*, Chefoo, 1882–91, p. 66.

The straw braid was used for the manufacture of hats and baskets. In the early days of the trade the braid had been sent to Canton where it was made into hats for export. But soon the foreign merchants found that it was better to ship the braid itself, and the Canton hat industry declined. The United States was the earliest market, but by 1870 London had begun to take the bulk of the supply.[1] This made difficulties for the English straw plaiters who petitioned Parliament against the import of the cheap Chinese product. Their protests were unavailing, however, and the British product was displaced.[2]

The main problem of the foreign merchants was to induce the Chinese to turn out the quality of braid required in Europe and to keep up their standards during the period when trade was booming. The pressure which they could bring to bear on their Chinese suppliers was often ineffective, and they were obliged to undertake some of the processes themselves. For instance, local methods of bleaching were not satisfactory and much of the braid had to be re-bleached before it was fit for sale abroad.[3] The dyeing of the goods also needed improvement,[4] while malpractices such as damping to increase weight led to frequent complaints.[5] In fact, in 1887 buyers were reported to be turning their attention to European-made braid, which, although expensive, was of reliable quality.[6] The foreign merchants engaged in the braid trade at Chefoo presented a memorial to the *Taotai* in which they pointed out the damage done to the industry by poor quality, and in 1888 they underlined their complaint by refusing to buy for several months.[7] This had the effect of inducing the plaiters to improve their goods, at least temporarily.[8] They also seem to have become more adaptable, for a few years later it was said that they were willing to make any new kind of plait that was ordered.[9] In 1893, for the first time, split straw braid was made and exported from Chefoo. Straw-splitting tools, as used in England, had been imported for this purpose and the plaiters soon became accustomed to them and made duplicates for themselves[10].

At the close of the century the old complaints about quality revived, and these were given a new force because by this time Japanese

[1] *British Consular Trade Report*, Chefoo, 1870, p. 52; *Chinese Customs Report*, Chefoo, 1871–2, p. 51; 1877, p. 61.
[2] *ibid.*, Chefoo, 1874, p. 28.
[3] *Far Eastern Products Manual*, No. 213.
[4] *British Consular Trade Report*, Chefoo, 1883, p. 191.
[5] *ibid.*, Chefoo, 1883, p. 191, and 1891, p. 8. Cf. *Chinese Customs Report*, 1877, p. 61, for a favourable opinion.
[6] *British Consular Trade Report*, Chefoo, 1887, p. 3.
[7] *Chinese Customs Decennial Report*, Chefoo, 1882–91, p. 45.
[8] *ibid.* But for a less favourable impression, *see ibid.*, Shanghai, 1882–91 p. 324.
[9] *ibid.*, Chefoo, 1882–91, p. 66.
[10] *British Diplomatic and Consular Reports on Trade*, No. 1412, Chefoo, 1893, p. 7.

competition had appeared. 'No effort is spared', wrote the British consul in Chefoo in 1896, 'to convince the Shantung producers of the rapid strides Japan continues to make'; but their complacency was unshaken.[1] The Japanese success was ascribed to their better straw, more skilful labour and superior organisation. By 1901 the straw plait export of Tientsin was regarded as dying; 'the Chinese, by deliberate bad work-manship and bad quality of straw, have spoilt what might have been ... a steadily increasing and profitable line'.[2] By the end of the century most of the merchants of Tientsin had ceased to deal in straw braid; 'only a few, who gave long credit and did a retail business in the foreign markets, still held on'.[3] Another promising trade had succumbed through the inadequacies of its participants as soon as a competent rival appeared.

The Chefoo trade was more prosperous at the turn of the century, although its character had changed. In 1891 the export had been for the most part in the hands of the foreign merchants.[4] By 1898 nearly 25,000 piculs of braid out of the total of 32,000 piculs exported from Chefoo were sent on Chinese account. Direct business with Japan had arisen; in this case the initiative seems to have been shared between the Japanese and the Chinese.[5] Yet the Western merchants had not been entirely driven out of the trade, for in 1907, as a result of protests from abroad about poor quality, they are reported as having supplied the Chinese Chamber of Commerce at Tsinan, the provincial capital, with standard samples.[6] About this time the Chinese authorities, as well as Chinese mercantile bodies, began to interest themselves in the problem of standards. In 1910 an association of Chinese braid dealers was formed to supervise the business, and its members worked together with foreign firms to establish a uniform quality of braid and to promote new methods of bundling.[7] In the next year the practice of supplying 'short braid' was stopped by the combined efforts of foreigners and Chinese. By this time the location of the braid trade in this region had altered, for the construction of the railway in Shantung between 1899 and 1904 had diverted it from Chefoo to Tsingtao. In 1922 a straw-braid bleaching and dyeing factory was opened under German management at that port. Its work was so satisfactory that some Japanese braid was imported for processing before shipment to Europe and America.[8]

[1] *British Diplomatic and Consular Reports on Trade*, No. 1966, Chefoo, 1896, p. 7.
[2] *Chinese Customs Decennial Report*, Tientsin, 1892–1901, p. 536.
[3] *ibid.*
[4] *ibid.*, Chefoo, 1882–91, p. 45.
[5] *British Diplomatic and Consular Reports on Trade*, No. 2478, Chefoo, 1899, p. 6.
[6] *ibid.*, No. 4129, Chefoo, 1907, p. 6.
[7] *ibid.*, No. 4682, Kiaochow, 1910, p. 5.
[8] *Chinese Customs Report*, Kiaochow, 1922, p. 16.

6. HATS

The manufacture of hats at Ningpo reproduced many of the features of the straw-braid industry, but although very similar in origin its subsequent history was different. The basis for the industry was a local supply of raw materials, for the rice lands of the Ningpo area produced a type of sedge suitable for this manufacture. The material was woven into hats by women and children who carried on the work in their own homes. An export trade in these hats began as early as 1868.[1] By 1877 15,000,000 were being exported annually from Ningpo, and the industry then gave employment to thousands of persons.[2] The export trade had been started by foreign merchants who bought the goods wholesale, shipped them to Shanghai, whence they were dispatched to the United States and the United Kingdom. The expansion of the trade was followed by the usual result—carelessness in the production of the goods and a deterioration in quality.[3] In the eighties, however, one of the largest braid firms in France interested itself in this trade and sent an agent to Ningpo to foster it.[4] From that time the trade was transformed. The area had a plentiful supply of workers who had acquired skill in this manufacture, but the local materials were not wholly satisfactory for the products needed in foreign markets. So the French firm turned the local supply of skill to better account by introducing more suitable materials. These took the form of Japanese wood shavings 'which, being superior to the native rush in colour, texture and quality, produced a much finer finished article'.[5] By the first decade of the new century very little of the material used by the Ningpo hat workers was produced locally. Most of it was imported from Japan, Formosa and Madagascar. Thus, the trade ultimately came to depend for its continued existence in the Ningpo area entirely on the supply of cheap skilled workers who had acquired their special aptitudes at a time when local rushes were used. The French firms to whose initiative the expansion of the trade was largely due had the usual struggle to maintain quality. The importance of turning out clean goods was not readily understood by the producers, and at one time only 13 per cent of the hats offered were fit for sale abroad.[6] Yet, in spite of these difficulties, the firm was able to market large quantities of Ningpo hats throughout the world under the names of leghorns, panamas and

[1] *Far Eastern Products Manual*, No. 93.
[2] *British Consular Trade Report*, Ningpo, 1877, p. 113.
[3] *ibid.*, Ningpo, 1888, p. 3.
[4] *ibid.*
[5] *Chinese Customs Decennial Report*, 1902–11, Ningpo, vol. II, p. 65.
[6] *ibid.*

manillas.[1] This trade continued to flourish until the outbreak of the Sino-Japanese War. Ningpo did not remain the only centre of hat manufacture, for a Chinese-owned panama hat factory was established in Chengtu in Szechwan. In 1921 it employed about 200 workers. At that time its management was reported to be very progressive and to be building up an export trade.[2]

7. HAIRNETS

Among the so-called 'muck and truck' trades there were many which deserve notice here, not so much because they were large in size, but rather because their inception and organisation throw light on the commercial relations between foreigners and Chinese. The hairnet trade is an instance. Before this manufacture was introduced into China, most of it was carried on in Germany and Austria, and the main market was the United States. In the years just before the First World War it became evident that the Central European merchants had begun to obtain some of their supplies of hairnets from China, for a London dealer discovered that a parcel of cheap nets which had been consigned from Strasbourg was Chinese in origin. The result was that by 1914 London firms had made contact with Chinese sources of supply and were buying direct from Chefoo where the trade was centred.[3] After the First World War there was a boom in hairnets which had the effect of raising the wages of the Chinese women workers in this trade to a level higher than that of their husbands. As with all Chinese goods, the problem was to maintain quality, and while some firms found a solution, many inferior nets were manufactured and exported. Indeed, the ultimate decline in the trade during the twenties was attributed to the bad quality of some of these supplies as well as to the world-wide changes in fashion.

The chief interest in the trade lies in its organisation. The reason why the trade was located in China was partly because that country could supply large quantities of hair, but mainly because her labour was cheap. Both these causes, of course, had their root in the poverty of the Chinese people. But China could not supply technical skill and still less aptitude in chemical processes. These were essential for producing hairnets, and so the trade came to rest upon a combination of Western technical and chemical skill and cheap Chinese labour and materials. The organisation of the trade reflected these conditions. The hair, sold to the Western merchants by the Chinese dealers who collected it, was sent to Europe and the United States, where it was softened,

[1] *British Diplomatic and Consular Reports on Trade*, No. 5201, Ningpo, 1912, p. 10.
[2] *Far Eastern Products Manual*, No. 93.
[3] *Chinese Customs Report*, Chefoo, 1915, p. 361.

bleached and dyed. It was then returned to China, where the merchants gave it out to the Chinese domestic workers for manufacture into nets for export. It is noteworthy that although Chinese firms in Shanghai had tried to carry out these bleaching and dyeing processes, they failed to achieve satisfactory results.[1]

[1] *Far Eastern Products Manual*, No. 92.

CHAPTER V

THE ORGANISATION OF THE
IMPORT TRADE

1. Cotton Goods

During the century that followed the Treaty of Nanking the organisation of the import trade changed even more than that of the export trade. The changes could be attributed mainly to three causes. First, as the Chinese gained experience of foreign trading methods and foreign goods, they were able to participate successfully in many commercial operations from which ignorance had hitherto excluded them. Consequently, the earlier ways of organising particular types of business ceased to be economical and gave place to others. Secondly, the types of imports themselves changed, as was shown in Chapter II. Finally, the sources of supply for many goods altered, and new men brought new methods. These adjustments could be observed as having taken place in particular classes of goods no less than in the import trade as a whole, and the trends in the organisation of the cotton trade well illustrate the general development.

It has been shown that after the Treaty of Nanking the import of cotton manufactures into China, chiefly from Great Britain, increased rapidly, and by the opening of the last quarter of the nineteenth century these goods took first place on the import list. At first, this business was entirely in the hands of the large merchant houses who bought and sold on their own account. These houses set up branches, not merely in the larger ports, but in the smaller ports also when these were opened to trade. Sometimes the goods were imported direct into these small centres, and sometimes they were trans-shipped from Shanghai or Hongkong; but in any event they remained the property of the foreign merchants until they were sold to the Chinese dealers at the last Treaty Port through which they passed. The technical skill and commercial knowledge needed for the piece-goods trade could, however, readily be acquired by the Chinese dealers. So, by the sixties, these, with their local experience and low distributive costs, were superseding the foreigners in all stages of the trade which did not require contacts abroad—that is to say, in all stages except the actual processes of import. The trans-shipment trade passed into Chinese hands; direct importing into the smaller ports ceased; and the branches that foreign firms had established there were gradually closed. Even the larger centres were affected. For instance, by 1872 about half the shirtings

90

and T-cloths that arrived in Hankow were consigned to Chinese merchants.[1] During the eighties the foreigners' share of the trade in Amoy steadily diminished. By 1891 no foreign piece-goods merchants remained in Foochow or Chefoo; for the trade had been taken over by the Chinese.[2]

Even in the business of importing from overseas, there were changes in the functions performed by the foreign merchants. Many of them ceased to buy and sell on their own account, and much more business was done on commission. By the nineties it had become a usual procedure for the foreigner to import on behalf of Chinese dealers and to charge a commission on the transactions. An alternative method of doing business was for the Chinese to contract with the foreign merchant to buy a certain quantity of goods at a fixed price and for the foreigner then to place orders with the manufacturers overseas and to obtain their profit from the difference between the cost price to them and the agreed price fixed with the Chinese customer.[3] This does not mean that foreign merchants no longer engaged in any speculative transactions. Indeed, some of them continued to import piece-goods on their own account and to dispose of them at the weekly auctions which became a familiar feature of the commercial life of Shanghai. The first merchant house to adopt this method of sale was Maitland and Company, a Manchester firm, which held its first Shanghai auction in 1873.[4] Others soon followed this example, and it was estimated that in 1914 about half the cotton piece-goods imported into China were disposed of in this way.[5] Yet even these speculative transactions were limited to the chief port, and the foreign merchants no longer concerned themselves with marketing in the smaller centres of trade, as had originally been their practice.

Meanwhile an import of cotton yarn had developed—for the use of China's handloom weavers. At first supplies came mainly from India, and then, as Japan built up her spinning industry during the later nineties, that country became the chief source of yarn supply. This trade stimulated the export to Japan of Chinese raw cotton from which some of the yarn was made. The yarn import trade, however, was short-lived, for the rise of power-spinning in China itself which began at the turn of the century checked the growth of imports. During the First World War they actually declined. In the twenties they dwindled rapidly and they became insignificant by the early thirties. Japan was able to replace her yarn exports to China by exports of piece-goods,

[1] *Chinese Customs Report*, Hankow, 1871–2, p. 53.
[2] *Chinese Customs Decennial Report*, Foochow, 1882–91, p. 416; and *ibid.*, Chefoo, 1882–91, p. 46.
[3] *Report of Committee on British Trade in Hongkong*, 1896, Witnesses 3 and 12.
[4] H. D. Fong, *Cotton Industry and Trade in China*, vol. I, p. 264.
[5] W. F. Spalding, *Eastern Exchange, Currency and Finance*, p. 365.

for power-looms were introduced much later than power-spinning machinery. Before 1914 Japan's piece-goods exports had been very small, but during the First World War she captured a large share of the market and much of this she retained throughout the next decade. By the later twenties Japan was supplying two-thirds of China's imports of cotton piece-goods.

This shift in the source of supply from Western countries to Japan had further effects on the organisation of the trade. The Japanese, because of geographical propinquity, were able to make prompt deliveries, and because of their lower distributive costs they were able to compete with the Chinese merchants in sections of the piece-goods trade from which the high-salaried Westerners had long been excluded.

They often undertook the marketing of cottons in the smaller cities, instead of selling them at the major ports as did the Westerners, and in this way they made close contact with their customers. To some extent, therefore, the methods of trade in these goods reverted to that followed in earlier times, a reversion that was associated with the change in the source of supply. During the thirties even the Japanese could not hold their trade in competition with China's growing cotton industry and their imports dwindled rapidly. By 1935 only an insignificant trade was left to Western countries, faced as they were by both Japanese and Chinese competition. In such trade as remained to the West the functions of the foreign merchants were still further limited, for the Chinese wholesalers began to enter into direct relations with overseas cotton manufacturers and so tried to circumvent the foreign merchant altogether.[1] Consequently the auction system and what remained of true merchanting on the part of Western firms almost disappeared,[2] and such business as still went through Western merchants was conducted on commission.

2. Raw Cotton

In the century under review, raw cotton figured prominently in both China's import and export trades. In the early nineteenth century it was imported from India by 'country' ships. Then from the 1880's raw cotton began to be exported from China on a considerable scale to supply the new spinning industry of Japan. Thereafter, while China continued to export short-staple cotton, she imported other growths. Most of these imports were handled by foreign houses, among which the three great Japanese cotton merchant firms were prominent.[3] The forty foreign concerns which in 1932 were engaged in this business in

[1] Arno S. Pearse, *Cotton Industry of Japan and China*, p. 222; and H. D. Fong, *Cotton Industry and Trade in China*, p. 261.
[2] H. D. Fong, *ibid.*, p. 266.
[3] See pp. 204–5, *infra*.

Shanghai organised themselves into the Indian Cotton Imports' Association of China. One of the functions of the association was to negotiate agreements about freights with the P. and O., the Nippon Yusen Kaisha and the Osaka Shosen Kaisha.

Most of the exports of raw cotton passed through Tientsin, where in the early 1930's they were handled by thirty-three foreign exporters. The six Chinese participants in this business were engaged for the most part in exporting to Shanghai and other Chinese ports.[1]

3. Machinery and Civil Engineering Products

The sale of capital goods in all countries requires comparatively few intermediaries between the producer and the final customer, and it was to be expected that when Western countries began exporting machinery to China, the Western firms should retain distributive functions which they tended to lose in the consumer-goods trades. In China there were special reasons why this should be so. During the last years of the nineteenth century, when imports of machinery first became significant, and indeed, down to the present time, China was technically backward, and in acquiring, setting up and operating mechanical equipment she had to lean heavily on the knowledge and experience that the Westerners alone could supply. Furthermore, Chinese firms interested in obtaining equipment often lacked the resources necessary for the initial investment, and so they then relied upon the foreigners to furnish long-term credit. Consequently the Western merchants retained the bulk of the machinery imports in their own hands even at a time when Chinese merchants had taken over many of their functions in the consumer-goods trades. Before the outbreak of the Sino-Japanese War in 1937 there were only two or three Chinese firms of machinery importers, and their volume of business was very small. On the other hand, when the Chinese Government entered the market as a buyer of capital goods, its agents sometimes dealt with the foreign producers and so by-passed both Chinese and foreign merchants. These purchases first became important in connection with the expenditure of the Boxer Indemnity Fund.

An active part in cultivating the Chinese market was played by the overseas producers of machinery themselves. Sometimes they worked through their own branches and sometimes through agents who were often firms of general merchants. Occasionally a number of manufactures formed a joint subsidiary. In 1932, for instance, eight British engineering companies together established a new concern, Dorman Long and Associates (China) Limited, to carry out large heavy engineering projects. The great merchant houses for their part were not slow

[1] H. D. Fong, *Cotton Industry and Trade in China*, p. 53. Among the foreign exporters there were nineteen Japanese and eight British firms.

93

in entering this new line of trade. Some of them had long imported equipment for their own use in their dockyards and other installations, and from this it was an easy transition to trade in machinery required by other concerns in China. Thus Jardine Matheson were among the leading importers of machinery. Because of the specialised nature of this business, however, they organised it separately from their general import trade and worked in close association with overseas manufacturers. At first an engineering department, and after 1923 a subsidiary company, the Jardine Engineering Corporation, looked after this side of the firm's interests. The corporation had its own staff of Chinese and foreign engineers and, in addition, had attached to it representatives of many of the British, American and Swiss engineering firms whose agencies it held.

The demand on the part of the Chinese for these goods was created both by foreign example and by foreign precept. In the last quarter of the nineteenth century the chief customers for imported machinery were foreign firms located in China, and it was by observing the operation of equipment in the foreign-owned factories and transport enterprises that the Chinese normally made their first acquaintance with mechanised production. In civil engineering the same process was at work. For instance, Dorman Long's first contracts for steel frames for buildings in China were made with foreigners in Shanghai. Chinese contracts of a similar type (e.g. for the Bank of China building in 1935) followed.

Foreign importers and engineering firms took active measures to arouse interest in modern equipment among the Chinese. Illustrated price lists were often found to be of little value; but, as it was said, a 'demonstration of what a machine can do . . . tended to lead to immediate business'.[1] A British firm, Messrs. John Bourne and Company, presented a valuable collection of optical apparatus to a polytechnic in Shanghai in 1876,[2] and in 1901 a leading foreign merchant house in Shanghai opened a showroom in which various machines were placed, with a small engine to drive them, so that they could be observed in operation.[3] An American firm offered in 1912 to donate the complete equipment of the technical department of Hongkong University, and also to provide teaching staff for ten years.[4] Subsequently British manufacturers made valuable gifts of machinery to the same institution.[5] In the early years of the twentieth century many foreign firms actively

[1] *British Diplomatic and Consular Reports on Trade*, No. 2912, Trade of China, 1901, p. 55.
[2] *British Consular Trade Report*, Shanghai, 1876, p. 23.
[3] *British Diplomatic and Consular Reports on Trade*, No. 2912, Trade of China, 1901, p. 55.
[4] Speech of Chairman (Mr. Douglas Vickers) at Inaugural Dinner of the British Engineering Association, 3 December 1912. Printed in Supplement to *Annual Report of China Association*, 1912–13.
[5] *Annual Report of China Association*, 1913–14, pp. 52–61.

canvassed for orders all over China. The eagerness of the Germans in pursuit of this business was noted by contemporary observers, who were apt to contrast the German enterprise with the lethargy of the British. For instance, it was reported that a Russian brick-tea factory in Hankow had been equipped with German electrical plant 'simply because the Germans came up from Shanghai to see after the order, whilst the English firm only wrote a letter'.[1] The vigour of German competition at this time and the alarm and self-criticism to which it led among the British have already been commented on.

It was recognised by the foreigners that a substantial increase in the demand for machinery depended to a great extent upon a rise in the number of Chinese technicians with experience of mechanised production. Consequently, foreign engineering firms found it to their interest to provide opportunities for training Chinese. After the First World War overseas manufacturers arranged for Chinese industrial trainees to obtain experience in their works. In the early twenties a number of Chinese were sent to England for practical instruction in the maintenance of textile machinery, and in 1932 the Federation of British Industries instituted a scheme for training Chinese engineering apprentices in England. The Jardine Engineering Company also sponsored a scheme for sending Chinese students for training in British factories, and American manufacturers offered even more opportunities of this sort than did the British. These training facilities could be regarded, in one sense, as an instrument of international competition, for men who had received their engineering instruction in a particular country and had become well acquainted with the type of equipment in use there were likely, when they came to place contracts for Chinese establishments, to turn to the sources of supply and types of product familiar to them.

During the later twenties and early thirties these educational efforts on the part of foreign firms began to bear fruit. It has been estimated that some 80 per cent of the machinery imported into China during that period was sold to Chinese concerns. A considerable number of Chinese technicians were, by this time, to be found in managerial posts, and so the initiative in the placing of orders for engineering products tended to pass to the Chinese firms whom they advised. For business in the older types of machinery, it now became the practice for a Chinese to approach the foreign importer with inquiries for the type of machine that he required. For technical innovations and specialities, the Chinese naturally continued to depend on the enterprise of the foreign firms in bringing these to their notice.

The process by which modern technical methods were imported into China stands in marked contrast to that in Japan. In that country it was by set Government policy that Japanese students were sent abroad

[1] J. Walton, op. cit., p. 125.

for training, modern technical schools and colleges established and foreign technicians engaged. In China only sporadic efforts were made on the initiative of the Government to learn from Western example. Foreign specialists were seldom officially appointed except when their employment was part of the terms of a foreign loan contract (as with the railways), and their engagement was left to private concerns, Chinese or foreign. Similarly, the State took little part in organising the technical education of students in foreign countries and what was done derived almost entirely from private enterprise, mainly the enterprise of foreign firms.

The functions of the foreigners did not cease with the sale of the equipment. In accordance with normal engineering practice the manufacturers or importers of machinery usually arranged for it to be installed by foreign engineers who were often members of their own staff. These also gave preliminary instruction in the use of the equipment. Thus, the plant of the Canton Mint, supplied by a Birmingham firm (Messrs. Ralph Heaton and Sons) in 1899, was set up by foreign engineers and mechanics. One of these, the superintendent, continued to be employed by the Mint long after the original contract had expired.[1] Similarly, foreign experts installed the machinery at the Chengtu Mint in 1897.[2] Again, at Wenchow in 1913, the Chinese-owned Pu Hua Electric Light Company bought its plant from Messrs. Anderson Meyer and Company of Shanghai, and had it erected by one of that firm's technical experts.[3] The contract (signed in 1931) by which the China Electric Company (a subsidiary of the International Telephone and Telegraph Company) was to supply the equipment for extending the telephone facilities at Canton, provided that the foreign firm should install the new plant and erect the appropriate buildings.[4] In the textile industry, too, it was usual for British companies engaged in the machinery trade to give initial instruction in its use. These are instances of a very general practice.

There was also the problem of maintenance. Large Chinese undertakings in later years were usually quite capable of servicing their own machines, and they employed their own specialist staff, Chinese or foreign, for this purpose. This applied to the textile industry, for example. Nevertheless, the importers were often called upon to provide maintenance and service facilities for the smaller concerns.

At times foreign importers and manufacturers gave generous credit to Chinese buyers of machinery. German salesmen, who were very active at the beginning of the century, were accustomed to offer inducements in the form of long credits and loans on condition that the buyers

[1] *Chinese Customs Decennial Report*, Canton, 1882–91, p. 577.
[2] *ibid.*, Canton, 1892–1901, p. 136.
[3] *Chinese Customs Report*, Part II, Wenchow, p. 1008.
[4] E. Bing-Shuey Lee, *Modern Canton*, p. 74.

obtained further supplies, as required over a period of years, from the same source.[1] This was of considerable benefit to the Chinese undertakings. 'The Chinese nowadays', reported a British consul in 1913, 'are constantly endeavouring to obtain machinery on extended terms of payment and offer only the flimsiest security. They appear to be of the opinion that suppliers of machinery should be ready and willing, not only to supply machinery at net cash prices on extended terms, but in addition to provide the working capital for the industrial undertaking.'[2] The generous credit terms offered by the German merchants were made possible by the support accorded by the large manufacturers, such as Krupps, the A.E.G. and Siemens-Schuckert, and by the close connection between German industry and finance. British firms, unlike the Germans, were seldom ready to offer long-term credit facilities unless reputable bank guarantees were given, or unless the client's standing was beyond question. Sometimes, however, they were obliged to modify their practice under the spur of competition. For example, when in the 1930's Anglo-German rivalry for contracts was renewed, Jardine Matheson agreed to extend credit over a period of four years in connection with an order from the Nanchang Electricity and Water Works Company. The price was £104,000 and the terms of payment were 20 per cent on the signature of the contract and the balance in sixteen quarterly instalments, with interest at 6 per cent per annum. Because of the Sino-Japanese War and subsequent events, the full amount was never paid. This was true of many transactions in which long credit was given.

When compared with the trade of the leading industrial nations in engineering products, the imports of such goods into China remained small even during the thirties. But the significance of this trade for Chinese economic development was much greater than the volume might suggest. For these machinery imports represented the beginning of industrial investment in China and signalised the intrusion of capitalistic methods of production into her primitive economy. The technical consequences, moreover, were not limited to those derived immediately from the installation of the imported machines, for the Chinese copied some of them and so created an engineering industry of their own.

4. Chemical Fertilisers

In certain parts of the Far East, notably Japan, the yield of the land has been greatly increased by the application of chemical fertilisers, and the United Kingdom Trade Mission to China in 1946 was informed that the production of food crops in China could be increased by

[1] *British Diplomatic and Consular Reports on Trade*, No. 5489, Changsha, 1914, p. 5.
[2] *ibid.*, No. 5376, Shanghai, 1913, p. 8.

30 per cent by this means.[1] The opportunities for creating a market for chemical fertilisers were not neglected by foreign companies, and the steps taken by them to build up a trade were typical of the methods of sale, employed from the early years of the present century, for the new classes of goods which were then being put on the China market. In 1901 Brunner Mond and Company embarked on a policy of pushing sales of their fertilisers in the district round Chinkiang on the lower Yangtse. Their agents gave demonstrations of the effectiveness of their products on the wheat-fields of that area. Half a field was fertilised chemically, the other half was dealt with by the farmer in the traditional way, and the results were observed.[2] Again, at Canton in 1908, a British firm was reported to have made a successful attempt to introduce sodium nitrate as a fertiliser,[3] and there were other examples.

By the later twenties the market had been widened to include many provinces where artificial fertilisers a few years previously had been entirely unknown.[4] This was due chiefly to the sales compaigns of the importing firms, mainly British and German. For instance, Imperial Chemical Industries set up divisional and district offices in many cities of China and appointed Chinese distributors or agents in the small inland towns. Agents were also employed to travel about the country and canvass the farmers. In 1933 I.C.I. began a large-scale programme of field fertiliser experiments which were carried out in many parts of East and Central China. Jardine Matheson, which began selling chemical fertilisers in 1931, set up an extensive organisation for the purpose and conducted sales campaigns. Its principal Chinese agent ran an experimental farm, and the results of the experiments were made known to the ordinary cultivators through the company's sub-agents. The British and German firms were later joined by Americans; while the Japanese became important suppliers during the thirties.

In 1929 about 80 per cent of China's imports of chemical fertilisers consisted of ammonium sulphate. Half of this came from the United Kingdom and was supplied by Imperial Chemical Industries, while a quarter came from I.G. Farben Industrie. At this time efforts were made to popularise other types of fertilisers. Thus, I.G. Farben tried vigorously to introduce a fertiliser called nitrophoska, but this was not successful except in Shantung.[5] Small quantities of Chilean nitrate were sold in Hopeh, but attempts to put this on the market in the Canton delta came to nothing.

[1] *Report*, p. 73.
[2] *British Diplomatic and Consular Reports on Trade*, No. 2797, Chinkiang, 1901, p. 5.
[3] *ibid.*, No. 4386, Trade of China, 1908, p. 73.
[4] United Kingdom Department of Overseas Trade, *Report on the Commercial, Industrial and Economic Situation of China*, June 1926, p. 36.
[5] United Kingdom Department of Overseas Trade, *Report on Economic Conditions in China*, to September 1929, p. 56.

In spite of these merchandising efforts the amount of artificial fertiliser sold in China remained very small. In 1939 it amounted in China Proper to only 140,000 tons.[1] Most of the fertiliser, moreover, was sold in a few provinces, especially Kwantung, Fukien and other coastal areas. The inland market remained insignificant. The failure to enlarge sales was attributable only in part to the cost of inland transport and the poverty of the peasants, for the Government must bear a large part of the responsibility. Whereas in Japan the State had successfully encouraged the use of chemical fertilisers, with remarkable results for rice production, the Chinese governments, both central and provincial, actually threw obstacles in its way. Thus, for a long time certain chemical fertilisers were classed as war material, and so the import trade was hampered by the cumbersome formalities that attended the issue of import permits.[2] Provincial governments for their part regarded this trade as a welcome source of revenue, and they imposed heavy local customs dues on consignments sent into or through their territories.[3] The unenlightened policy of the authorities, therefore, thwarted the efforts of the foreign firms to develop a large market in these products.

5. Glass

Another illustration of the methods pursued by foreign manufacturers in creating markets in China is afforded by the activities of Messrs. Pilkington Brothers Ltd., the glass manufacturers. This firm began trading in China in 1902, and between 1923 and 1937 it conducted its affairs in that country through a subsidiary company with headquarters in Shanghai. During the twenties and thirties it employed three foreigners on its China staff. These handled the business with architects, civil engineers and large building contractors, and through them an attempt was made to bring new types and improved qualities of glass to the notice of users in the chief cities and so to enlarge the market for the firm's products. Chinese salesmen handled transactions with dealers both in the ports and up-country. The firm's chief market was in Shanghai, but its goods were also sold in North China and as far up the Yangtse as Chengtu.

6. Mineral Oil

Mineral oil from hand-dug wells has been known in China for many generations, but the quantity used was always small and the Chinese domestic consumer normally depended upon native vegetable oils for illuminating purposes. In the fourth quarter of the nineteenth century

[1] *Report of the U.K. Trade Mission to China*, 1946, p. 72.
[2] *British Diplomatic and Consular Reports on Trade*, No. 5216, Trade of China, 1912, p. 16.
[3] United Kingdom Department of Overseas Trade, *op. cit.* (1929), p. 56.

99

kerosene began to be imported by foreign merchants, and it quickly superseded vegetable oil, especially after a cheap tin lamp had been put on the market. Later, petrol, diesel oil and other oil products were brought in; but even as late as 1936 nearly half of the 1,160,000 tons of oil imported consisted of kerosene. Although electric lamps became competitive with oil lamps in many cities they were not available to the great mass of the population.

The methods by which the oil was marketed were typical of those that came to be employed for selling many new types of foreign goods, especially proprietary goods, in the early years of the present century. The two chief oil companies that operated in China were the Royal Dutch Shell and Standard Oil. The Royal Dutch Shell alliance was formed in 1907 and its interests were represented in China by three separate organisations, the Asiatic Petroleum Company (South China) Limited, the Asiatic Petroleum Company (North China) Limited, and the Compagnie Asiatique des Petroles which operated in Yunnan. The Standard Oil Company of New York became Socony Vacuum Oil Co. Inc., which merged its Far East organisation with that of Standard Oil Company (New Jersey) in 1933 to form Standard Vacuum Oil Company. These companies set up an elaborate distributive organisation which aimed at extending the sale of mineral oil throughout the country. Their network of agents, under company supervision, ensured a wide distribution, and the improved techniques of transport and storage which were introduced helped to keep the price low even in remote areas.

Efficient transport was an essential condition for sale over the vast expanse of China. The difficulties faced by the importers of mineral oil were very similar, though on a larger scale, to those that confronted the exporters of Chinese vegetable oil. New methods for the bulk storage and transport of oil had, however, been devised in the West during the later years of the nineteenth century and the early years of the present century, and the foreign oil companies were quick to introduce them into China. Originally the oil was imported in tin containers, but it was not long before oil tankers and storage tanks became the chief method of bulk transportation and storage. Tanks for storing kerosene were opened at the main ports of China during the nineties. For instance, in 1894 Lapraik, Cass and Company established three tanks at Amoy with a total capacity of 300,000 gallons, and it was noted at the time that these were not as large as similar installations that already existed at Shanghai and Swatow.[1]

At first the importers were content to sell their oil to the buyers at the larger ports who resold to the smaller dealers. Gradually the importers assumed wider functions in the distribution of their products. They set up depots and storage facilities at an increasing number of

[1] *British Diplomatic and Consular Reports on Trade*, No. 1578, Amoy, 1894, p. 3.

ports and inland points, and they assumed control over the inland distribution of the oil, first by the use of small river tankers, later by railway tank cars, and finally by motor tank trucks. These modern means of conveyance, of course, never covered the whole of the country. Ox-carts, pack-horses, camels, wheelbarrows and human porterage were still needed for distribution over the large areas where there was neither water nor rail transport. The tin containers in which the oil had normally been packed in the early days of the trade remained an important means of distribution, although they were supplemented by 20 or 40 litre returnable metal drums. These, however, were economical only within a restricted radius of the depots because of the time taken for their return, and for the remote areas the old type of container was still necessary.

While supplies to Government authorities and to some of the larger private consumers were sold direct by the head or branch offices of the oil companies, the greater part of the sales was made through the companies' Chinese agency organisations. Each branch office appointed selling agents to cover its territory. These agents were local Chinese merchants; some were specialists in oil, others did a general business. The oil consigned to them remained the company's property until sold, and the agent was officially required to remit the proceeds of the sale within two weeks, although in practice a longer period was allowed. It has been estimated that throughout China stocks equivalent to a consumption of from four to five months were held at the companies' risk. The companies had a large number of itinerant stock-checkers and inspectors to supervise the agents and to promote sales. At first these inspectors were foreigners. In later years Chinese were employed in these posts, although periodical tours of the agencies still continued to be made by members of the foreign staffs.

CHAPTER VI

BANKING AND INSURANCE

1. Banking

The native financial institutions of China appear to have been reasonably adequate to the functions which they had to discharge before the modern era; but they were not fitted for handling the international financial transactions that resulted from trade with Western countries. The European merchants, therefore, themselves had to create what was lacking, for their trade could not develop in the absence of efficient machinery for financing it. But economic institutions have a life of their own. In the political and economic conditions that existed in China throughout the nineteenth century, it was inevitable that once foreign banks had begun to participate in the China trade they should extend the range of their activities. In the end they cast their net over a wide diversity of financial activities and they became, in their own right, important agencies of Western enterprise in the Far East. This, however, was far from being their only function. At times, also, they discharged on behalf of the Chinese Government responsibilities that are normally restricted to central or official banks, and for many years they supplied China with the financial machinery necessary for coping with the financial problems associated with the modernising of her economy. The growth and the activities of the modern banks can hardly be understood without some acquaintance with the condition of Chinese currency and banking in the early years of the modern era, and this will now be briefly sketched.

The Chinese currency at that time was in a state of quite remarkable chaos and muddle. The currency used for the majority of transactions was then the copper cash (i.e. a copper coin with a square hole in the middle to permit stringing). The minting of cash had been a Government monopoly for over two thousand years; there was no system of free coinage and the value of the cash had never been fixed in terms of copper. So, although nominally the value of all cash was the same, by the nineteenth century there were in existence innumerable types which differed from one another in weight and fineness. There was also a large quantity of counterfeit coins. The cash circulated in the form of *tiao* (i.e. a certain number of cash strung together on a cord), and commodity prices were normally quoted in *tiao* or fractions thereof. But the *tiao* themselves varied in the number and type of cash of which they were composed, and a high proportion of commercial transactions consequently required the services of money-changers.

The use of silver for currency purposes began later than that of copper, and it would seem that only after the Ming dynasty was there a substantial amount of it in circulation. At first it circulated only in ingot form, the unit being the tael (or Chinese ounce), and the casting of these ingots was left to private foundries and was unregulated by law. If China can be said to have had a standard unit of currency in the nineteenth century, then the tael has the strongest claim to that distinction. Yet it was not uniform throughout China. Different places, and even different trades, used different scales. The Treasury at Peking measured its transactions in terms of a different tael from that used for customs dues, and these both differed from the Shanghai tael. In recent times, it has been estimated, there were more than 170 leading currency taels in China. The differences affected both weight and fineness. The range of variations in weight in the present century was from about 540 grains to 583 grains. The variations in fineness were also considerable, and silver ingots which attained or exceeded a certain standard of fineness were known as *sycee*.[1]

In the nineteenth century, the tael was mainly a unit of account and bankers' money. Actual payments were normally made in silver dollars. These were originally brought to China by Spanish and Portugese missionaries in the sixteenth century, but they did not begin to fill an important rôle in China's currency until after 1757 when Canton was opened to foreigners. Then these Carolus dollars poured into China in payment for her tea and silk exports, and they circulated widely not only in Kwangtung but in all the south-eastern coastal provinces.[2] When the minting of the Carolus dollars ceased in the early 1840's,[3] its place was taken by the Mexican dollar[4] which became the chief coin in which business transactions were settled, especially in the provinces of Southern and Central China. Other foreign minted silver coins also circulated during the nineteenth century; viz. the Hongkong dollar which was widely used in Kwangtung and Kwangsi, the American trade dollar, the Saigon piastre and, later in Fukien and South Manchuria, the Japanese silver yen. China did not begin to mint her own dollars until 1890. These various dollars differed slightly from one another in silver content and, although they usually exchanged at parity, on occasions some commanded a premium over others.[5]

The obstacles which this confusion of currency presented to the

---

[1] Sometimes this term was used to describe silver ingots, regardless of the standard of fineness.
[2] E. Kann, *The Currencies of China*, p. 127.
[3] *ibid.*, p. 128.
[4] The Spanish dollars had actually been minted in Mexico.
[5] *See* p. 215, *infra.*

development of trade were indeed formidable, for there was no fixed relationship between any of these different types. There were the copper cash, of varying weight and content, including numerous counterfeit cash; *tiao* which varied widely in the number and type of cash of which they were composed; and several brands of taels and silver dollars. In practice the inconveniences were less than might have been expected, since in the early part of the modern era China was composed of numerous self-contained communities. Furthermore, when it was necessary to translate one *tiao* into another, or to sort out the various types of cash, there was plenty of cheap labour to perform this task. For internal trade, then, the currency chaos merely made its modest contribution to the general inefficiency with which economic affairs were conducted; it did not bring commerce to a standstill. For the larger business transactions that took place between the great trading centres, however, the inconveniences were considerable. Since the silver dollar, though normally used for making payments, was not the standard currency, its value in terms of taels (known as the *yangli*) varied from day to day, and as there were several kinds of taels, the value of which was fixed in terms of silver, a multiple exchange transaction was necessary for most debt settlements between different trading centres; namely, first, a translation of the dollars into taels at one trading centre at the local *yangli*, second, an exchange of one kind of tael into the other, and third a conversion of the second tael into dollars at the *yangli* prevailing in the second centre.[1] This state of affairs continued until brought to an end by the abolition of the tael in 1933, when for a short time the silver dollar became the standard coin.

The condition of the currency reflected the indifference of the Chinese Central Government to what is usually regarded as one of the primary duties of government in the economic sphere. Yet this traditional indifference may well have had less deleterious effects on the Chinese economy and on international commercial relations than the kind of active monetary policy which was the most likely alternative. As long as each local tael represented a clearly defined amount of silver of a specified fineness, the Chinese price-level had some sort of anchor, and in dealings between foreigners and Chinese the currency risk was limited to variations in the gold price of silver bullion. So, in spite of the clumsiness of the tael standard, the foreign business men in 1933 were generally opposed to its abolition, for they feared that its replacement by the Chinese dollar would afford opportunities for debasement which would be eagerly seized upon if military governments obtained control of the provincial mints.

These fears appeared to be amply justified by the experiences of the

[1] Much useful information on this and other aspects of China's monetary system has been gleaned from Hou Shou-Tung, *The Currency and Banking Problems of China.*

previous thirty or forty years. Thus, the Chinese dollars minted after 1890 varied considerably from mint to mint, and even though attempts were made by the Republic to introduce uniformity in silver content, these were never completely successful. Other coins, such as subsidiary token silver coins, the minting of which also began after 1890, were grossly over-issued, so that they were exchanged for dollars at much less than their face value. The same was true of copper coins minted after 1900 with the object of replacing the old copper cash. The provincial mints poured these into the market with the result that the cent pieces had no fixed relation to the dollar, and their value fluctuated from day to day. The worst effect of Government intervention in the currency, however, was seen in the note issues of the provincial government banks. The notes were issued, for the most part, to finance the war lords who obtained control of many of the provincial governments after the death of Yuan Shih-Kai.[1] They enjoyed only a local circulation and were often heavily depreciated in terms of silver.

The condition of China's currency has been described at some length partly in the hope of throwing light on the problems that faced the foreign merchants in conducting their trade. The currency chaos also helps to explain China's very slow economic development and her prolonged resistance to the stimulus of foreign contacts. Domestic transactions were turned, in effect, into foreign transactions in the sense that an exchange operation was necessary for nearly all of them, and it was often an exchange operation between unstable and depreciated currencies. A retail trader who bought his supplies in local taels and sold them in dollars and *tiao*, or in later times, fractional silver or copper coins, would be accepting risks of fluctuations in the value of all these currencies which were largely independent of one another. Large concerns were afflicted no less than small traders. Thus the Shanghai Tramway Company lost 29 per cent of its total revenue in December 1920 through the depreciation of the copper coins in which the fares were paid. In some public utility services, as on the railways, it was normal to charge the customer a premium in order to cover the supplier against the risk of currency depreciation.[2] It is obvious that a confusion of currency which might be merely inconvenient in a country of self-sufficient local communities raised a most formidable barrier to large-scale economic development.

It is not surprising that the business of money-changing became the leading activity of many of the native banking institutions of the country. These will be now described. The native banks that flourished in the early days of the modern era were of several types. First, there were the so-called Shansi banks which conducted exchange operations

[1] Yuan, the first President of the Chinese Republic died in 1916.
[2] Hou Shou-Tung, *The Currency and Banking Problems of China*, pp. 56-8.

between one part of the country and another, having built up an exten-sive branch and agency system for the purpose. The Shansi banks appear to have had their origins among the merchants of that province whose business required them to transmit money from one part of the country to another. At one time these banks held much of the revenue of the central and provincial governments to which they sometimes granted credit. They entered upon a period of decline in the early years of the present century when the establishment of provincial government banks robbed them of their function of holding the provincial revenues and, weakened by several crises, they received a final blow from the losses sustained as a result of the Revolution of 1911. Another type of bank of rather later origin, the cash shop bank,[1] developed from money-changers. Indeed, money-changing until recent times remained the chief business of the smaller cash shop banks. The larger banks, however, conducted operations similar to those of commercial banks in the West. They devised a credit instrument known in Shanghai as the 'native bank order' and their loans were usually made in these orders. The bank order circulated like a bank-note in the business community, although it was payable not at sight but usually about ten days after issue. To a large extent it occupied among the Chinese business men the place that deposits subject to cheque occupy in the West. An elaborate system of clearing was devised to handle the 'orders', and the bankers' guild strictly regulated the business in them. The cash shop banks were owned by individuals or partners with unlimited liability. Their advances were made on the basis of personal knowledge of their clients, and they enjoyed a high reputation for integrity. They seem to have served China well so far as her internal trade was concerned, but neither they nor the Shansi banks were equipped to finance foreign trade, and from the beginning Western merchants had to evolve their own financial methods for this purpose.

The financing of the China trade by the East India Company and the Agency Houses during the early decades of the nineteenth century has al-ready been described (see Chapter II). Even after the Treaty of Nanking the Agency Houses continued to do a large part of the exchange business, and efforts to create special English banks for the East were for some time unsuccessful. A few Anglo-Indian banks, established in the forties primarily for foreign exchange transactions, had branches at Canton and Hongkong; but the extension of their business was handicapped by their lack of corporate status. The first of them to overcome this obstacle was the Oriental Bank Corporation.[2] This concern started in a small way in Bombay in 1842, transferred its headquarters to London

---

[1] Both these and the Shansi banks were often known as 'native banks'.
[2] A. S. J. Baster, 'The Origins of the British Exchange Banks in China', in *Economic History*, January 1934, p. 143.

in 1845 and obtained a charter in 1851. Once this precedent had been set, the way was cleared for other banks also to obtain the privilege of incorporation. This they did, in spite of the opposition of the East India Company and some of the Agency Houses.

The foreign exchange business thus came to be shared among the Company, the Agency Houses and a number of new banks. The facilities provided by the last-named were particularly useful to the smaller and newer merchant firms that entered the China trade after the middle of the century, and the success of those firms in the face of the competition of the older houses owes much to these new institutions. Among the most important banks founded at this time was the Chartered Bank of India, Australia and China. This was established in 1853 in London by a group of East India merchants, shipowners and members of Parliament.[1] In 1858 the Chartered Bank opened a branch at Shanghai, although it still regarded the China trade as an appendage of the Indian trade.

Other Western banks, most of them Anglo-Indian in origin, opened branches in Hongkong during the next few years. But all these banks were controlled from abroad and their directors lacked local knowledge. Consequently a desire grew up among the Western business men in China for a bank of their own, with its headquarters on the spot and organised to meet the special needs of the China trade. This desire came to fruition in 1864, when, on the initiative of Thomas Sutherland, agent of the P. and O. at Hongkong, a meeting of merchants was held in that colony and a provisional committee elected to form a bank to be chartered under the Ordinances of Hongkong. It was to be called the Hongkong and Shanghai Banking Company; two years later 'Corporation' was substituted for 'Company' in the title. The minutes of this meeting record that 'the local and foreign trade in Hongkong and at the Open Ports in China and Japan has increased so rapidly within the last few years that additional banking facilities are felt to be required. The banks now in China being only branches of corporations whose headquarters are in England or in India, and which were formed chiefly with the view of carrying on exchange operations between those countries and China, are scarcely in a position to deal satisfactorily with

[1] It received a Royal Charter authorising its establishment 'for the purpose of carrying on in London under the management of a Court of Directors by means of banks and branch banks the business of banking in any part of our colonies and dependencies in Australia and New Zealand, in the islands of Ceylon and Hongkong, or at any other port, town, city or place in China where a Consulate is or may hereafter be established or which may be under the superintendence of the principal Superintendent of Trade at Hongkong . . . and for this purpose of establishing agencies in the chief ports of India and in any of our colonies or possessions eastward of the Cape of Good Hope . . . and in other chief ports or places of trade in the East in order to conduct the business of exchange deposit and remittance in connection with their other establishments'.

the local trade which has become so much more extensive and varied than in former years. This deficiency the Hongkong and Shanghai Banking Company will supply, and it will in fact assume the same position with relation to this Colony as the Presidency Banks in India or the Banks of Australia in their respective localities.'

The Bank began business simultaneously in Hongkong and Shanghai in 1865. Its provisional committee was a cosmopolitan body, including representatives of the British, American, German and Parsee houses, and its first chief manager was a Frenchman. At first its shares were taken up mainly by persons resident in China and Japan.[1] The Bank retained this cosmopolitan character until the last years of the nineteenth century when national rivalries in China grew keen. During the First World War its directorate became almost entirely British.[2]

The Hongkong Bank (to use its popular name) was founded in prosperous days for the Eastern trade. The American Civil War had given a great stimulus to the export of raw cotton from Bombay, and British capital was poured into the Anglo-Eastern banking and trading concerns. At the same time, Shanghai was enjoying a period of great prosperity, partly because of its new trade with Japan and partly through the opening of the Yangtse ports. The boom ended in the financial crisis of 1866 when Overend and Gurney, and with it many Eastern firms, failed. At the beginning of 1866 eleven European banks were operating in Hongkong; within a year six had gone out of business. The young Hongkong and Shanghai Banking Corporation succeeded by able leadership in weathering the storm, and indeed benefited from the high mortality among its competitors. By 1868 it was already regarded as 'the most important public company in China'.[3] The Bank had some difficulties during the seventies; but, with the downfall of the Oriental Bank Corporation in the next decade, its predominance was secure.

The British banks had a cosmopolitan outlook; their presiding motives were commercial; and they treated customers of all nationalities without discrimination. So, although up to 1890 the British banks had few competitors in China, the trade of other nations in the Far East was not prejudiced thereby. Later, several non-British banks were established. Some of these were influenced by political considerations in the conduct of their business, and they were sometimes used as instruments of government policy. One of the earliest of these newcomers was the Deutsch-Asiatische Bank, a subsidiary of a group of

[1] A. S. J. Baster, 'The Origins of the British Exchange Banks in China', in *Economic History*, January, 1934, p. 148.
[2] The Bank's capital was originally 5 million Hongkong dollars. At present (1953) it stands at 20 million Hongkong dollars with a published Reserve Fund nearly five times its capital.
[3] *A Retrospect of Political and Commercial Affairs in China 1868–1872*, published by the *North China Herald*, p. 99.

German banks. It was followed by the Yokohama Specie Bank, which opened a branch in Shanghai in 1892. Before the end of the century, the Russo-Chinese Bank and the French Banque de Chine had begun business in China. A few years later came the Banque Belge pour l'Étranger, the Franco-Belgian ·Crédit Foncier pour l'Extrème Orient, the Nederlandsche Handel-Maatschappij, and two American banks, the Cathay Trust Company, controlled by the Guarantee Trust of New York, and the International Bank Corporation, which later became a subsidiary of the National City Bank of New York. Other foreign banks that became important in China included branches of the financial institutions owned by the Japanese *Zaibatsu*, and also the Oriental Development Company, a semi-official bank established by the Japanese Government in 1908 for financing enterprise in Manchuria.

Some Sino-foreign banks were also established. The Russo-Chinese Bank, and its successor, the Russo-Asiatic Bank, and also the Banque Industrielle de la Chine, fall into this category, as part of their capital was supplied by the Chinese Government. Both operated under foreign laws, however, and were considered 'to all intents and purposes foreign banks'.[1] The Sino-foreign banks established in later years were of a different type. The Chinese share of their capital was supplied not by the Chinese Government, but by individual Chinese or by Chinese banks, and they were subject to Chinese law. One joint enterprise of this kind was the Chinese-American Bank of Commerce, in which the Chase National Bank of New York had a substantial holding. At first Chinese and American interest held equal shares, but in the mid-1920's the Chinese obtained control.[2] The advantages and limitations of Sino-foreign banks were discussed by an American consul at about that time. He wrote: 'The strength of such institutions lies in the fact that they can take a greater part in the internal affairs of China than outright foreign banks, but their weakness is that, for the most part, they operate under Chinese law and cannot evade the forced political demands made upon them, and cannot avoid mixing in the internal politics of China with which the country's finances are almost hopelessly interwoven.'[3]

According to the China Bankers' Year Book, there were at the end of 1932 thirty-two foreign banks operating in China (including Hongkong). Most of them were branches or subsidiaries of institutions which had headquarters abroad, but the Hongkong and Shanghai Banking Corporation constituted, of course, a noteworthy exception. These banks confined their operations to the chief cities. Just before the outbreak of war in 1937, European banks had branches in about twelve

[1] F. E. Lee, *Currency, Banking and Finance in China*, p. 85.
[2] *ibid.*, p. 87. [3] *ibid.* p. 90.

cities in China Proper, besides others in Mukden, Harbin and Dairen. The Japanese banks had branches in many of the smaller cities of Manchuria as well as in the major centres. There is no record of the existence of any foreign bank in Chungking, or elsewhere in Szechwan, before the outbreak of the Sino-Japanese War.[1] The financing of foreign trade remained, as it had begun, the chief function of the foreign banks. In the absence of a local discount market, there was a need for types of bank credit which would cover the period between the export of the goods and the payment for them on delivery, or between the arrival of imports and the receipt of payment from the Chinese dealer. The great Agency Houses and their successors had, of course, large resources of their own; but without bank credit the lesser merchants could hardly have established themselves. In 1873 the British consul at Canton remarked how 'a trade which was in the hands of the few has drifted into those of the many' because while formerly a large capital was essential, it had later been rendered unnecessary by bank advances on shipments.[2] Trade indeed followed the banks, or at least the expansion of one depended on the presence of the other. Thus, it was remarked that the initial increase in the export trade of Tientsin was closely associated with the opening of a branch of the Hongkong Bank in that city in 1881.[3] Even as late as 1930 it was estimated that at least 90 per cent of China's foreign trade was financed through the foreign banks.[4]

These did not limit themselves to financing the merchants during the period when the goods were in transit across the ocean. In the export trade advances were made to cover the period between the purchase of the goods and shipment. Frequently an exporter already in possession of the merchandise would be granted a credit to enable him to pack and prepare it for export. In the words of the Feetham *Report*: 'a considerable proportion [of the goods for export] are financed by foreign banks during the time they are being sorted and packed in Shanghai, which may mean a period of many weeks before the goods are placed on board ship'.[5] In the import trade the accommodation provided by the banks to the foreign importer made it possible for him to extend credit to his Chinese customers. This credit was often for a period of from thirty to ninety days; in the case of capital goods the period was frequently much longer. The title to the goods, on their arrival at the port, was sometimes retained by the bank which had granted the import credit and the goods themselves were placed in a specified go-down. As payments were received from the Chinese brokers or

[1] *China Yearbook*, 1937, pp. 536–7.
[2] *British Consular Trade Report*, Canton, 1873, p. 6.
[3] *British Diplomatic and Consular Reports on Trade*, No. 2487, Tientsin, 1899, p. 12.
[4] R. Feetham, *Report to the Shanghai Municipal Council*, pp. 304–5.
[5] *ibid.*

dealers to whom the importer was selling, the goods were released piecemeal.

Most of the advances of the foreign banks for financing the export and import trade were made to foreign firms. Credit was also given, however, to Chinese merchants who were trading in imported goods, or who were concerned with the collection and preparation of goods for export. As early as 1869, the delegates of the Shanghai Chamber of Commerce reported that Chinese were getting a share in the local trade in imported goods and in Chinese products for exports, and they added that this development was being assisted by loans made by foreign banks on the security of the goods and on river shipments. 'The capital so used is highly remunerative to the shareholders of the banks, though the native banks are so strong as to prevent this from becoming an important branch of foreign business.'[1] Loans from foreign banks to Chinese tea dealers at Foochow appear to have been customary around 1881.[2]

The direct advances to Chinese merchants constituted a smaller part of the foreign banks' business than the credit which they gave to cash shop banks. These, with their intimate knowledge of their clientele, were prepared to make advances on personal credit alone, while the foreign banks required security. But the latter found it a safe and profitable business to supply the cash shop banks with short loans, either by taking up their bank orders or by giving them 'chop loans', which were equivalent to money at call, on the guarantee of their compradore. The 'chop loans' made by foreign to Chinese banks that were outstanding at the outbreak of the Revolution of 1911 in Shanghai amounted to nearly 9 million taels.[3]

The fact that the foreign banks throughout our period monopolised the financing of foreign trade (and indeed all other international financial business) meant that they in effect constituted the foreign exchange market. As long as China retained the silver standard, the functions which they had to perform in this field were very important, for fluctuations in the exchange rates on gold standard countries were of considerable amplitude, and those rates were matters of profound concern to all engaged in the China trade, foreigners and natives alike. As London was the centre of the world's silver market as well as, before 1914, the pivot of international finance as a whole, the British banks were well placed for dominating the foreign exchange business in China. It was through them, and especially through the Hongkong Bank, that the effects of changes in the gold price of silver were communicated to

[1] *British Consular Trade Report*, Hankow, 1869, p. 223.
[2] *ibid.*, Foochow, 1881, p. 8.
[3] *British Diplomatic and Consular Reports on Trade*, No. 4966, Shanghai, 1911, p. 4. The Revolution occasioned a run on the Chinese banks; foreign banks came to their aid by delaying demand for repayment of the outstanding 'chop loans'.

China, and foreign exchange dealings and international arbitrage constituted until the end of our period their chief preoccupation. Until 1935
the daily exchange rates published by the Hongkong Bank were accepted
as official rates by the market in Shanghai. The banks also played a
leading part in the financing of trade and the remittance of funds between
the chief commercial centres within China itself; as we have seen, these
internal transactions, because of the variations in the value of the tael
and dollar, involved what would be regarded elsewhere as foreign
exchange operations. The foreign banks furthermore participated
largely in the business that arose through the remittance of funds to
China by Overseas Chinese. This was a most important source of
foreign income for China, and it was the basis of the large triangular
trade by which funds sent to South China by Overseas Chinese financed
the import surplus of that region with the Yangtse Valley and so
permitted the latter to sustain an import surplus of foreign goods via
Shanghai. Thus, the indirect influence of the foreign exchange business
of the foreign banks on the Chinese economy extended far beyond the
Treaty Ports and the adjacent areas to which their direct operations
were largely confined.

This is not all. The foreign banks were not merely the channel
through which the flow of silver to and from China took place and
fluctuations in the gold price of silver were determined. They also
supplied China with an important part of its currency in the form of
their notes. These notes, together with the silver dollars which before
1890 were all minted abroad, made up the most reputable media of
exchange in China. The note-issuing right of the banks did not proceed
from the Chinese Government, but from the charters which they had
received from their home governments.[1]

Although the conditions governing the right of note issue varied from
bank to bank, most of the notes were backed by ample silver reserves.
The Chartered Bank, for instance, had a legal obligation to keep a specie
reserve equivalent to at least a third of its notes in circulation; in actual
fact, it kept sufficient silver dollars at Hongkong and the Straits to cover
fully half of its note circulation and in addition held in coin the
equivalent of a third of the liabilities to branch customers in respect
of their current accounts. The practice of other foreign banks was
similar.

Foreign bank-notes circulated not merely in the concessions and their
immediate neighbourhood but also in more distant parts. Similarly,
the notes issued in Hongkong, in terms of the Hongkong dollar, were
widely accepted in China itself. Even in 1937, when the notes of
modern Chinese banks had begun to replace the foreign-issued notes,

[1] Notes issued in Hongkong were subject to the regulations of the Hongkong
Government.

between thirty and forty million Hongkong dollar notes issued in the Colony by the three largest British banks were estimated to be circulating in South China.[1] In Yunnan and Kwangsi, notes issued by the Banque de l'Indo-Chine circulated, and in Canton those issued by the International Banking Corporation.[2] With the spread of nationalist feelings, political objection was taken to the circulation of these foreign bank-notes, and at one time their prestige was diminished through the suspension of payments by the Banque Industrielle in 1921. Yet foreigners were not slow to point out that 'in the capital of China itself the only bank-notes accepted at par were the notes of the foreign or Sino-foreign banks, while the notes of the Peking branches of the two Government banks, the Bank of China and the Bank of Communications, stood at 76·50 to 77·50 per cent respectively of their face value'.[3] During the 1930's the standing of the Government bank-notes improved and the volume of foreign notes in circulation diminished.

All these foreign notes were issued in terms of the tael, the Chinese dollar or the Hongkong dollar, but there were certain issues that were made in terms of foreign currency. These came mainly from the Japanese banks in China. The Bank of Chosen, the central bank of Korea, issued gold yen notes which during the twenties circulated in the Liaotung Leased Territory and the South Manchuria Railway Zone. The Yokohama Specie Bank's silver yen notes also had a wide currency in the same regions.[4] Before the Japanese occupation of Manchuria, the amount of gold yen notes in circulation was about 50 million and that of the silver yen notes between 5 and 10 million. Gold yen notes issued by the Bank of Taiwan, the central bank of Formosa, circulated in the province of Fukien.

The foreign banks had a large deposit business. Apart from the accounts needed by the foreign business community in China, wealthy Chinese found it convenient to place their liquid resources with those banks. When conditions were disturbed in China, there was an obvious advantage in holding deposits with banks that enjoyed extraterritorial rights. 'At Changsha, during troubled political times, many Chinese were accustomed to rush to the former American branch bank there with their deposits, for the reason that the bank afforded protection, and also because the foreign bank did for nothing what Chinese banks made a charge, and usually at such times an excessive charge, for

[1] The Hongkong and Shanghai Banking Corporation, the Chartered Bank of India, Australia and China, and the Mercantile Bank of India. Their total Hongkong note issue in June 1937 amounted to H.K. $188·5 million. The proportion issued by the Hongkong and Shanghai Banking Corporation was usually over 90 per cent. *See* F. M. Tamagna, *Banking and Finance in China*, p. 106.
[2] *ibid.*
[3] F. E. Lee, *op. cit.*, p. 85.
[4] Hou Shou-Tung, *Japanese Bank-notes in Manchuria, passim.*

doing.'[1] The liquid resources so made available to the foreign banks were profitably employed by them and were drawn from a wide area, In some cities where considerable deposits were made there was little local demand for loans. These funds were remitted to the great trading centres where the bank used them in the financing of foreign trade.

The business of the foreign banks was not limited to short-term lending nor to operations normally undertaken by commercial and exchange banks. It included industrial finance and the provision of long-term credits. In this way the banks participated in most of the new industrial enterprises of Shanghai and, while foreign concerns in particular leaned heavily upon them, they were involved also in many Chinese undertakings. For instance, between 1897 and 1901 the Russo-Chinese Bank made large advances to the Yah-Wong Cotton Spinning Company of Shanghai; by December 1901 the overdraft was nearly 380,000 taels.[2] The loans made by the Hongkong and Shanghai Banking Corporation to the China Merchants' Steam Navigation Company afford another example of long-term credits given by foreign banks to Chinese commercial ventures—in this case to an official enterprise. Yet although the business of the banks was by no means exclusively conducted with foreign nationals, it was naturally with the foreign-owned concerns in China that they became most heavily committed. Every bank or group of banks tended to form the nucleus of a national business group. 'The entire British business community in China', it was remarked in 1919, 'was dependent in some degree on the credit facilities of the Hongkong and Shanghai Banking Corporation',[3] and other banks had similar spheres of influence among their nationals.

Until the rise of modern Chinese banks the foreign banks, especially the Hongkong Bank, formed an essential link between the Chinese Government and foreign capital markets. Whenever the Government borrowed abroad, it used the foreign banks to float the loan and, subsequently, as its agent in servicing the debt. Payment of indemnities to foreign Powers and the construction of railways were the chief, though not the only, occasions for Government borrowing abroad. Foreign loans first became important in 1895 when China found it necessary to raise funds to pay the indemnity to Japan which was due in gold.[4] Later came the Boxer Indemnity and the railway loans. By 1914 loans to the amount of about £120 million had been floated; of this amount about £37 million represented those raised for railway construction. They usually carried rates of interest of between 5 and 8 per cent, and many were issued at well under par. Undoubtedly the

[1] F. E. Lee, *op. cit.*, p. 110.
[2] *Chinese Customs Decennial Report*, Shanghai, 1892–1901, p. 515.
[3] T. W. Overlach, *Foreign Financial Control in China*, p. 47.
[4] *See* p. 24 *supra*.

Chinese Government often had to borrow at very high rates, but it must be remembered that as a borrower it was a bad risk, and that in the event many of its loans went into default. The hard terms consequent on this risk were aggravated by the organisation of potential lenders into monopolistic groupings or Consortia. On the occasions when China was able to play off one set of lenders against another more favourable terms were secured.[1]

The lenders usually demanded specific security for the loans. Many of them were secured on the customs revenue and the salt revenue, which were under foreign management, while the railway loans were generally covered by a first mortgage on the railway properties. The foreign banks that undertook the flotations were entrusted with the servicing of the loans and so became responsible for safeguarding the interests of the bondholders. Their function as exchange banks came into operation in this capacity; for, although the funds from which the interest and amortisation payments were made were, until 1929, collected in silver, the bondholders had to be paid in gold.

It was in connection with the servicing of foreign debt that the banks came to undertake another function normally entrusted to a central or government bank, namely the holding of certain of the Chinese public revenues. During the Revolution of 1911 customs revenues were remitted to Shanghai and paid into foreign banks there in order to prevent funds from falling into the hands of unauthorised military and political leaders. This arrangement continued until after China obtained tariff autonomy in 1928. The banks which held these revenues (the Custodian Banks) were originally the Hongkong and Shanghai Banking Corporation, the Deutsch-Asiatische Bank and the Russo-Asiatic Bank. These were chosen because of their connections with loans secured on the customs revenues; for the payments due on these loans were subtracted from the revenues before the net surplus was handed to the Chinese Government. In 1917, when China joined the Allies in the First World War, the Deutsch-Asiatische Bank's share of the revenues was transferred to the Hongkong Bank. In 1926 the Russo-Asiatic Bank went into liquidation, and so the Hongkong Bank became the sole depository of the customs revenues. In the same way, under the Reorganisation Loan Agreement of 1913, it was laid down that the revenues of the newly established Salt Administration were to be paid into designated foreign banks as in the case of the customs revenue. The regular inflow of large sums in silver into the Custodian Banks put them in a very favourable position for giving forward

[1] See Chap. VIII and H. B. Morse, *International Relations of the Chinese Empire*, vol. III, Appendix A; S. F. Wright, *Hart and the Chinese Customs*, p. 652 *et seq.*; T. W. Overlach, *op. cit.*, J. V. A. MacMurray, *Treaties and Agreements with and concerning China*; P. H. B. Kent, *Railway Enterprise in China*.

quotations for silver, and this gave rise to complaints from the other banks.[1]

The activities of foreign bankers in China, like those of foreign merchants, were from the outset closely dependent upon the services of compradores. In all relations between the banks and the Chinese business community they were indispensable, and even the Japanese found it necessary to employ them. Before entering the service of a foreign bank, a compradore had to be vouched for by Chinese of standing and reputation, and he was required to deposit a guarantee fund with his bank in the form of cash, marketable securities, or titles to real estate. In return he undertook to engage and guarantee all Chinese employees of the bank. In his capacity as cashier he was responsible for examining all coin brought to the bank, and every transaction with the Chinese clientele was performed through the compradore and with his guarantee. Should a Chinese client default on a loan the compradore had to make good the loss. Another of his functions was in connection with native bank orders. Every such order received by a foreign bank was referred to the compradore for identification, and once an order had been accepted on his advice he became responsible for its collection. In a sense this function was similar to that of the bill-broker in the London money market *vis-à-vis* the joint stock banks, and the compradore was as sensitive to the 'smell' of a native bank order as his counterpart was to that of a bill of exchange. The compradore's department was a distinct and almost independent section of the bank's organisation. He was remunerated partly in the form of a salary and partly in commission on all items of business that passed through his hands. His was a key position in the development of foreign banking in a country distinguished by the bewildering complexity of its currency, a social and economic system unfamiliar to the Western business men and a language which few of those who traded with it attempted to learn—at any rate until very recent times. As a British consular report stated in 1901: 'it speaks very highly indeed for the business integrity of the Chinese that almost all European banks and mercantile houses in China conduct their business without having in their employment one single white man capable of checking in the slightest degree—be it even to the extent of reading simple numerals—documents submitted by native shroffs concerning transactions running into thousands of pounds'.[2]

Like the compradores in the merchant firms, those employed by the banks lost much of their importance during the thirties as certain of the

[1] The loans secured on the Customs revenues were honoured until 1939; the Salt Gabelle loans defaulted intermittently; most of the railway loans fell into arrears between the two World Wars.
[2] *British Diplomatic and Consular Reports on Trade*, No. 2912, Trade of China, 1901, p. 54.

conditions to which they owed their origin disappeared. With the modernisation of part of the Chinese economy and with the increase in the number of Western-educated Chinese and of Chinese-speaking Europeans, the barriers of language and custom that had formerly separated Western and Chinese members of the business community were lowered, and so the compradore to a large extent lost his *raison d'être*. In particular, the rise of various types of modern Chinese banks, which conducted their affairs on the same lines as Western banks, together with the decline in the importance of the cash shop banks, robbed the compradores of some of their leading functions. Finally, the abandonment by China of the silver standard in 1935, the adoption of a managed currency system and the nationalisation of the silver stocks deprived the compradores of their responsibilities in connection with the currency in which banking transactions were conducted.

These changes deserve some attention, since they led also to a decline in certain of the activities of the foreign banks themselves. Among these changes the rise during the present century of various types of modern Chinese banks can be regarded as the most significant from this point of view. This is not the place to describe the evolution of modern Chinese banking in detail. A brief description of the place they came to occupy in China's financial system is sufficient for our purpose. By the early thirties China had over 140 modern banks. These included a Central Bank, established in 1928; two chartered banks or semi-official banks, viz. the Bank of China which could trace its origin to 1904, and the Bank of Communications, founded in 1908; several provincial government banks; and a large number of ordinary commercial banks. The Central Bank of China was given charge of the Government revenues, but it did not succeed during the thirties in fulfilling the rôle of a central bank as understood in Western countries. The Bank of China was probably the largest of the Chinese banking institutions and was chartered for the purpose of taking part in foreign exchange business. In that field it competed strongly with the foreign banks, and it also became important for its commercial banking business. The Bank of Communications, originally founded to hold the revenues of the railways and the Post Office, was by the thirties supposed to act as an industrial bank and to furnish industry with long-term loans. In fact, its activities in this field were not very extensive. The provincial government banks held the provincial revenues and financed the provincial governments; but they were of little value to the business community. The other banks operated in much the same way as commercial banks in Western countries, and many of them had a substantial business. The Central Bank, the chartered banks and the provincial banks all issued notes, and this was true also of many of the commercial banks.

117

Thus by the thirties there was a substantial number of modern banking institutions owned and managed by Chinese, and the foreign banks suffered from their rivalry. By this time, moreover, the foreign banks had lost their former privileges. For instance, with the formation of the Central Bank, the Hongkong and Shanghai Banking Corporation ceased to be holders of Government revenues. Between 1928 and 1932 the transference of the salt and customs revenues to the Central Bank was completed, while the Boxer Indemnity Funds by that time had been either remitted or brought under the control of Sino-foreign boards of trustees who deposited them for the most part in the Government banks. Meanwhile, the decline of the cash shop banks during the depression of the early thirties had adversely affected the business of the foreign banks which had been accustomed to make advances through them to the Chinese sector of the economy. As time went on the modern Chinese banks attracted an increasing share of the deposits of Chinese business men and competed with the foreign banks in many types of business. Although the latter still played a leading part in the placing of China's foreign loans, they no longer monopolised this business. For instance, during the six years before the Sino-Japanese War, two foreign loans were issued through foreign banks, but in each case Chinese banks were associated with the operation. In 1934 a group of Chinese banks, Government and private, co-operated in establishing the China Development Finance Corporation. This set out with the twofold aim of developing the capital market in China and of attracting foreign capital into Chinese enterprises, and it acted as the agent of the Chinese banks in their collaboration with foreign institutions. Thus in 1936 it was associated with the British and Chinese Finance Corporation in the issue of the Shanghai-Hangchow-Ningpo Railway Completion Loan, to the amount of £1 million, on the security of the completed part of the line. The China Development Finance Corporation also negotiated other railway loan agreements with foreign interests, British and French, and it collaborated with Americans in formulating plans for financing industrial developments.[1]

During this decade important changes occurred in the Chinese currency. In 1935 the Chinese Government formally abandoned the silver standard, nationalised the stocks of silver and set up a managed currency. Henceforward, although the circulation of foreign bank-notes continued, the notes issued by the Government banks became the sole legal tender, and the foreign banks also lost their position at the centre of the foreign exchange market. In spite of the nationalistic sentiment of the time, the transference of these functions to the Chinese banks appears to have taken place smoothly and with goodwill on both sides.

[1] *North China Herald*, 19 September 1947, Speech by T. V. Soong. *See*, also, E. M. Gull, *British Economic Interests in the Far East*, pp. 163–4.

This was especially noticeable in connection with the operations that attended China's abandonment of the silver standard. T. V. Soong, the Minister of Finance, acknowledged the help rendered by the foreign banks when this step was taken. 'In the task of introducing the present currency system', he said in 1937, 'the Government has been able to rely upon the sympathetic consideration of foreign governments and financial institutions in China. This has been most helpful in inspiring public confidence and in strengthening the currency position.'[1]

It is evident that by the outbreak of the Sino-Japanese War the foreign banks had long ceased to dominate the financing of the modern sector of the Chinese economy, except in the field of foreign trade where they remained pre-eminent. Even in that field they were challenged. Thus, modern Chinese banks by 1937 were trying to capture the remittance business of the Overseas Chinese in competition with both foreigners and the old-style Chinese banks. It was with this aim that the Bank of China and the Bank of Communications established branches in South-east Asia. In 1936 the former opened its first branch in Singapore and two years later its first branch at Batavia. By 1941 it had eight branches in Java alone.[2] Although it is probable that the Western banks still had the bulk of the remittance business, they now had to fight for it against determined competitors.

2. Insurance

Long before modern insurance companies were formed, Chinese merchants had employed devices for spreading risks on goods in transit, and the merchant guilds had taken a prominent part in effecting insurance, of a kind, for their members.[3] These arrangements, however, were less systematic and widespread than the corresponding practice of marine insurance in Western countries. The need for other types of insurance, especially life or accident insurance, was smaller in China because the family and clan accepted responsibility for the individual. When Western merchants came to China they had, therefore, to provide themselves with insurance facilities as with most other services ancillary to merchanting.

In the days when it took months to communicate with Europe, it was difficult, if not impossible, for risks to be covered by insurance companies situated in London. A few of the Calcutta insurance offices appointed agents in Canton, but there was great convenience in having losses payable in China. Hence local insurance societies were formed.

[1] Speech at the Annual General Meeting of Bank of China, *North China Herald*, 7 April 1937.
[2] Mou Shou-Yu, *History of the Economic Development of the Chinese in the East Indies* (in Chinese), p. 419.
[3] For an example of the guilds' part in insurance against piracy in 1869, *see* G. R. G. Worcester, *The Junks and Sampans of the Yangtze*, vol. I, p. 47 n.

The first of these was the Canton Insurance Society, founded in 1805. Its shares were held by the managing agents in Canton and their correspondents in Calcutta and Bombay, and every five years the Society was wound up and re-formed. It was managed alternately by Dents and by the Beale-Magniac-Jardine firm until 1835 when these two concerns decided to end the arrangement.[1] The Society remained in Jardine Matheson's hands and after reorganisation became the Canton Insurance Ltd. In 1866 Jardine founded another company, the Hongkong Fire Insurance Company Ltd. Both these concerns undertook marine, fire and accident insurance. Dents, for their part, founded in 1835 the Union Insurance Society of Canton, which in 1841 transferred its head office to Hongkong. For many years this Society also used to liquidate itself periodically—in fact, every three years. 'In this way the shareholders, who were also the clients of the Society, operated for their own benefit.'[2] In 1874 the practice came to an end, the Society opened an office in London and, ceasing to be a concern that provided a system of mutual insurance for traders who were also its shareholders, it grew into a great specialised insurance company with world-wide activities.[3] These structural changes within the great China merchant houses are of some general interest, for the vertical disintegration of self-contained businesses into a number of specialist firms is, of course, a characteristic feature of commercial development.

Chinese merchants were not slow to appreciate the value of the new insurance arrangements. As we have already noted, it was the unwillingness of the foreign companies to insure junks which frequently persuaded the Chinese to ship their goods by foreign vessels. Thus the advance of foreign shipping in China waters and foreign insurance companies went hand in hand. In 1863 the British consul at Tientsin remarked that the 'principle of marine insurance annihilates the native craft. "Can you insure?" is a question which the Chinese merchants invariably put.'[4] A British traveller to Chungking in 1868 was asked about insurance by Chinese merchants in that city. 'After I had explained as well as I could the system on which they worked in Europe, I was somewhat startled by one of my visitors becoming quite enthusiastic; he entered into a long conversation with his companions which ended by their offering to provide 30,000 taels to start a company in [Chungking] if I would only undertake it in my own name, in order to secure it from the depredations of the mandarins who, they said, would not dare to squeeze a foreigner.'[5]

---

[1] M. Greenberg, op. cit., p. 171.
[2] A Brief Historical Record of the Union Insurance Society of Canton, Ltd., p. 6.
[3] ibid., p. 15 and passim.; cf. also, P. H. B. Kent, The Twentieth Century in the Far East, p. 216.
[4] British Consular Trade Report, Tientsin, 1863, p. 121.
[5] T. T. Cooper, Travels of a Pioneer of Commerce, p. 128.

In 1875 at least seven local foreign insurance companies were operating in China, with a total paid-up capital of about £570,000.[1] By then telegraphic communication had assimilated methods of conducting business and the rates of premium very closely to those in Europe. But the local companies held their own; for the convenience of being able to arrange the insurance of cargoes on the spot and the fact that many of the insurers were shareholders in the companies gave them an advantage over their distant competitors.[2] At a later date, however, some of the larger foreign export firms began to place their insurance in Europe through their head offices.[3] As the foreign merchants penetrated into new regions, they took their insurance business with them. Archibald Little, on establishing himself at Chungking in the 1890's, undertook insurance as well as shipping and trade. He specialised in covering cargoes on the dangerous river journey through the gorges between Chungking and Ichang. Wealthy Chinese merchants were usually not anxious to insure, preferring to divide their goods among several boats and to bear the risks themselves; but the smaller merchants, who often ventured their whole capital in a single cargo, made ready use of the insurance facilities that Little provided. It appears that at first he underrated the risks, and in 1893 it was 'currently reported that the losses exceeded the premia collected'.[4] Meanwhile, a number of Chinese companies were founded on the foreign pattern. As early as 1875 a purely Chinese underwriting concern was doing business in connection with the China Merchants' Steam Navigation Company.[5] But it was not until the 1930's that Chinese insurance companies became prominent. Even then few of them had the facilities to write hull insurance.

Marine insurance remained the chief, as it was the earliest, type of insurance undertaken by the foreign companies. Yet other forms of insurance were not neglected. Thus, fire insurance gradually became common in the Treaty Ports. At first it was the foreign-owned concerns which covered themselves. Then Chinese began insuring their property, and by 1937 most fair-sized Chinese factories in Shanghai, Hankow, Tientsin and Canton were covered. But in the small towns and country districts the situation was very different. There the poor construction of buildings and the lack of adequate water supplies and fire-fighting arrangements made the business too risky to be attractive. This was an early complaint. For instance, in 1876 one of the reasons given for the removal of the Russian tea factories into Hankow from the countryside was that in the city the property could be covered by

[1] *British Consular Trade Report*, Shanghai, 1875, p. 34.
[2] *ibid.*
[3] *British Diplomatic and Consular Reports on Trade*, No. 5399, Hankow, 1913, p. 12.
[4] *ibid.*, No. 1230, Chungking, 1893, p. 5, and No. 1396, Chungking, 1893, pp. 5–6.
[5] *British Consular Trade Report*, Shanghai, 1875, p. 34.

fire insurance—'which cannot be done in districts situated at a distance from foreign settlements'.[1] The obstacles to insurance operations up-country were increased after 1935 when the Chinese Government placed legal restrictions on the activities of foreign insurance companies outside the Treaty Ports. Life insurance in China as elsewhere began later than the insurance of property, and this branch of the business never made much progress. The family system weakened the inducement to take out life insurance, and at the same time the fact that births and deaths were not registered led to difficulties of identification on the death of a policy holder. In 1933 the number of life policies in China was estimated to be less than 30,000.[2]

[1] *British Consular Trade Report*, Hankow, 1876, p. 26.
[2] *North China Herald*, 7 June 1933. Report of First Annual General Meeting of the Tai Shan Insurance Company.

CHAPTER VII

WESTERN SHIPPING IN CHINA WATERS

IT has been shown in Chapter II that the expansion of Western commerce with China was from the beginning closely linked with the activities of foreign ships in Far Eastern waters. The links were not only those created by a mutual dependence of ships and trade, but at times they took the form of an integration of shipping and trading functions in the same firms. Both the East India Company and some of the merchant houses that succeeded to its empire were shipowners as well as traders, and their success in the buying and selling of goods was in a large measure dependent upon their capacity for organising the means of carriage over oceans and inland waters. The great shipping lines which, after the middle of the nineteenth century joined Europe and America with the Far East, generally owed their origins to the initiative of merchants, and some of them have retained associations with particular mercantile houses down to the present time. In the coastal and inland waters of China, the merchants' part in the inception and development of services was predominant.

In the early years of the modern era the ships that carried the cargoes between China and the West were sailing ships. This was, to later eyes, the romantic period when the great tea clippers made their easting and then raced home to London with each new season's crop. They survived until the opening of the Suez Canal in 1869 conferred a decisive advantage on the steamers, since sailing ships were not allowed through it. By then, however, steamship companies had long been competing for the trans-ocean trade. The first of these was the Peninsular and Oriental Steam Navigation Company, which came into being after protracted negotiations among the interests concerned with Oriental trade and communications, namely the British Government, the East India Company, and the merchant houses of London, Liverpool and Calcutta. In 1840 the P. and O. agreed to conduct a regular service to India with the aid of annual subsidies from the British Government and the East India Company, and in 1844 it signed a contract with the former to carry mails between Suez and Hongkong. This led to the institution of a steamer service between Ceylon and Hongkong to connect with the monthly service from Suez to Calcutta, with the result that the time taken for mail between England and China was reduced from five months to eighty days. In 1850 the service was extended to Shanghai, and in the following year it became fortnightly instead of monthly. When, shortly afterwards, the profitability of the service was threatened by the rise in the price of bunker coal at Eastern ports, the agents of the Line found a partial solution to the problem by opening up 'new coalfields which had been discovered in such places as Labuan and Formosa and by the purchase of steam colliers to transport these supplies to the Eastern depots'.[1]

By the middle sixties the P. and O. had been joined by the Messageries Impériales in the carrying of mail, passengers and cargo between Europe and Shanghai; while Alfred Holt and Company had a quarterly service from Liverpool.[2] Ten years later the Castle and Glen lines and Watts, Milburn and Company had entered the business, 'each with large steamers . . . constantly plying between Shanghai and England'.[3] The trans-Pacific steamship lines were later to appear; and the trade that had been carried on between the United States and the Far East by clippers was interrupted by the American Civil War. By 1874, however, the Pacific Mail Steamship Company was operating a bi-monthly service between Shanghai and San Francisco, and this soon met with competition from the Japanese Mitsubishi Company which began to run ships between Shanghai and Japan in 1875.[4] In 1886 an officially subsidised German line started a monthly service between China and Bremen.[5] By this time the trans-Continental railways of Canada and the United States had been completed, and the additional opportunities for carrying traffic across the Pacific led the Canadian Pacific Railway Company in 1887 to begin its service to China. Before the end of the century Japanese steamship services to America were in operation and liner services linked China with Australia and most other countries of the world. In the face of all these developments of ocean-going traffic, the Chinese themselves were passive spectators, unlike their neighbours, the Japanese, who were by then well embarked upon their career in the modern mercantile marine.

From time to time the older established shipping companies organised 'conferences' to control the rates, but their action led to vigorous complaints from the China merchants. In 1896 a witness before the Commission on British Trade in Hongkong alleged that freight rates from London were considerably in excess of those from continental European ports.[6] Archibald Little, the pioneer merchant in Szechwan, complained that his efforts to develop trade had not been seconded by British steamship companies, and that while the 'conference' rates had originally

[1] Boyd Cable, *A Hundred Years History of the P. and O.*, p. 135.
[2] *Chinese Customs Trade Report*, Shanghai, 1866, p. 11.
[3] *ibid.*, Shanghai, 1874, p. 104.
[4] *British Consular Trade Report*, Shanghai, 1875, p. 36; *see* p. 219, *infra.*
[5] *Chinese Customs Decennial Report*, Shanghai, 1882–91, p. 324.
[6] *Report on British Trade in Hongkong*, 1896, Witness No. 5.

been fixed for produce worth about £50 per ton, those same rates were later charged on goods worth only £10 to £15 per ton. 'Remonstrances are useless', he wrote, 'in the face of "conference" rates which leave a shipping agent in China tied up with red tape, and unable to meet the wants of shippers by reasonable reductions on cheap produce which cannot afford the high tariff rate agreed upon.'[1] Little stated that the rates to New York, which were not controlled by a 'conference', were from 30 to 50 per cent lower than those to the United Kingdom. Nevertheless, the 'conferences' during this period seem to have been unstable, and freight rates between China and the West were on the whole kept low through the constant invasion of the market by new-comers to the shipping business and through vigorous counter-measures taken by the merchants. Thus in 1879 an attempt by shipping companies to raise freights between Shanghai and London was broken by an association of merchants who chartered their own steamer.[2] By 1881 the same 'conference', which had been revived, consisted of five British and one French company.[3] It then attempted to tie shippers to the 'conference' ships by introducing the practice of deferred rebates; but shortly afterwards the rates were broken by the coming of new German competition.[4]

Even in the new century the 'conferences' were not always successful. For instance, a few years before the First World War, freight rates on tea exported from Hankow were low because of the competition of the Nisshin Kisen Kaisha with the European shipping companies. In 1913, however, this company joined the ring and rates were raised by 50 per cent.[5] Yet almost immediately the new price structure was destroyed. Two firms of merchant shipowners, the Danish-owned East Asiatic Company and Diederichsen and Company of Hamburg, partners in the Rickmers Line, decided to amalgamate their trade and shipping businesses, and '[were] thus able to outbid all competitors in this market (sc. at Hankow) and at the same time to undersell them in the home market'.[6] To meet this competition the 'conference' again had to reduce its rates.

In addition to this trans-ocean shipping, important services to Southeast Asia were developed. This traffic was of ancient origin and had formerly been conducted by junks, but by the seventies steamers had taken over much of the business. Besides the carriage of goods, these ships played an essential rôle in swelling the great wave of emigration from China to Siam, Malaya and the East Indies during the later years

[1] Archibald Little, *Gleanings from Fifty Years in China*, pp. 48–9.
[2] *British Consular Trade Report*, Shanghai, 1879, p. 200. For another such instance see *Chinese Customs Decennial Report*, Hankow, 1882–91, p. 169.
[3] *British Consular Trade Report*, Shanghai, 1881, p. 191.
[4] *Chinese Customs Decennial Report*, Shanghai, 1882–91, p. 324.
[5] *British Diplomatic and Consular Reports on Trade*, No. 5399, Hankow, 1913, p. 8.
[6] *ibid.*, No. 5551, Hankow, 1914, p. 8.

of the nineteenth century. The Westerners had been pioneers in organising this business, and they continued to hold much of it; but, in contrast
to their meagre share in the trans-ocean trade, the Chinese began to run
steamers on this route quite early in the modern era. In 1875 a Singapore
Chinese owned a line of steamers which ran between Amoy and
Penang.[1] By 1879 nine-tenths of the emigrants from Swatow to Singapore and Bangkok went by steamer; about half of them travelled on
ships belonging to Lloyd, Kho Tiong Poh and Company (presumably
a Sino-foreign firm), and the rest on vessels of the Holt line or on other
large steamers specially chartered for the purpose.[2] Later, German
shipping companies entered this trade. In 1901 the Norddeutscher
Lloyd Steam Navigation Company bought fifteen steamers from the
Scottish Oriental Steamship Company. These ships, which averaged
about 100 tons each, for some time enjoyed a virtual monopoly of the
emigration business between Swatow and Bangkok, and they had a
large share of the traffic to the Straits Settlements.[3] In 1906 the
Japanese Nippon Yusen Kaisha tried unsuccessfully to establish a rival
service. Then, in 1908, some Chinese and Siamese merchants combined
to form a new company to compete with the Norddeutscher Lloyd on
the service from Swatow to Bangkok and the Straits. Six ships were
chartered and Jardine Matheson acted as agents at Swatow. The
Customs Decennial Report for 1902–11 for Swatow listed six firms which
owned, or held agencies for, steamers engaged in the carriage of
emigrants from that port. These included two companies with Chinese
names. There were no fixed rates for passages, for the charge varied
from 1 dollar to 10 dollars according to whether competition was keen
or not.[4]

Dutch and German steamship companies took an important part in
carrying Chinese emigrants to the East Indies. For instance, a German
company during the nineties had a contract with the Deli Planters
Association to bring labourers to the tobacco plantations of North
Sumatra. By this arrangement the brokers, who had previously handled
the business, were circumvented and an effort was made to protect the
interests of the Chinese emigrants themselves.[5] The same cannot be
said of the emigrant traffic to Peru and Cuba. Conditions on some of
the steamers on this route were deplorable and emigrants were sometimes persuaded to embark by force or fraud. The Chinese customs
officials were unable to control the traffic because of the great power

[1] *Chinese Customs Trade Report*, Amoy, 1875, p. 249.
[2] *ibid.*, Swatow, 1879, p. 219.
[3] *British Diplomatic and Consular Reports on Trade*, No. 2443, Swatow, 1899, p. 4.
[4] *Chinese Customs Decennial Report*, Swatow, 1902–11, vol. II, p. 118.
[5] *British Diplomatic and Consular Reports on Trade*, No. 876, Pakhoi, 1890,
pp. 7–9; No. 898, Kiungchow, 1890, p. 7; No. 1997, Swatow, 1896, p. 8; No. 2620,
Swatow, 1900, p. 11.

conferred by extraterritoriality on the consuls of the Treaty Powers who, at some Chinese ports, were agents of, or were otherwise interested in, the ships concerned.[1] The British, Americans, Germans and French imposed and enforced regulations on ships of their nationalities, but vessels under other flags were sometimes quite uncontrolled.

For the purpose of this study the participation of Western ships in the coastal and river trade of China is even more interesting than their ocean-going activities. It was the growth of smuggling via Lintin and along the China coast that had helped to undermine the Canton Commercial System. After 1842, the more extensive operations of these foreign ships in Chinese waters—now more respectable but still without any legal sanction—can be attributed to the impact of the foreigners' technical superiority in shipping on the existing transport requirements of the Chinese traders; for it was to the mutual interest of the foreign shipowners and the Chinese that these vessels should ply in the home waters. The Western sailing ships were faster and more agile than the junks which had hitherto carried the traffic along the China coast, and their turn of speed not merely shortened the voyages but also enabled them to show their heels to the pirates who infested the coastal waters. Furthermore, their cargoes, unlike those of the junks, were accepted for coverage by the newly formed foreign insurance companies in Hongkong and other ports. So, in the early days of the modern era, Chinese merchants showed themselves eager to charter foreign sailing vessels. It was reported from Swatow in 1863 that there had been a great increase in the number of small ships under continental European flags, and that 'nearly all the vessels employed in the trade of the port, exclusive, of course, of steamers, were chartered by Chinese merchants'.

Steamships also made an early appearance in this trade. In 1835, only fifteen years after steamship service across the English Channel had started, Jardines put a steamer into service on the China coast. This vessel was intended to carry passengers and mail between Lintin, Macao and Whampoa; but after a few trips the Chinese authorities forbade her to enter the Canton River, and her owners sent her to Singapore. In spite of set-backs of this kind, many new ships were introduced into the coastal and river trade during the period that immediately followed the Treaty of Nanking. Subsequent treaties made reference to these activities and legalised them, notably the Treaty of Tientsin in 1858 which permitted British ships to trade up the Yangtse. The 'most favoured nation' clause, of course, extended this right to ships under the flags of the other Treaty Powers, and by 1862 twenty steamers were plying regularly on the river.[2] Foreign shipowners seldom lost much time, after the opening of a port, in establishing a

[1] *Chinese Customs Trade Report*, Amoy, 1874, p. 162.
[2] *British Consular Trade Report*, Kinkiang, 1862, p. 54.

regular service from it to Shanghai and Hongkong, and in this way the smaller ports became linked to the ocean routes. In the early years even the ocean-going vessels often called at these smaller ports, but as time went on, this practice became less usual and they limited their calls to Shanghai and Hongkong. There was an exception in the case of Tientsin which remained a port of call for ships *en route* from Japan to Europe via Shanghai.

The ships operating in the coastal and river trade were owned by numerous concerns, many small ones and a few great ones with famous names. Jardines were pioneers in this as in so many other economic activities in China. Their ships were run by several subsidiary or associated companies until 1881 when these were merged in a public company, the Indo-China Steam Navigation Company. Butterfield and Swire, as we have seen, founded the China Navigation Company to take over its ships in Chinese waters.[1] Most of the shipping firms were British, although other nationals also participated. Until 1877, for instance, one of the leading shipping companies to operate in Chinese water was the Shanghai Steam Navigation Company, a subsidiary of Russell and Company, an American firm. In that year its fleet was sold to the China Merchants' Steam Navigation Company, a Chinese-owned concern which had been founded a short time before by a group of officials. The C.M.S.N.C. passed through many vicissitudes and under varying degrees of Government control.[2] Chinese merchants were sometimes reluctant to make use of it because the Government authorities were inclined to mark down the largest shippers for 'squeeze'.[3] The foreign shipping companies, on the other hand, could keep their records secret from the Chinese officials and thus protect their clients. This experience demonstrates the handicaps imposed on Chinese enterprise by an indifferent or venal government, and also, in the legal and political conditions that existed in China throughout much of this period, the essential importance of extraterritorial privileges for the success of foreign ventures.

Among the major influences exercised by foreign firms on the economic development of China, the services which they operated on the Yangtse have a high place, for, by seizing the opportunities offered by this great waterway, these firms opened up the heart of China to trade. At the outset there were technical as well as legal and political difficulties to overcome. The swift-flowing and shoal-infested Yangtse

---

[1] *See* p. 35, *supra.*
[2] In 1933 the company was reorganised as a completely State-owned body and received a loan of £400,000 from the British Boxer Indemnity Fund for the purchase of new ships. *See Chinese Economic Journal*, June 1934, 'China's Foreign Trade', p. 600.
[3] *North China Herald*, 11 April 1878. Quoted in J. E. Orchard, *Contrasts in the Progress of Industrialisation in China and Japan*, p. 42.

was not an easy river to navigate. The problems to be faced were found to be similar to those on the rivers of North America, and good use was made of the experience gained in that continent. 'American-built steamers are preferred', it was reported in 1862; '. . . they carry cargo on deck and therefore load and discharge with greater speed, facility and safety. Paddle-wheel vessels are superior to screw steamers for navigation of the Yangtse. The former make better way against the current; and in the event of touching the ground, the reversing of the paddle wheels is found to be more effective than that of the screw.'[1] A year later it was stated that 'steamers of large carrying capacity [were] continually arriving from America' for the Yangtse service, and that this brought the rates down.[2] These American vessels sometimes made the run between Shanghai and Kiukiang in less than 48 hours in contrast to a week taken by ships unadapted to the river.[3] The suitability of American steamers gave the American concerns a decided advantage, and the Shanghai Steam Navigation Company, which was American-owned, had a substantial share of the business in the early days of Yangtse steam navigation. The British-owned China Navigation Company (Butterfield and Swire) was another pioneer in the river trade, and the Chinese Merchants' Steam Navigation Company also became important soon after its foundation. In 1874, apart from some ocean-going steamers which came up the river to ship tea in season, these three companies were carrying on almost all the river-steamer traffic between Hankow and Shanghai.[4] But they did not retain this predominance for long. In 1879 Jardine Matheson began its service on the Yangtse,[5] and by then several smaller foreign firms were also running steamers.[6]

Up to 1878 no steamers had penetrated beyond Hankow. In that year, however, the China Merchants' Steam Navigation Company began to run a steamer to Ichang, a venture in which Butterfield and Swire had a share. At first this service could not be maintained during the winter because the water was then too low. The C.M.S.N.C.'s attempts to adapt a ship for the winter service on this run was unsuccessful, and the British consul at Ichang tried in vain to interest some of the leading British companies in the project.[7] Then, in 1884, Archibald Little tackled the problem and with his small steamer, the Y-Ling, he succeeded in maintaining a service throughout the year.[8] Soon afterwards the big companies followed Little's example.

[1] *British Consular Trade Report*, Kiukiang, 1862, p. 54.
[2] *ibid.*, Kiukiang, 1863, p. 72.
[3] *ibid.*, Kiukiang, 1864, p. 169.
[4] *Chinese Customs Trade Report*, Hankow, 1874, p. 34.
[5] *ibid.*, Chinkiang, 1879, p. 86.
[6] *British Consular Trade Report*, Kiukiang, 1878, p. 100, and 1879, p. 96.
[7] *ibid.*, Ichang, 1881, p. 28.
[8] Foreword by R. S. Gundry to A. Little's *Gleanings from Fifty Years in China*, p. vi.

This success opened a new vista—a steamer service on the upper Yangtse, from Ichang to Chungking. On one part of this stretch, between Ichang and Wanhsien, the river runs through narrow gorges, and dangerous rapids impede navigation. The dauntless Little again led the way. He persuaded some friends to help in providing the capital for a specially designed stern-wheel steamer which was built to his order on the Clyde.[1] This vessel, the *Kuling*, arrived at Ichang in 1888. The Chefoo Convention, however, had laid down that traffic with Chungking should be carried by Chinese-built boats, and that only after Chinese steamers had taken cargo to Chungking and back were foreign steamers to be permitted to do so. The authorities, therefore, refused to allow the *Kuling* on the upper Yangtse and the vessel was sold. In 1895 this restriction was abolished by the Treaty of Shimonoseki. Thereupon Little designed and built a small steam launch, entirely from his own resources. In this vessel, 'acting as his own captain and engineer', he reached Chungking in 1898, although he had to be helped over the worst rapids by trackers.[2] After this encouraging start some friends agreed to join Little, and they had a larger steamer built. This ship, the *Pioneer*, made her first run between Ichang and Chungking in June 1900. Then the Boxer troubles broke out and the British authorities commandeered her to bring British subjects down the Yangtse. In the same year a German ship tried to make the trip to Chungking but was wrecked. This loss, and the interruption caused by the Boxers, delayed the coming of a regular service on this run. Eventually the credit for it went to a Chinese company. Captain Plant, who had commanded the *Pioneer* on her trip to Chungking in 1900, designed a suitable ship and 'interested a number of influential Chinese in his scheme'. In 1908 a purely Chinese company was floated, styled the Szechuan Steam Navigation Company, with a capital of 200,000 taels; 40 per cent of this sum was subscribed from official funds, and the balance was raised from private persons.[3] Plant supervised the construction of the vessel at Thorneycroft's works at Southampton.[4] When in service this craft towed alongside a flat on which cargo and passengers were carried. In 1909 the ship, and the flat, made their first run to Chungking and in the following year fourteen trips were made.[5] After the First World War several foreign companies put ships into commission on the Chungking run.

As with the ocean-going traffic in its early days, competition in coastal and river shipping was keen, and the large number of participants and the diversity of their interests provided a safeguard against the introduction of restrictive practices. Favourable terms were, therefore,

---

[1] Cornell Plant, *Glimpses of the Yangtze Gorges*, p. 46.
[2] Foreword to A. Little's *Gleanings from Fifty Years in China*, p. vii.
[3] *Chinese Customs Decennial Report*, Chungking, 1902–11, vol. I, p. 262.
[4] *ibid.*, Ichang, 1902–11, vol. I, p. 274.   [5] *ibid.*, Chungking, 1902–11, vol. I, p. 262.

still offered to shippers, in spite of efforts that were made from time to time to bring the rates under control. For instance, in the eighties the C.M.S.N.C. and two British companies combined to monopolise the Yangtse steamship trade; 'but the energy of Mr. McBain, a British merchant of Shanghai, who [had] two steamers on the line which by reduced rates continually [secured] full cargoes, [had done] much to discourage this expectation'.[1] A few years later a Commissioner of Customs at Wuhu on the lower Yangtse reported that steamer rates had fallen very heavily because of keen competition.[2] In 1893 the C.M.S.N.C. obtained a monopoly of the service from Wenchow to Ningpo and Shanghai as the two British companies had agreed to keep out; but this provoked a small 'opposition' British steamer to enter the trade with Wenchow.[3] The British consul, Bourne, in a report on the trade of Central and South China, published in 1898, gave his opinion that competition on the Yangtse had led to 'excellent terms being offered to Chinese shippers whose interests the companies go to great lengths to serve', and that as a result Chinese were able to get goods carried from Shanghai to Hankow as cheaply as the foreigners could.[4] A few years later the British consul at Hankow reported that the German and Japanese shipowners, who had recently entered the Yangtse service, had not joined the ring which the British and Chinese companies were trying to preserve. Although [as he added] there was no 'such open war of rates' as might have been expected with twenty-two steamers plying between Hankow and Ichang, it is abundantly clear that monopoly was highly vulnerable in this traffic.[5] During the First World War the German lines ceased to operate, and their activities were never resumed. The British, Japanese and other foreign companies, as well as the Chinese, maintained their business until the outbreak of war in 1937. American shipping was of negligible importance in the China coastal trade and on the Yangtse after the 1870's when Russells had sold their ships to the Chinese.[6]

The organisation and conduct of the coastal and river shipping business throws some useful light on the relations between Chinese and foreign enterprise. In the first place, this was a field in which Chinese and foreigners, especially in later years, were accustomed to co-operate closely, both in the capitalisation of the shipping concerns and in the

[1] *British Consular Trade Report*, Wuhu, 1888, p. 2.
[2] *Chinese Customs Decennial Report*, Wuhu, 1882–91, p. 251.
[3] *British Diplomatic and Consular Reports on Trade*, No. 1406, Wenchow, 1893, p. 1.
[4] *ibid.*, Miscellaneous Series, No. 458, p. 23.
[5] *ibid.*, No. 2795, Hankow, 1901, p. 5.
[6] In 1936, of the coastal and inland tonnage (excluding junks) entered and cleared at Chinese ports, 41 per cent was British owned, 35 per cent Chinese, 16 per cent Japanese, and under 1 per cent American. The corresponding proportions for ocean tonnage in the same year were 36 per cent British, 21 per cent Japanese, 9 per cent Chinese and 7 per cent American. E. M. Gull, *op. cit.*, p. 162.

organisation of the services. A high proportion of the shares of many of the foreign controlled companies was held by Chinese, and Chinese directors sat on their boards. A notable instance is Jardine Matheson's Indo-China Steam Navigation Company. In other cases, the association was legal rather than administrative or economic. Thus, Chinese-owned companies were sometimes registered in Hongkong in order that they might enjoy the protection accorded to foreign concerns. Secondly, until about 1930, almost all the officers of the merchant steamships, both Chinese and foreign-owned, in China waters were foreigners. After that time Chinese companies began to employ their own nationals as officers. The crews, on the other hand, were all Chinese. Finally, the foreign-owned shipping companies were by no means concerned exclusively, or even predominantly, with the carriage of foreign-owned goods. On the contrary, throughout the modern period, the greater part of the cargoes of foreign vessels engaged in China's domestic trade was carried for the account of Chinese merchants. According to a business man of great experience this was particularly so in the nineteenth century. Later, with the growth of the distributive networks set up by foreign firms in the newer proprietary goods trades, the foreign-owned share of the cargoes increased, but never to the extent of raising it above that of the Chinese.

CHAPTER VIII

RAILWAYS, CIVIL AVIATION AND PUBLIC UTILITIES

1. Railways

The great industrial and commercial development of the Western world during the nineteenth century was made possible by the contemporaneous improvements in transport, for in the absence of steamships and railways very narrow limits would have been set to the growth of specialised areas of raw-material production and of large-scale manufacturing industry. Railway transport was of special importance in the great continental land masses and, with the experience of the economic expansion of Europe and America, it was natural that foreigners concerned with China's trade should soon realise that without cheap internal transport the vast hinterland could never be brought within the orbit of the modern economic system. As we have seen, the long waterways offered certain opportunities which were not neglected; but there were huge areas of China which could be opened up only by improved methods of land transport, and in the nineteenth century this meant railways.

Railway construction in China raised a new set of problems for foreign enterprise. This was to be expected, for even in the Western countries the construction and operation of railways had given rise to novel issues of economic policy. In the first place, railway construction in China was only feasible if capital as well as expertise could be provided by the foreigners, and when a large fixed investment of this character was involved the Chinese Government had perforce to abandon its traditional aloofness. Secondly, the means by which the land needed for the lines could be acquired raised awkward questions, for there were complications caused by the status of the foreigner in China and by the conditions under which his economic activities were conducted. The treaties gave him various privileges, such as the right to create trading and residential centres from which his commercial enterprises might radiate, the right to travel in the interior, and the right to operate craft on the rivers; but before a railway system could be constructed those who built the lines had to acquire strips of land across the face of the country. Whereas trade had meant merely the formation of a few compact foreign enclaves, railways often meant the creation of extensive foreign zones of control. Not unnaturally the Chinese were suspicious of this extension of foreign privileges and influence, and when foreign Governments began to interest themselves in railway projects in China, these suspicions were seen to be well founded, for the railways could with justice be regarded as the spearheads of imperialism. This was not all. Plans for railway construction provoked, in the early days, the opposition of the massive conservatism of the Chinese, not merely because railways were an obvious and ever-present demonstration of Western penetration, but because they offended against ancient beliefs and cherished traditions. The scars made by the railway engineers across the land and the belching monsters of speed that disturbed the countryside were held to destroy the *Feng-shui* of the localities through which they passed (that is, the benevolent influences exerted by kindly nature).[1] To countenance such innovations was impious.

Yet for many years Chinese conservatism and Chinese nationalism alike had to retreat on this front before the persistent foreigner. The original policy of refusing all rights for railway construction soon had to be abandoned. The policy which succeeded to it, of trying to keep railway building and railway operation in Chinese hands, was defeated by China's dependence on foreign capital and by the political weakness of the Government. Railway construction became caught up in the struggle between rival Powers for influence or control in China, and it thus came to form part of the diplomatic as much as of the economic history of the period. When the 'battle of the Concessions' was over and the Government, in China Proper at any rate, seemed at last to be in a position to organise the railway development of the country, the civil war of the twenties broke out to disrupt the existing railway system and destroyed the possibilities of extension. A few years after the establishment of the Kuomintang Government in 1926, plans were made for the rehabilitation of the railways, but few of these had been realised when the Sino-Japanese War broke out in 1937. For thirty years after the Revolution of 1912, it was only in Manchuria, where most of the railways were under foreign control, that the system was efficiently operated for long periods.

It is not the purpose here to describe the history of railway development in China, as this would mean an incursion into political history. Our more limited concern is with the foreigners' part in providing capital for railway construction and in the actual building and operation of the various lines. It was in the early sixties that the first stirrings began. Sir MacDonald Stephenson, who had been prominent in railway construction in India, had his attention drawn by a retired partner of Jardine Matheson to the opportunities presented by China for similar ventures. Stephenson visited China and drew up a scheme for a comprehensive railway system, but he failed to enlist the support of the Chinese authorities. Soon afterwards, in 1865, a company was formed

[1] Sir Meyrick Hewlett, *Forty Years in China*, pp. 55–6.

134

under the auspices of Jardine Matheson to build a railway from Shanghai to Woosung, a distance of twelve miles. Chinese as well as Europeans held shares in this company which embarked on the delicate task of acquiring land for the project under the pretext that it proposed to make a road. After many delays the land was obtained and the line built.[1] In the meantime Richard Rapier, of Ransomes and Rapier of Ipswich, though ignorant of Jardine Matheson's plans, had for some years had it in mind to present the Emperor of China with miniature engines and carriages in the hope of enlisting his support for railway development. The Emperor was not interested, and so in 1874 Rapier built a small engine which he proposed to send to China when a suitable moment arrived. The promoters of the Woosung Railway heard of it, and it was sent to China for experimental service on the new line. The railway was opened in July 1876. Two larger engines were sent out and these ran regularly. The Chinese authorities were, however, bitterly opposed to the railway, for which their consent had not been obtained, and they were determined to destroy it. They therefore contracted to buy the line from the company in three instalments. When in October 1877 the final payment was made, they took over the railway and, although it had been running profitably, they dismantled the equipment, tore up the rails and threw them into the river.[2]

By this time there were many persons in China who took a more favourable view of the railways than the authorities had done—so much so that the next railway schemes were worked out by Chinese themselves. A project for a line in Formosa came to nothing, but in 1878 the Kaiping Coalmining Company (then a Chinese concern with a British engineer) received permission to build a railway to link the mines with a canal. This short line was the nucleus from which the Imperial railways of North China ultimately developed. From this time onwards the Chinese Government seems to have become reconciled to the necessity of railway construction, although it still had misgivings. Its policy was now to keep the building of railways in Chinese hands; but this foundered on its inability to mobilise Chinese capital for the purpose. Foreigners, therefore, had to provide the funds required, and with foreign capital there went, in greater or less degree, foreign control.

This foreign control was most evident in what are known as the 'concessioned' lines. These were built and subsequently operated by foreign companies which were often sponsored by foreign Governments and sometimes became instruments of political and economic penetration. They were formally distinguished—although in practice the

---

[1] The acquisition of the land meant 400 separate purchases; each plot had to be fenced as it was bought. R. S. Lewis, *Eighty Years of Enterprise, 1869–1949*, pp. 19–24.

[2] Rapiers retrieved much of this equipment and shipped it home to Ipswich. *See* R. S. Lewis, *op. cit.*, p. 24.

distinction was not always clear-cut—from the lines built with the proceeds of foreign loans for the account of the Chinese Government. A few lines were built with capital subscribed by Chinese, but at the end of 1934 it was estimated that nearly four-fifths of the capital invested in Chinese Government Railways had come from abroad.[1] This was exclusive of the amount invested in foreign-owned 'concessioned' lines and in lines belonging to mines or industrial plants.

The chief 'concessioned' lines were those in Manchuria (the Chinese Eastern Railway and the South Manchuria Railway), the French line in Yunnan and, before 1923, the German railway in Shantung. 'The history of Manchuria since 1895 has been, in the main, one of international rivalry over the construction and operation of railways and ancillary enterprises', and although we are not here concerned to recount the details of this complicated phase of international politics, an outline of events is necessary for our purpose.[2] The railway development in Manchuria owes its inception to the terms of a secret treaty, the Li-Lobanov Treaty, signed by Chinese and Russians in June 1896. By Article 4 of this treaty the Chinese gave the Russians the right to build a railway across northern Manchuria to Vladivostock, and in the following September a contract between the Chinese Government and the Russo-Chinese Bank, which was under the control of the Russian Ministry of Finance, provided for the setting up of the Chinese Eastern Railway Company. This was to build and operate the line and it was given exclusive rights of administration over the lands needed for the construction, operation and protection of the railway. In 1898 Russia obtained the lease of the southern part of the Liaotung Peninsula and the right of building a branch line to connect Port Arthur with the C.E.R. By 1903 these lines were open to traffic, and by the end of the next year the Russians had built over 1,500 miles of railway in Manchuria and had founded the modern cities of Harbin and Dairen. All this represented a heavy investment of fixed capital, most of which had, in fact, been supplied by French investors.

The defeat of Russia in the Russo-Japanese War led to the transference of the southern part of the railway to Japan, while the northern part of the system continued in Russian hands. Between 1905 and 1917 the Russians made no further attempt to extend their railways in Manchuria. After the Russian Revolution the Chinese Eastern Railway came under the control of White Russians for a period, while the Russo-Chinese Bank (now the Russo-Asiatic Bank) was reorganised in 1920 under French auspices and concluded an agreement with the Chinese Government for the future management of the line. This had little practical

[1] Cheng Lin, *The Chinese Railways*, p. 80.
[2] Based largely on F. C. Jones, *Manchuria since 1931*, Chap VI.

effect, and a Sino-Soviet agreement of 1924 and subsequent arrangements with Chang Tso-Lin led to the setting up of a Sino-Soviet board of directors for operating the line.[1] Effective control returned to Russia.

The part of the C.E.R. that had been transferred to Japan was managed after 1906 by the South Manchuria Railway Company, which became henceforth an official instrument for promoting the political and economic interests of Japan. Capital was furnished partly by the Japanese Government and partly by the great business houses of Japan, and eventually the company became engaged in a great mass of mining, industrial and transport activities in Manchuria as well as in public utilities and political and social administration. By 1932 its properties were worth 200 million yen, and it had 110,000 employees. In a word, it had become the greatest single enterprise on the continent of Asia,[2] and its success in developing the resources of Manchuria can be measured by the fact that Dairen, which the company greatly enlarged, had by 1932 become second only to Shanghai in the volume of its foreign trade. Between 1906 and 1932 the company built many new railway lines, and through its links with the trans-Siberian Railway and the Korean Railways it afforded a through service between Japan and Europe. The amount of freight carried on the S.M.R. rose from 1·3 million tons in 1907–8 to 18·5 million tons in 1929–30, and the number of passengers carried from 1·5 million to 10·4 million.

The Japanese thus solved the problem of railway construction in China by establishing in Manchuria a railway zone in which they exercised political control; their railways were, of course, regarded as a means for the realisation of ambitious political aims. The Chinese responded by building a competitive system of their own. The first Chinese-owned line in Manchuria was financed by British capital and built by the British and Chinese Corporation. This formed the nucleus of the railway properties operated by the Chinese State Railways in Manchuria. Other lines, including some built by the Japanese, were acquired by this body and new lines were constructed during the twenties in an attempt to compete with the S.M.R. The Japanese financed some of these lines and the S.M.R. even carried out contracts for their construction. By 1931 there were about 3,600 miles of railways in Manchuria, divided into three competitive systems, viz. the C.E.R. with over a thousand miles, the S.M.R. with 700 and the Chinese State Railways with 1,900 miles.

After the overthrow of Chinese authority in Manchuria in 1931, the Japanese established the Manchukuo administration and seized the

---

[1] Chang was Military Governor of Mukden under Yuan Shih-Kai. After Yuan's fall he made himself master of Manchuria and eventually declared his independence of the Central Government.

[2] Unless any greater existed in Soviet Asia.

Chinese-owned railways, the management of which was entrusted to the S.M.R. An era of great activity in railway construction then followed, and the Russians, confronted with developments which, damaging as these were to the C.E.R., they were powerless to prevent, decided to sell their railway to Japan. This sale was completed in 1935 and the S.M.R. was thus able to take over the management of the whole railway system of Manchuria. Further lines were constructed and by 1939 the total length of the railways in Manchuria was 6,250 miles. As has been said, 'The railway network, while primarily strategic in design, made possible the intensive exploitation of the agricultural and mineral resources of Manchuria.'[1] Indeed, if the political implications of these events and policies are ignored and attention concentrated on the economic results, it is clear that Japanese enterprise made an impressive contribution to the growth of an efficient transport system in Manchuria and so to the massive economic development of that country. The migration of large numbers of Chinese to Manchuria began only after railway construction had started and the greater part of the new population settled in areas contiguous to the railways. Before 1932 the only mineral resources worked on a considerable scale were those on the railway zones, and the growth in the great export of soya beans had been made possible by the transport facilities that foreign enterprise had provided. After 1932 the immense industrial developments in Manchuria must be regarded as part of the economic history of the Japanese Empire rather than of China, although after many vicissitudes the Chinese Government came into possession of the results.[2]

The great economic expansion of Manchuria stands in marked contrast to the experience of China Proper in the thirty years before the outbreak of the Second World War. But the success of the Japanese had been achieved only by imposing their dominion, first over the railway zones and then over the whole of Manchuria, and inasmuch as this success was won, at any rate during the thirties, by means that sapped the power of the Chinese Government to introduce economic reforms in the country as a whole, it was won in some degree at the expense of economic progress in the rest of China.

The other 'concessions' may be referred to very briefly. The line in Yunnan owed its origin to an agreement between China and France in 1898 by which the latter obtained the right to extend the Indo-China Railway into that province. French financial interests combined to take advantage of this concession and established for the purpose the Compagnie Française des Chemins de Fer de l'Indo-Chine et de Yunnan. The French Government of Indo-China made over the railway rights to this new concern. The construction of the line began in 1904 and was

[1] F. C. Jones, *Manchuria since 1931*, p. 114.
[2] But *see* the qualification of this statement in the note on p. 29, *supra*.

completed in 1910. It ran through mountainous and malarial country and was regarded as a fine engineering achievement. The German right to build railways in China also dated from 1898. In 1900 the Shantung Eisenbahn Gesellschaft was formed and a line from Tsingtao to Tsinan, the provincial capital, was completed four years later. During the First World War the Japanese took over the line; by an agreement of 1923 it was transferred to the Chinese Government.

The distinction between the 'concessioned' railways and the Chinese Government lines built with foreign loans, though legally clear-cut, was not always obvious in the actual administration of the properties. In the earlier contracts for building railways for the Government the foreign underwriting syndicates were given close control over the construction and operation of the lines. This was true of some of the Chinese-owned lines in Manchúria, e.g. the Peking–Mukden line, built between 1897 and 1905. A loan of this type was usually secured on a first mortgage of the property. The foreign syndicate which represented the bondholders appointed and controlled the staff and supervised the financial management until the loan was repaid. After 1908 the Chinese Government was able to obtain better terms. In that year it made a contract with combined German, British and French interests for the construction of a railway from Tientsin to Pukow. The foreign loan was secured not on the railway receipts but on certain provincial revenues, and it was laid down that 'the construction and control of the railway [would] be entirely vested in the Imperial Government of China'. Other railways for which foreign money was provided on these terms included the Shanghai–Hangchow–Ningpo, the Hankow–Canton and the Lunghai railways.[1]

The foreign companies with which the Chinese Government concluded the contracts were usually syndicates that represented several financial interests, and after obtaining the contracts they proceeded to float the loans in their home capital markets. The British and Chinese Corporation, for instance, was formed jointly by the Hongkong and Shanghai Bank and Jardine Matheson. The French Banque de l'Indo-Chine, the Banque Belge pour l'Étranger, the Deutsch-Asiatische Bank and the Russo-Chinese Bank were other leading participants in these activities. Many other concerns from time to time angled for Chinese railway contracts, and syndicates were occasionally formed to represent the financial interests of several companies. The Chinese Central Railways Limited was formed by French interests in association with the British and Chinese Corporation and the Pekin Syndicate. The Banque Belge pour l'Étranger obtained part of its funds from French and Russian sources.

Besides these organic unions of the financial interests of several

[1] The line from Haichow, on the coast of Kiangsu, westwards to Shensi.

countries, looser associations, known as Consortia, were organised for collective bargaining with the Chinese Government. These were much resented by the Chinese because they restricted the choice of markets in which to raise the loans. The first Consortium was formed in 1911 when British, American, German and French financial groups combined to offer China terms for the Hukwang Railway Loan. The Chinese Government tried to circumvent this Consortium by approaching independent British interests, but this attempt failed. In 1913 the American group was persuaded by President Wilson to withdraw from the Consortium as he considered that its activities constituted an infringement of China's sovereignty. After the First World War, however, American financiers took the lead in forming a new Consortium, in partnership with British, French and Japanese interests, for they feared that if there were no Consortium, Japan would obtain a monopoly of Chinese railway development. In the event, the political situation in China during the early twenties prevented railway construction in China Proper, and, in spite of efforts to protect the interests of the foreign bondholders, the majority of the loans fell into default.

A foreign syndicate in charge of construction of a line always employed foreigners in managerial and technical positions. For the building of the Peking–Hankow Railway (financed by nominally Belgian interests) some forty Frenchmen, thirty Belgians, twenty-five Italians and twelve other foreigners were employed and, in addition, much of the work was given out to foreign subcontractors, chiefly Italians.[1] Italian contractors, many of whom had experience of similar work in eastern Europe and Africa, also worked on the French 'concessioned' railway in Yunnan.[2] In many cases, however, the earthwork was done mainly by Chinese contractors 'who thoroughly understood their business' and required little or no foreign supervision.[3]

The control exercised by the foreign syndicates over the construction and operation of the railways was a condition of technical efficiency in the days before good Chinese engineers were available. Yet, from the standpoint of efficient operation, the methods by which the Chinese railways came into being had one serious disadvantage, for each line was built and operated as a separate unit. Thus, no railway *system* came into being—only a number of lines, 'each as distinct as if existing on separate islands'.[4] During the First World War foreign control over the railways was relaxed and the Chinese authorities were able to make

---

[1] *Chinese Customs Decennial Report*, Hankow, 1892–1901, p. 306.
[2] A. Little, *Across Yunnan*, p. 65.
[3] H. Stringer, *The Chinese Railway System*, p. 188.
[4] J. E. Baker (at one time Adviser to the Chinese Ministry of Railways), 'Transportation in China', *Annals of the American Academy of Political and Social Science*, vol. 152, November 1930, p. 168.

administrative changes. 'An effort was now made to weld these lines into a system. Within ten years the work had been practically accom-plished.'[1] This meant that most of the chief cities were now connected with through trains, even though these had to pass over different lines. Through tickets, baggage and freight services were introduced; accounts and statistics were standardised, and rolling stock was interchanged. This progress was interrupted by the civil war of the 1920's. The newly unified Chinese railway system was once again split up into sections, this time according to the regions held by the various military factions. The consequences were disastrous. 'An estimate made early in 1926 covering the period 10 September 1924 to 31 December 1925 was to the effect that as a result of military disturbances the loss of tonnage on Government lines represented a value of approximately 800 million dollars—a sum more than twice as large as the total foreign debt on the same lines.'[2] This applies, of course, to China Proper. In Man-churia, as we have seen, the railways, largely under foreign control, were prospering.

The Kuomintang Government, after establishing itself in Nanking in 1926, undertook the rehabilitation of the railways. In this they were helped by the agreement on the use of the remitted British Boxer Indemnity Fund, much of which was spent on railway equipment, including, for example, the materials for the completion of the Hankow–Canton Railway. Construction of new lines also seemed feasible once again after the long lapse caused by the First World War and the internal disturbances of the following decade. The Chinese Govern-ment was now in a position to take a less obviously subordinate rôle in this type of enterprise, and railway construction became a sphere in which foreigners and Chinese could co-operate as equals. By the 1930's modern Chinese banks were well established, and they and the Govern-ment-sponsored China Development Finance Corporation collaborated with foreign interests in raising the new loans then projected. For instance, in 1936, the C.D.F.C., in association with the British and China Corporation, and the Hongkong and Shanghai Bank, floated a joint loan for the extension of the Shanghai–Hangchow–Ningpo Railway, and shortly afterwards these concerns collaborated in other railway loans. Similarly, the C.D.F.C. and the French Groupe Uni (the Bank of Paris and the Netherlands, the Banque de l'Indo-Chine, Lazard Frères and the Sino-French Bank) together undertook responsibility for financing the proposed Chungking–Chengtu and the Nanning–Indo-China Border Railways.[3] The realisation of most of these projects was thwarted by the war with Japan. Nevertheless, some of them were

[1] Baker, *loc. cit.*, p. 169.
[2] Presumably Mexican dollars. Baker, *loc. cit.*
[3] *North China Daily News*, 19 September 1947, Speech by T. V. Soong.

completed, including the extension of the Hangchow Railway to Nanchang.

The famous Chien Tang Bridge was among those built to carry this line. By this time Chinese experts had become fully competent to direct large civil engineering works, and foreigners and Chinese co-operated intimately in the construction of this bridge. The Chinese head of the Government Bridge Department was in charge of the work. He and his staff prepared the first design but later accepted an alternative submitted by Dorman Long which had the contract for the super-structure. A local Danish firm was responsible for the substructure, and Dorman Long used them as subcontractors for the erection of the steelwork. The Chien Tang Bridge took three years to build, and then had to be blown up by the retreating Chinese forces a few weeks after its completion. Just before the outbreak of the Sino-Japanese War, plans were being made for a road and railway bridge across the Yangtse at Hankow. The preliminary designs were prepared by the Chinese Government. It is probable that if this project had been carried out British interests (principally the Hongkong and Shanghai Bank) would have joined with the Chinese in financing it, and that British engineers would have been called on to assist, as had happened with the Chien Tang Bridge. This technical and financial co-operation is an example of the new economic relations between Chinese and foreigners that came into being during the thirties. At the administrative level there were also changes. In the early days the operation of the railways had normally been supervised by foreign engineers; but later on qualified Chinese were able to take their place, and by the thirties very few Westerners were still employed on the Chinese railways.

2. Civil Aviation

The introduction of civil air services into China occurred at a time when co-operation between Chinese and Westerners at the entrepreneurial and administrative levels had become more common than in the past. Consequently, from the beginning, the growth of civil aviation was accompanied by a close association between Western firms and Chinese in the operation of the services. As the Chinese Government had, by this time, abandoned its former attitude of indifference towards commercial and industrial affairs and was, in fact, actively intervening in economic processes, it was with the Government or with officially sponsored bodies that the Westerners found themselves in collaboration.

The civil air service may be said to have had its beginning in 1929 when the Chinese Ministry of Communications signed a contract with an American company, Aviation Exploration Inc., a subsidiary of the Curtiss Wright Aeroplane Company, for the joint operation of air services in China.[1] A new concern, the Chinese National Aviation Corporation, was formed with a capital of N.C. $10 million of which the Chinese Government provided 55 per cent and the American company the remainder. Four of the seven directors, including the president and one of the vice-presidents, were nominated by the Chinese Government which thus had a controlling interest. At first pilots and executives were all Americans, and their relations with the management were not cordial. During the first year the service was irregular and the corporation lost heavily. In 1931 the Curtiss Wright Aeroplane Company sent out one of their men to reorganise it, and two years later they sold their interest to Pan-American Airways. This concern poured personnel, equipment and funds into the C.N.A.C. From then on it prospered, and before the outbreak of the Sino-Japanese War it was paying its own way without any Government subsidy.[2] The employment of Chinese pilots began in 1934. These, however, were all American-born Chinese, and it was not until 1936 that C.N.A.C. had any China-born pilots. Thereafter the number increased steadily. Chinese were also trained as ground mechanics and engineers. The corporation used American planes, and one of the results of its formation was that the British lost the China market for aeroplanes, aviation fuel and equipment.

By 1937 C.N.A.C. was operating a network of services which linked the main cities of China. From Shanghai air lines radiated westwards to Chengtu, north to Peking, and south to Canton and Hongkong with many intermediate stops, and there was also a service between Chungking and Kunming. The C.N.A.C. services were linked with the world air routes. The Chinese Government prohibited foreign air lines from entering China, partly because of the implications of extraterritoriality and partly from fear that the Japanese might use air lines as a means of political penetration. Nevertheless, connections were made with the services of Air France as a result of a contract signed in 1936 which allowed the Chinese Corporation to operate to Hanoi. In the following year, when the C.N.A.C. Canton line was extended to Hongkong, it became linked with the services of Imperial Airways. During the war many new services were begun. These maintained contacts between the largest cities of Free China and they provided after 1941 the only link with the Western world. C.N.A.C. enjoyed a high reputation for technical efficiency, especially in maintaining the difficult 'hump' service from Kunming to Dinjan in Assam which was said to operate at a higher altitude than any other civil air service in the world at that time.

Another joint concern came into existence in 1931. This was the Eurasia Aviation Corporation, a Sino-German concern formed by a

[1] *China Handbook*, 1937–45, pp. 256–60.
[2] *Far Eastern Review*, May 1937. Article by Dai Enki on 'Aviation in China.'

contract between the Chinese Ministry of Communications and the Deutsche Lufthanse A.G. Its purpose was the operation of air lines between Shanghai and Berlin, primarily for carrying mail. The Chinese Government provided two-thirds of the capital and the Germans the rest,[1] although the Chinese Government obtained funds for half its share by borrowing from the Deutsche Lufthanse at 7 per cent.[2] The managing board consisted of six directors nominated by the Chinese Government and three by the German company. So, in this case also, control was in the hands of the Chinese.

At first the pilots and chief mechanics were all Germans, but Chinese were trained both for air crews and for ground duties. Some of them were sent to Germany for advanced training and for experience in European air services. The corporation was equipped with Junkers. It had been originally planned to run a line from Shanghai via Peking to Mongolia and thence to connect with the air lines to Europe. The Japanese invasion of Manchuria in September 1931, however, meant that the terminus had to be shifted to Peking. An alternative route could not be operated because of political difficulties in Sinkiang; but services were maintained to link Shanghai, Peking and Nanking with Lanchow and Lcyang. Later the corporation operated a line between Peking and Canton via Chengchow, Hankow and Changsha. This line was subsequently extended to Hongkong. In 1935 a Sian–Chengtu service was inaugurated and in the next year this was extended south to Kunming. When the Chinese Government severed relations with Germany in August 1941, the Eurasia Aviation Corporation came completely under Chinese control. Two years later it was reorganised as the Central Air Transport Corporation.

Until 1941 almost all China's civil air transport was in the hands of these two Sino-foreign companies. Both of them were registered under Chinese law and, although they enjoyed independence in administration, they came under the general supervision of the Ministry of Communications. Neither company relied in any way on extra-territorial rights. Both were successful and at the outbreak of war in 1937 they were operating on 13,826 kilometres of air routes, and carried passengers, freight and mail.

3. Public Utilities[3]

When foreigners were given the right of residing and trading in China, this concession, as already shown, had consequences which neither Chinese nor foreigners foresaw when it was first granted. Thus Western

[1] *China Handbook* 1937–45, p. 260.
[2] *China Quarterly*, autumn 1939. Article by Chang Kia-Ngau, 'Development of Civil Aviation in China.'
[3] *See also* Appendix E on Telegraphic Communications.

merchants whose business was primarily the buying of Chinese goods for export were led inevitably to concern themselves with the organisation of production and with the provision of shipping and financial facilities. Public utilities fall into this class of derivative activities. When Westerners took up residence in the ports they wished to assure for themselves the amenities of life which their compatriots at home enjoyed, and at the same time their trading, manufacturing and transport undertakings could not be conducted efficiently without services of the type normally provided in the West by municipal authorities or public corporations. The Chinese authorities were at first neither interested in, nor capable of introducing, these public utilities. So the foreign business community was bound to take the initiative, and the forms of organisation which it established for the services were naturally similar to those found in Western countries. As in other branches of economic life, Chinese entered the field after they had become familiar with Western models; but since these undertakings required heavy capital investment it was to be expected that foreign interests should predominate until very recent times. Among the public utilities for which foreign enterprise was responsible were electricity, gas, water and local transport services; these were, of course, confined to a few of the larger centres of foreign settlement. It is not proposed to describe the evolution of all these services; we shall give only one example.

China's first electricity generating plant was set up in Shanghai by a German firm in 1882,[1] and three years later there is reference to the supply of current for street lighting by this undertaking.[2] In 1893 the plant was bought by the Municipal Council of the International Settlement which operated it until 1929. Then the undertaking was sold to the American and Foreign Power Company which worked it through a subsidiary, the Shanghai Power Company. According to the terms of the sale the company was to have a monopoly in the Settlement for forty years, and then the Council was to have the right to buy back the plant. Half the dividends above 10 per cent per annum were to be applied to the reduction of the rates, and local residents were to be given an opportunity of investment in the concern.[3] The Western District Power Company, in which the Shanghai Power Company had a majority holding, was formed to distribute the current.[4] In 1937 the Shanghai Power Company had a generating capacity of 183,500 kilowatts out of a total capacity in Shanghai of 263,000 kilowatts.[5] The rest was in the hands of five other companies. Four of these were Chinese;

[1] *Far Eastern Review*, January 1940. Article by C. C. Wong, p. 26.
[2] *British Consular Trade Report*, Shanghai, 1885, p. 6.
[3] C. F. Remer, *Foreign Investments in China*, p. 287.
[4] *Chinese Economic Journal*, May 1937, 'Electrical Enterprises in China.'
[5] *Report of the U.K. Trade Mission to China*, 1946, p. 95.

the other was the Compagnie Française de Tramway et d'Éclairage Électrique de Shanghai which supplied the French Concession.[1] Important generating plants were also established in Tientsin. In 1937 the largest of them was the Tientsin Tramway and Lighting Company, a Belgian undertaking with a capacity of 22,000 kilowatts. The British, French and Japanese municipal councils also operated plants. The only Chinese electricity company in Tientsin bought its power from the British concern.[2] At Hankow the position was similar. There, in 1937, three out of the four power companies were foreign; the largest was the British-owned Hankow Light and Power Company. There had been some early attempts to introduce electricity generation into Canton. In 1890 a syndicate composed chiefly of wealthy Chinese residents in San Francisco established a plant.[3] Its equipment, however, was unsatisfactory; the company which owned it under-capitalised; and in 1899 the concern was liquidated. Another plant, set up at Canton in 1898 also failed. Its properties were acquired by a foreign company which for some years also appears to have met with considerable difficulties.[4] Other plants were established by large mining and industrial concerns to supply their own needs for power.

Even in 1936 electricity generating in China Proper was on a very modest scale, for production in that year was less than 2,500 million kilowatt hours, about one-tenth of the production of Japan and about half that of Belgium. The larger electricity plants were concerned almost entirely with supplying foreign settlements and concerns. Outside these privileged areas and undertakings the poverty of the Chinese, the small demand for industrial power and in most areas the difficulties of fuel supply, meant that there were few opportunities for the development of a successful large-scale industry, although many small local power plants existed. The insecurity which existed in China, except in the foreign concessions, was not conducive to heavy investment by foreigners in large fixed plants and installations.

It was otherwise in Manchuria. There the generation of electricity had begun in 1902 with the setting up of a small generating station at Dairen by the Chinese Eastern Railway Company. After 1906 this plant passed into the hands of the South Manchuria Railway Company, and during the next two decades that company built a number of small plants while others were started by a joint Sino-Japanese concern. The current was used mainly for lighting and traction. In 1926 the Japanese formed the South Manchuria Electricity Company to promote electricity generation outside the S.M.R. and as a result of these developments the total quantity of electricity supplied in South Manchuria

[1] *Chinese Economic Journal*, May 1937, *loc. cit.*
[2] *loc. cit.*
[3] *Chinese Customs Decennial Report*, Canton, 1882–91, p. 564.
[4] *ibid.*, p. 196.

nearly trebled between 1924 and 1932.[1] In that year the output of current, though it compared favourably with the contemporary output in China Proper, was still small, for the demand for industrial power had not yet become substantial.

As soon as the Japanese took over the country a remarkable growth began. Their ambitious plans for Manchurian economic development could not be realised without an expansion in the supply of power, and they at once set about the reorganisation of the industry and the construction of new plants, both thermal and hydro-electric. In 1934 the Manchukuo Electric Power Company was formed as a joint Manchukuoan-Japanese Corporation to handle the production and transmission of all thermo-electric power, apart from the S.M.R. undertakings. It increased the capacity of the existing plants and built new ones, notably at Fushun and Kanchingtze. By 1939 the thermo-electric capacity of Manchuria had been raised to 500,000 kilowatts[2] compared with 894,000 for China Proper in 1937. The major innovation accomplished by the Japanese was, however, the development of hydro-electric power. Two great enterprises were begun in 1937, the Yalu River Dam and Power Station at Suiho and the Sungari River Dam and Station near Kirin. The first of these was undertaken under the joint auspices of the Governments of Manchukuo and Korea, and it was intended to supply power to the North Korean industrial region as well as to Manchuria. The work of construction was in the hands of the Japan Nitrate Fertiliser Manufacturing Company which had numerous interests in Korea, and most of the machinery was of Japanese manufacture. The dam was completed in 1941 and by 1944 a generating capacity of 460,000 kilowatts had been created. By the same year the Sungari project had been carried through to a point at which a capacity of 300,000 kilowatts was available. These undertakings ranked with the greatest engineering works in the world, and the Yalu River Dam exceeded in size the Great Boulder Dam of the United States. Besides these, other hydro-electric and thermal power stations were built during the war, and by 1945 the total capacity of the Manchurian thermal and hydro-electric stations was in the neighbourhood of 3 million kilowatts.[3] This was probably about fifteen times greater than it had been in 1932. Alone among the countries of continental Asia, Manchuria as a power producer could now rank with European industrial countries.[4] These results had, of course, been achieved through turning Manchuria into part of the Japanese Empire and developing the country to serve the strategic and economic interests of Japan.

[1] *Japan-Manchukuo Year Book*, 1936, pp. 840–1.
[2] *Report of the U.K. Trade Mission to China*, 1946, p. 192.
[3] F. C. Jones, *Manchuria since 1931*, pp. 156–8.
[4] Unless Soviet Asia's power production at that date was of a similar order.

There were a few other foreign-owned public utilities which were important enough to require mention here. The Shanghai Gas Company was founded by British interests in 1863 and was still operating after the Second World War.[1] Other British-owned public utilities included the Hongkong and China Gas Company, the Shanghai Waterworks Company, and the Shanghai Electric Construction Company. The Waterworks Company was registered in 1880 to supply water to the foreign settlements in Shanghai. The Shanghai Electric Construction Company owned and operated 18 miles of electric tramway and 21 miles of trackless trolley routes in Shanghai.[2]

[1] E. M. Gull, *op. cit.*, p. 80.
[2] *Stock Exchange Year Book*, 1952.

CHAPTER IX

MINING

1. Coal

Western mining enterprise in China encountered problems similar to those found in the course of railway development. For both types of undertaking land and rights over its use had to be acquired outside the concessions. Where foreigners were involved and unfamiliar methods introduced the xenophobia of the local population was excited. Mechanised mining, whether by foreigners or by Chinese seduced by foreign example, offended against deep-seated traditions and beliefs, for it was held to disturb the natural balance of the elements. The risk that attended an investment in great specific capital projects was, moreover, augmented by the political insecurity of the country, especially by the weakness of the Central Government in the face of hostile or rapacious provincial authorities. Further, the successful operation of a mining enterprise always depends upon the existence of efficient carriage to a market, and since China lacked an adequate railway and canal system, those responsible for sinking the mines had also, as a rule, to concern themselves with introducing new means of transport. This extension of the physical area of operations increased the vulnerability of Western-owned undertakings. On the other hand, the more alert Chinese, both among officials and private business men, who were interested in modernising the mining industry, lacked capital and technical and administrative experience in operating modern undertakings.

These obstacles delayed the introduction of Western mining methods into China long after the great coal resources of the country had become widely known, and down to the end of our period they narrowly restricted the area of operations in China Proper. They were also the explanation why, after several false starts, coal-mining in China, in so far as it was successful, rested upon close co-operation between Chinese and foreign interests within the various operating concerns themselves. In other words, modern coal-mining was essentially a joint undertaking. This applies mainly to China Proper, for Manchuria, in this as in so many other respects, stands apart. There the development of the coal resources was largely controlled by foreigners, and after 1932 it became an integral part of the great industrial expansion fostered by Japan and so is to be regarded as a part of Japan's rather than of China's economic history.

Interest in the means employed for modernising China's coal industry must not be allowed to obscure the fact that even in the middle thirties

149

the output was still very small. That of China Proper ranged between 18 and 21 million tons, about half the output of Japan and about two-thirds the output of Belgium. Even then China was still on balance an importer of coal, for many of the coastal towns found it cheaper to bring supplies from overseas than to obtain them from domestic sources. The Manchurian output in 1936 was about 13·6 million tons, and so produced only about one-third less than the rest of China.

As with most commodities, the foreigners first interested themselves in the merchanting of coal which was produced by primitive methods in Chinese-owned mines. For instance, in 1865 the Commissioner of Customs at Hankow reported that 'the energy of a French merchant at this Port and his personal researches among the coal districts have resulted in his furnishing a superior article and in his succeeding in keeping a large stock always on hand'.[1]

The next stage was reached when prospecting began. Several Westerners who visited the interior during the middle decades of the nineteenth century reported the existence of mineral resources, but their evidence was vague. Then, in the 1870's, the Shanghai Chamber of Commerce commissioned an experienced geologist, Baron Richthofen, to make an extensive survey. His reports were informative and provided a sound basis for the plans for many of the mining projects undertaken in later years. He visited many Chinese mines and speculated on the results that could be obtained from them by the introduction of Western methods. In the Chinghwa district of North Honan, for example, he found that about a hundred mines were being worked and he estimated their output of coal at between 200,000 and 300,000 tons a year. 'Work', he wrote, 'is done through vertical pits which are from 120 to 400 feet deep; their shape is cylindrical, with a diameter of five feet. The sides are secured by wicker work. A large windlass turned by eight men, serves for hoisting; the coal is raised in baskets containing 120 to 130 catties each.[2] If the mines were worked by steam and power and connected with Su-Wu by a tramway, then the anthracite of Tai-hang-shan (sc. the mountain range in the region) might be delivered cheap enough at Tientsin to compete with that from Fang-shan-lien near Peking, to which it is superior in quality.'[3] In the near-by plain the coal bed sank to a greater depth and, 'as at 400 feet below the surface too much water is encountered to allow the Chinese to proceed any further, these portions of the coalfield will be reserved till such time as more perfect methods of mining and intercommunication are introduced'.[4] On the other side of the Tai-hang-shan lies the coal and iron

[1] *Chinese Customs Trade Report*, Hankow, 1865, p. 39.
[2] 1 catty=1⅓ lb.
[3] Baron Richthofen, *Letters 1870–82*, p. 38.
[4] *ibid.*, p. 39.

field of South Shansi which Richthofen described as 'one of the most remarkable coal and iron regions in the world'; but he added that it lacked water communications and would present difficulties to railway construction.[1]

While foreigners were exploring the coal resources of China and, at the same time, were becoming ever more conscious of the obstacles in the way of their exploitation, certain Chinese mineowners were attracted by the possibility of introducing modern machinery. In 1875 a Chinese mineowner of Weihsien in Shantung imported a mining pump; but the local authorities immediately banned it, and so made it impossible for him to continue to work all his pits.[2] Other mineowners succeeded in obtaining Western mining machinery and using it without obstruction. In such cases it became usual for foreign experts to be engaged. But the ventures did not always prosper. For instance, in 1888 a Cantonese who had formerly been compradore to a foreign firm in Hankow bought 10,000 taels' worth of boring and pumping machinery for his mine near Tatung on the Yangtse. At the same time he engaged a foreign engineer on a three-year contract. 'The results, unhappily, proved unsatisfactory and the engineer was discharged three months after the date of his arrival with a year's pay and his return passage to England. After his departure the machinery, some of which had never been put together, all fell into disuse and gathered rust.'[3] The mineowner, who died in 1892, was reported to be 'an amiable old gentleman for whose venture one could have wished success'; but his son, though perhaps equally amiable, was less enterprising, for he proposed to 'continue the working with native appliances'.[4] In another instance modernisation was planned by the provincial authorities of Shantung. In the middle eighties foreign experts were engaged by the Governor, Chang Yao, to advise on operations in the Tzu Chuan mines and to install some foreign machinery. When Chang Yao died the work stopped; but it was reported that the new Governor 'had obtained the Imperial sanction to continue working this mine by foreign methods and that he intended recommencing operations energetically with the assistance of foreign experts'.[5]

These examples show that there were Chinese who were alive to the advantages of modernising the mining industry. Unfortunately, obstruction from the more conservative authorities, lack of skilled management, inadequate transport, and political insecurity handicapped their efforts no less than those of foreign entrepreneurs. It was not until the twentieth century that an advance was made and, when it came, it

[1] ibid., p. 43.
[2] British Consular Trade Report, Chefoo, 1875, p. 28.
[3] Chinese Customs Decennial Report, Wuhu, 1882–91, p. 268.
[4] ibid.
[5] ibid., Chefoo, 1882–91, p. 69.

was the result of co-operation between foreigners and Chinese in joint concerns. The way was opened by changes in the legal status of foreigners engaged in this type of enterprise. After the Boxer Rising the Powers insisted upon a more satisfactory definition of the rights of their nationals in this field. Articles were inserted in the commercial treaties by which China promised to 'recast her present mining rules in such a way as, while promoting the interests of Chinese subjects and not injuring in any way the sovereign rights of China, will offer no impediment to the attraction of foreign capital nor place foreign capitalists at a greater disadvantage than they would be under generally accepted foreign regulations'. This vague statement of principles had little immediate practical effect; but after the Revolution of 1911 the Chinese Government promulgated rules, in conformity with the principles, to define the part that foreigners might take in mining. Mining rights in China were to be reserved for Chinese subjects and to nationals of the Treaty Powers in business jointly with Chinese subjects. Foreigners were not to hold more than half the shares of a mining concern.[1] In 1930 new regulations were issued which provided that at least 51 per cent of the capital of a mining company had to be Chinese owned and that the chairman, manager and over half the directors were to be Chinese citizens.[2]

These rules had a considerable effect in shaping the structure of mining concerns in China. The best illustration of the course of events that led to the establishment of successful Sino-foreign mining companies is provided by the history of the Kailan Mining Administration and the firms from which it arose. In 1874 Li Hung-Chang, then Governor of Hopeh, commissioned a British subject to buy machinery and engage foreign engineers for coalmines near Tzechow in South Hopeh. This scheme came to nothing; but the equipment was used for the mines at Kaiping near Tientsin. These mines belonged to the Chinese Engineering and Mining Company and had been opened at the instance of Tong King-Sing, founder and head of the China Merchants' Steam Navigation Company, who was anxious to get a Chinese source of supply of coal for his steamers. By 1879 this mining concern was employing 'nine competent English engineers and foremen', and was said at that time to be operating 'on a rather large scale'.[3] The problem of transporting the coal was solved by the construction of a canal and a railway. The canal, about 21 miles long, was the first in China to be built on European principles. It was fitted with gates and substantial iron and stone bridges. A 6½-mile railway linked the colliery with the head of the canal; this had the distinction of being the first railway in China, with

---

[1] J. Arnold, *China. A Commercial and Industrial Handbook*, p. 230.
[2] *Chinese Yearbook*, 1938, p. 397.
[3] *Chinese Customs Trade Report*, Tientsin, 1877–9, p. 272.

the exception of the ill-fated line near Shanghai torn up by the order of the Government. A deep shaft was then sunk; but in 1883 work had to be temporarily stopped because an official successfully memorialised the Throne to the effect that the shaft would be deleterious to the Imperial Tombs some 60 miles away.[1] The undertaking met with other misfortunes, and its management was not always alert. Thus, although it had a monopoly of mining within ten li (3½ miles) of the colliery, it took no action to prevent others from mining coal within this area, which the company had drained. Further, it lacked vigour in developing its ancillary undertakings, and at one time its 'coal-washing, brick-making and tile plants, patent-fuel machinery and quarries were quite idle, entirely owing to want of energy in opening up a market'.[2] The railway worked satisfactorily, but the canals and river that linked it with Tientsin were scarcely navigable for the coal barges. At certain seasons the concern found difficulty in getting labour, and the mining school was ill-conducted. So the annual output of coal remained small and the company's financial affairs fell into confusion.

'No foreigner', wrote the British consul at Tientsin in 1883, 'has ever had the faintest control over the financial affairs of the Company; . . . in my opinion native systems of bookkeeping are entirely useless for large works even if those connected with them were fully to be trusted.'[3] Despite these misfortunes and deficiencies—which may well have been exaggerated by contemporary Western observers—by the late eighties coal from the Kaiping mines was being widely marketed. In 1891 the company had four steamers employed in carrying coal to Port Arthur and Weihaiwei and three in carrying it to Canton.[4] By 1899 the coal output at Kaiping exceeded 500,000 tons. 'The best coal in the old mines', it was reported in that year, 'has apparently been exhausted, but from the new mines at Linsi an enormous output is looked for, and it is mainly for their benefit and that of other mines to the eastward that harbour works are being carried out to improve these new harbours at Chinwangtao at a cost of about £100,000.'[5] This was obviously a substantial venture, and its proprietors were by no means lacking in enterprise. The capital structure of the company at this time is some-what obscure, but it would appear that foreign financial support had been attracted. Thus there is evidence that a British firm of financiers had interests in the company and that a loan of 450,000 taels had been received from the Deutsch-Asiatische Bank.[6]

During the Boxer troubles the Company's property was occupied by

---

[1] *British Consular Trade Report,,* Tientsin, 1881, p. 128.
[2] *ibid.,* Tientsin, 1883, p. 273.   [3] *ibid.*
[4] *Chinese Customs Decennial Report,* Chefoo, 1882–91, p. 74; Canton, 1882–91, p. 564.
[5] *British Diplomatic and Consular Reports on Trade,* No. 2487, Tientsin, 1899, p. 14.
[6] E. Teichman, *Affairs of China,* p. 274.

foreign troops and its director-general (Chang Yen-Mao) feared that it might be confiscated. He therefore took steps to forestall this action and sought to strengthen the Company's ties with foreign interests. A certain Mr. Detring was appointed attorney and general agent of the Company, and Detring in turn appointed Herbert Hoover,[1] previously chief engineer of the Chihli Bureau of Mines, as general manager under Bewick Moreing and Company, a British firm which now assumed control. In December 1900 a new Company styled, like the original, the Chinese Engineering and Mining Company Limited, was formed in London and registered under British law by the foreign interests now in charge of the Chinese company. In February 1901 Chang Yen-Mao assigned to the new Company all the property and rights of the old concern, and a memorandum was drawn up to set out the terms of the transfer. The new company had a capital of £1 million, of which £375,000 was allotted to the original Chinese shareholders, and it assumed all the liabilities of its predecessor. In these transactions the conduct of the Westerners did not escape criticism. According to the official Chinese account Chang signed the agreement under pressure and the original stockholders were unfairly treated. The dispute gave rise to litigation in the British Courts, and in 1905 the High Court in a judgment, which was upheld on appeal, decided that the British Company had broken the terms of the memorandum. It also passed strictures on the conduct of some of the Westerners involved.[2]

Nevertheless progress under the new management was very considerable. The Company improved the port of Chinwangtao,[3] built another five miles of railway,[4] installed electric light in the mines[5] and expanded the ancillary activities of the company, such as the manufacture of cement, tiles and similar products. In 1906 it joined with the Imperial Railways of North China in establishing an engineering and mining college.[6] In 1909 the annual output of the Company's collieries exceeded 1,360,000 tons.[7]

In the meantime another Company had been formed, namely the Lanchow Mining Company, set up in 1908. This concern was sponsored by local officials and employed German engineers as advisers.[8] It began operations in the same area as the Chinese Engineering and Mining Company, with which it vigorously competed. This rivalry came to an

---

[1] Later President of the United States.
[2] *Memorandum on the Kaiping Mining Case.* Prepared from documents and memoranda in the possession of the Chinese Government, pp. 72–93.
[3] *Chinese Customs Decennial Report*, Tientsin, 1892–1901. p. 538.
[4] *ibid.*, Chinwangtao, 1902–11, vol. I, p. 184.
[5] *British Diplomatic and Consular Reports on Trade*, No. 4152. Trade of China, 1907, p. 91.
[6] *ibid.*, No. 3916, Tientsin, 1906, p. 11.
[7] *ibid.*, Miscellaneous Series, No. 680, 1911, p. 3.
[8] *Chinese Customs Decennial Report*, Shanghai, 1902–11, Shanghai, vol. I, pp. 180–1.

end in 1912 when the two Companies became associated. Each of them retained its legal existence, but a joint body, the Kailan Mining Administration, took over the management of the collieries, the transport and marketing services and the subsidiary businesses. The Administration was controlled by a board of six, three from each company. The Chinese Mining and Engineering Company was entitled to 60 per cent and the Lanchow Company to 40 per cent of the annual profits up to £300,000; profits above that sum were to be divided equally. For nearly thirty years this joint administration worked successfully. By 1922 the annual output had risen to over 4,000,000 tons,[1] and this remained the normal level of output until the outbreak of the Sino-Japanese War. In 1936 the Kailan mines produced about a third of China Proper's bituminous coal output.[2] It supplied 60 per cent of the coal consumed in Tientsin, while places as distant as Hankow largely depended upon it for their coal supplies.[3] The Administration employed about 40,000 workers and held mining rights over some 600,000 acres. It performed with efficiency many duties of a public nature. It housed about a tenth of the labour force;[4] it provided all pits with baths and established clubs and primary and secondary schools. It interested itself in afforestation.[5]

Transport between the mines and the port of Chinwangtao continued to present difficulties throughout this period. In the 1920's the Chinese Government Railway, which carried the coal on the last stage of this journey, was short of rolling stock. The Administration thereupon financed the purchase of 18 locomotives and 600 forty-ton coal wagons, selling these to the railway on a hire-purchase system. According to the terms of the sale, this equipment was to be used solely for the purpose of carrying coal belonging to the Administration until the last instalment had been paid; but the railway was accused of having diverted a number of the locomotives to other uses, and local military leaders seized six of them.[6]

While the Kailan Mining Administration began as a Chinese Company and later passed into Sino-foreign ownership with foreigners predominant in the management, another mining company, the Pekin Syndicate, was a Western concern which started mining operations on its own before linking itself with a Chinese Company. The Syndicate

[1] United Kingdom Department of Overseas Trade, *Report on the Economic, Commercial and Industrial Situation in China*, July 1922, p. 36.
[2] *The Times*, 9 December 1946. Report of the Annual General Meeting of the Chinese Engineering and Mining Company.
[3] *Chinese Economic Journal*, April 1937, 'China's Coal Production and Trade', p. 395.
[4] *The Times*, 9 December 1946.
[5] *Chinese Customs Report*, Chinwangtao, 1921, p. 9.
[6] *Shanghai Evening News*, 8 April 1931. Article by H. G. W. Woodhead. Quoted by E. Ware, *Business and Politics in the Far East*, p. 93.

was formed in London in 1897 chiefly through the exertions of an Italian, Commendatore Luzatti. The following year Luzatti obtained a sixty-year concession to mine in certain areas of Honan and Shansi with permission to build railways as necessary. These rights were conceded in agreements with the authorities of the two provinces concerned. The Honan Agreement, which we may take as typical, laid down detailed conditions. These are worth recounting since they throw light on the Government's policy towards foreign enterprise in China at this time. Thus, it is clear that they were intended not merely to afford a general protection to Chinese interests, but in particular to compel the Western company to share its undertaking with Chinese. Each mine was to have one foreign and one Chinese manager. The foreign manager was to control the mining operations, while his Chinese colleague supervised the relations between Chinese and foreigners. The accounts were to be kept by Western methods; the foreign manager was given control over receipts and payments; but the Chinese manager was to audit them. The Syndicate was to pay compensation for any damage it should cause, whether by subsidence or otherwise, and it was to avoid disturbing shrines in the course of its operations. The Syndicate agreed to pay the Government 5 per cent on the cost of extraction as a producer's tax. There were also regulations to govern the allocation of profits. The first claim on them was to be a payment of 6 per cent on the capital invested and the next 10 per cent was to be put aside as a sinking fund until the invested capital was wholly repaid. On any profit above this, the Chinese Government was to receive 25 per cent. At the end of sixty years the mines with all the plant, materials, buildings, lands, railways and bridges were to be handed over gratuitously to the Chinese Government.[1]

Two go-betweens were to be appointed to prevent discord between the Syndicate on the one hand and the Chinese people and officials on the other. One of these go-betweens was to be nominated by the Government, and the other, also a Chinese, by the Syndicate. Chinese were to be given preference in employment. 'On first opening the mines', the agreement stated, 'foreigners must of course be employed as mining engineers and foremen but later on . . . the Syndicate should arrange to select for such positions any Chinese who may be proficient in mining, engineering or managing work.'[2] Chinese were to be entirely employed in subordinate positions and natives of Honan were to be given preference. Fair wages were to be paid; and regulations modelled on those of Europe and America were to be drawn up to govern pensions, compensation for injuries and hours of work. These regulations were subject to

[1] J. V. A. MacMurray, *Treaties and Agreements with and concerning China, 1894–1919*, vol. I, p. 131 *et seq.*
[2] *ibid.*, p. 133.

the approval of the Chinese Government. The Syndicate agreed to establish a school of engineering and mining to train young Chinese for positions in the mines and railways, and Chinese were to be given opportunities of becoming shareholders.

Within a few months of the signing of this agreement the Syndicate sent out an expedition to report on the concessions and to estimate the cost of railways to the Yangtse and the Wei River and of other works necessary to development. The survey led to the conclusion that 'the coalfields and iron ore deposits contained within the concessions of the Pekin Syndicate are of enormous extent and value ... the demand for this coal in China itself is now large and there are reasonable grounds for the assumption that it will besides command an extensive export sale'. The quantity of iron ore available was reported to be 'practically unlimited'. After analysing samples, experts considered it 'to be of excellent quality for smelting purposes and to yield as much metal as good Spanish ores . . . The excellence of the ore, the abundance and proximity of cheap fuel suitable in its raw state for smelting purposes, the lowness of wages and the certainty of a large demand' gave reason for thinking that the establishment of an ironworks would be worth while. Finally, the construction of railways to connect the mines with navigable waters was likely to be achieved without great expense.[1]

This optimistic report did not lead to immediate action because of the outbreak of the Boxer troubles; but in 1902 a mining camp was pitched in the Chinghwa Coalfield of North Honan. A railway was built to connect this coalfield with Taokow on the Wei River. On its completion in 1905 the ownership of the railway passed to the Chinese Government for which the Syndicate ran it on commission. There was, as always, opposition from local interests. In Shansi this was so vigorous that in 1908 the Syndicate surrendered its rights in the province in return for compensation in a sum of 2,750,000 taels; while in Honan a Chinese company, the Chung Yuan Company, obstructed the Syndicate's operations and was alleged to have violated its concessionary rights. These difficulties found a solution similar to that reached by the Kailan Mining Administration. In 1915, by an agreement between the Syndicate and the Chung Yuan Company, a new company, the Fu Chung Corporation, was formed to market all the coal produced by both mining concerns. The new corporation's capital of one million silver dollars was subscribed in equal shares by the two participants. For the next eighteen years the two producing companies marketed their coal through this joint sales organisation, and in 1933, they reached a new agreement by which control over the actual mining operations was to be undertaken by a joint organisation called the Chung Fu Joint Mining

[1] *Report* by Mr. J. G. H. Glass, November 1899, pp. 41–2.

Administration.[1] This made the similarity with the K.M.A. very close.

During the twenties and early thirties the mining activities of this concern were disrupted by political upheavals. In 1927 General Feng Yu-Hsiang (the chief rival of Chiang Kai-Shek) confiscated the Chung Yuan Company's property and prevented the Syndicate from operating its mines. Most of the foreign staff were withdrawn at the order of the British Legation and the majority of the Syndicate's 12,000 Chinese employees were thrown out of work.[2] Throughout these years some workers were kept on to supply electric light and water to the neighbourhood, and this 'helped to relieve in a practical manner the distress which was so prevalent all around Chiaotso'.[3] In March 1931 employees of the Pekin Syndicate paraded the streets with tablets which eulogised the colliery manager and two of his Chinese staff.[4] Yet this expression of goodwill did not allay the endemic local hostility, and in 1933 students from Chiaotso colleges and schools demonstrated against the Syndicate. Attempts to reopen the mines, although supported by the Central Government, were thwarted by provincial officials. When eventually in 1934 work was resumed, the mines were found to be waterlogged, and pumping was necessary for several months before mining could start. In 1936, when the mines were working full time, 1,350,000 tons of coal were sold.[5] The next year the property of the joint administration was seized by the Japanese.

Apart from the two major concerns, there were several smaller ventures in which foreigners took part. The Pekin Syndicate owned coalmines in Szechwan, but these were on a much smaller scale than its undertakings in Honan. Another Sino-British concern, the Tung Hsing Coalmining Company, operated at Mentoukow, near Peking. That restless innovator, Archibald Little, tried his hand in mining as in so many other ventures; but in this case the obstacles to be overcome proved to be too formidable. In 1898, in association with some Chinese, he began to work the Kiangpei mines at Lung Wang Tung, thirty miles from Chungking.[6] At first he enjoyed a fair measure of success although his operations were on a small scale. When Little retired from China the mines passed to a Sino-British company, the Kiangpei Ting Coal and Iron Mining Company, which ordered plant from abroad and planned to build a light railway to the nearest waterway.[7] 'Matters

[1] *Stock Exchange Yearbook* 1950, vol. II, p. 3256.
[2] *Oriental Affairs*, September 1931, p. 125.
[3] *North China Herald*, 7 April 1931.
[4] *ibid.*
[5] Chairman of Pekin Syndicate at Annual General Meeting, 27 July 1937. Quoted in E. M. Gull, *op. cit.*, p. 195.
[6] *China Association Annual Report*, 1908–9, pp. 82 *et seq.*
[7] *British Diplomatic and Consular Reports on Trade*, No. 3943, Trade of China, 1906, p. 104.

progressed well and the output of good marketable coal was very satisfactory until May 1908 when a difference of opinion relating to the
interpretation of the terms of their concession caused the company to
cease operation.'[1] It was the old story of the refusal of provincial
authorities to act in accordance with obligations accepted by the Central
Government. This obstruction prevented the laying of the light railway
to the mines, even though the equipment had already arrived.[2] Finally,
in 1909, the company surrended the concession in return for compensation. From then on the mine was operated by a local and purely
Chinese concern which contented itself with primitive methods of coal
getting. The first attempt to introduce modern mining into Szechwan
thus ended in failure.[3]

Other nationals besides the British took part in the development of
Chinese mining resources. Before the First World War German interests
undertook large-scale coal-mining in Shantung. In 1902 the Schantung
Bergbau Gesellschaft opened mines at Fangtze and Hungshan, and by
1910 the annual output of each of these collieries exceeded 200,000 tons.
At that time a European staff of 77 and nearly 6,000 Chinese workers
were employed.[4] Germans also collaborated with the Chinese Government in operating mines on the Hopeh-Shansi border. These were the
Ching Hsing Collieries which were managed by a German engineer, and
by 1910 produced 150,000 tons a year.[5]

In later years the Japanese became very prominent in this industry.
Some of their enterprises were located in China Proper, for example, the
Lu Ta Mining Company, a Sino-Japanese concern which began to raise
coal in Shantung in 1923. Their main activities, however, were in
Manchuria. Coal had been raised in that country by primitive methods
for centuries before the modern industrial era; but it was the Russians
who first introduced mechanised mining. This they did for the purpose
of serving the needs of the Chinese Eastern Railway. Output remained
quite small until after the Russo-Japanese War when the Japanese
inherited the famous Fushun Mines. In 1908 these passed under the
control of the South Manchurian Railway Company, and an era of
rapid expansion began. Output from these mines rose from under
500,000 tons in 1908 to over 3 million tons in 1920 and to about
7 million tons in 1930; this represented about three-quarters of the
whole Manchurian output.[6] By 1930 the S.M.R. were also operating
collieries at Yentai; while the Okura firm, in association with Chinese

[1] *Chinese Customs Decennial Report*, Chungking, 1902–11, vol. I, p. 268.
[2] *Annual Report of China Association*, 1909–10, p. 83.
[3] *Chinese Customs Decennial Report*, Chungking, 1902–11, vol. I, p. 268; *British
Diplomatic and Consular Reports on Trade*, No. 4489, Chungking, 1909, p. 9.
[4] *British Diplomatic and Consular Reports on Trade*, Miscellaneous Series, No. 680,
1911, p. 6.
[5] *ibid.*, p. 4.
[6] F. C. Jones, *Manchuria since 1931*, pp. 10, 154–5.

interests, worked a mine at Penhsihu to the south-east of Mukden, where 400,000 tons of good coking coal was annually produced. These three groups of mines were responsible for nearly all the coal then produced in South Manchuria, although the Chinese administration at Mukden operated small mines in Jehol and elsewhere and in North Manchuria the C.E.R. was responsible for a small output.[1]

Thus, before the Japanese occupation of Manchuria, nearly all the Manchurian coal was produced in the railway zones which were under foreign jurisdiction, and little had been done to develop the resources elsewhere. Indeed, the Chinese even tried to hinder the exploitation of the Fushun coal measures by arguing that the removal of the shale, which overlay the coal in that area, was not covered by the terms of the concession granted by the Chinese Government.[2]

After the Japanese had established Manchukuo, the pace of development quickened both in the older centres and in areas beyond the railway zones. In 1934 a semi-official concern, the Manchuria Coal Mining Company, was jointly capitalised by the Manchukuo Government and the S.M.R. to run all the collieries, except those at Fushun, Yentai and Penhsihu. As the expansion of the heavy industry both of Manchuria and of Japan Proper was dependent upon the enlargement of the fuel supply, vigorous efforts were made during the thirties to develop the resources. New mines were opened in areas beyond the old railway zones, and the former mining regions were more intensively worked. By 1936 output in Manchuria is estimated to have reached 13·6 million tons of which the Fushun Collieries produced about 9 million tons.[3] By then this concern was not only the largest in China but was considered to be the largest opencast colliery in the world. It is significant that whereas in China Proper the chief mining concerns were jointly owned and operated by foreigners and Chinese, the chief mines in Manchuria were, from 1908, under purely foreign ownership and control. Even there, however, a few joint enterprises existed, apart from the purely formal association of the Manchukuo Government and the S.M.R. in the Manchuria Coalmining Company.

2. Other Minerals

When foreigners began to take the initiative in the mining of iron ore in China, they met with the same difficulties as those they had encountered in coal-mining. To quote an example, in 1904 the London

[1] F. C. Jones, *Manchuria since 1931*, p. 155.
[2] E. B. Schumpeter (ed.), *The Industrialisation of Japan and Manchukuo, 1930–1940*, p. 403.
[3] *Report of the U.K. Trade Mission to China*, 1946, p. 185; and E. B. Schumpeter, *op. cit.*, pp. 408–9. The various estimates of the Fushun output differ slightly from one another.

and China Syndicate obtained mining rights in the South Anhwei iron belt; an agreement was made with the Governor of the province, and this received Imperial sanction. Nevertheless, as the Commissioner of Customs at Wuhu recorded, 'every possible obstacle was put in the way of the Syndicate's engineers; and though they continued the work of development, constructing broad roads for the conveyance of the iron ore towards the river . . . and actually sent a number of boatloads of ore to Wuhu, permission to ship it was refused'. Protracted negotiation followed; but 'the provincial obstructionists rejected the most reasonable proposals of the Syndicate, and eventually the redemption of the concession for £52,000 was arranged. This was a heavy burden upon an already impoverished province.'[1]

In this branch of mining the leading foreign participants were the Japanese who were responsible for the development of the Hanyehping Company. This concern had been established by Chang Chih-Tung as part of his ambitious scheme to found a centre of heavy industry near Hankow. Insufficient capital for the venture was available in China and loans were obtained from Japanese sources. In return the Company made an agreement in 1913 to ship to Japan 17 million tons of iron ore and 8 million tons of pig iron over a period of forty years.[2] By 1914 about 30 million yen had been borrowed from Japan, and the safeguarding of this interest in the Hanyehping Company was included among the 'Twenty One Demands' which Japan presented to China in 1915. The Chinese Government agreed that 'when the opportune moment arrives the Hanyehping Company should be turned into a joint Sino-Japanese concern, and it undertook meanwhile not to dispose of any of the rights or property of the Company or to allow any of the mines in the neighbourhood to be worked by other persons without the Company's consent'.[3] The Chinese Foreign Minister also gave an undertaking that his Government would not 'confiscate the said Company, nor, without the consent of the Japanese capitalists, convert it into a State enterprise, nor cause it to borrow and use foreign capital other than Japanese'.[4] After the First World War the fortunes of the Company declined and in 1928 the ironworks ceased production. Iron mining continued, however, and the ore was exported to Japan; but the output which had reached over 800,000 tons in 1920 fell to 70,000 tons in 1926, a year in which the Yangtse Valley was much disturbed. Later there was a recovery, and after new capital had been provided by the Japanese, output rose to 400,000 tons.

[1] *Chinese Customs Decennial Report*, Wuhu, 1902–11, vol. I, p. 385.
[2] C. F. Remer, *Foreign Investments in China*, p. 508.
[3] J. V. A. MacMurrary, *Treaties and Agreements with and concerning China, 1894–1919*, vol. II, pp. 1232–3.
[4] *ibid.*, p. 1229.

These mines were looked upon as a valuable source of supply for the Japanese iron and steel industry which could count on only small quantities of home-produced ores. During the thirties, however, developments in Manchuria far outstripped those of China Proper. As with coal, the mining of ore had been undertaken long before the foreign economic penetration of Manchuria; but large-scale operations had to await the creation of the Japanese sphere of interest in that country. They began with the establishment by Okura, in collaboration with local Chinese, of modern ore mines and blast furnaces at Penhsihu just after the Russo-Japanese War. Then followed, in 1918, the Anshan Iron Works set up by the S.M.R. to the south-west of Liaoyang to work the extensive orefields of that locality. By 1930, however, the ore produced was still under one million tons a year and was barely sufficient for the needs of the two ironworks which together turned out only 250,000 tons of pig iron. Most of the ore was of a very low grade, and it did not, moreover, respond to the usual methods of treating such ores. Experiments by the S.M.R. in new processes had a successful outcome in 1926, and the application of these results at length turned the iron industry of Anshan into an economical undertaking. After the creation of Manchukuo the Japanese made extensive geological surveys, and, in the course of these, they discovered large deposits of high-grade ore, especially in the Tungpiento region. In the late thirties these were exploited, partly for use in the Anshan and Penhsihu blast furnaces, and partly for export to Japan where the iron and steel industry was growing rapidly. By 1936 the total ore output of Manchuria had reached nearly two million tons and the pig iron production about 650,000 tons.[1] The subsequent development, which was enormous, belongs to the war-time history of Japan.

In the mining of other minerals foreigners played a less important part than in coal and iron mining. For instance, during the 1930's China produced about 70 per cent of the world's output of antimony,[2] but all this was mined by traditional methods because the xenophobia of Hunan, the chief producing area, led to the exclusion of foreigners from the actual mining operations. In the crushing and refining of the ore, foreigners had long found a niche. During the 1890's a French firm built an antimony ore works at Wuchang, where antimony, zinc and lead ores, purchased from the local authorities, were crushed and purified. 'The most modern machinery,' it was reported, 'comprising five crushing machines, 38 gigs, and five concentrating tables, imported from Germany and America, were day and night at work.'[3] In the first

[1] E. B. Schumpeter, *op. cit.*, pp. 404–8; F. C. Jones, *Manchuria since 1931*, pp. 158–60.
[2] United Kingdom Department of Overseas Trade, *Report on Economic Conditions in China*, 1933–5, p. 49.
[3] *Chinese Customs Decennial Report*, Hankow, 1892–1901, p. 305.

decade of the century about 3,000 tons of zinc and lead ores and 2,000 tons of antimony ore were crushed every year. Besides this, in 1905 a German firm, Carlowitz and Company, was operating a large smelting works at Wuchang.[1] At Changsha there were two Chinese smelters, but the ore was so crudely smelted that the waste ashes were found to contain 30 per cent of antimony. An enterprising foreigner made a profit by buying up these ashes.[2] Later the efficiency of the Chinese smelters was considerably improved. A Hunanese, who had been trained in Paris, bought new plant in 1908 and engaged two French engineers to supervise its erection at Changsha.[3] His concern, the Hua Chang Antimony Company, was given a local monopoly of antimony smelting for twenty-five years.[4] The operations were competently conducted and the venture was successful. At first it sold its output through a British firm;[5] but in 1914 it opened an office in New York and sold direct.[6] The same happened in the case of the other Chinese concerns, and the foreign exporters were dispensed with.[7] Some antimony was exported also from South China. In the first decade of the century a British firm in Wuchow was trying to work up the trade.

In 1900 a piece of mineral resembling coal was brought for inspection to the Customs House at Chinkiang on the Lower Yangtse. It had been 'discovered by a foreigner while riding among the hills . . . to the west of Chinkiang where there was plenty of it scattered about on the ground', and it turned out to be plumbago.[8] The local people thought it was coal of poor quality which would not burn. A mining expert surveyed the area and suggested that a company should be formed to market the mineral in Europe. There was a successful trial shipment to London and negotiations were opened between the company and the Chinese authorities. So far as can be gathered, however, nothing further came of this venture. The mining of tungsten, on the other hand, increased in importance with the growth in the special steel industry of Western countries. China became the chief source of supply of this mineral; but foreigners had little to do with its production.

[1] *British Diplomatic and Consular Reports on Trade*, No. 3708, Changsha, 1905, p. 7.
[2] *ibid.*, No. 4216, Changsha, 1908, p. 5.
[3] *ibid.*
[4] Nevertheless two years later another antimony smelting concern, the Imperial Smelting Works, was being built at Changsha. See *British Diplomatic and Consular Reports on Trade*, Miscellaneous Series, No. 680, 1911, p. 9.
[5] *British Diplomatic and Consular Reports on Trade*, No. 5119, Changsha, 1912, p. 14.
[6] *ibid.*, No. 5489, Changsha, 1914, p. 9.
[7] United Kingdom Department of Overseas Trade, *Report on Economic Conditions in China*, to September 1929, p. 38.
[8] *Chinese Customs Decennial Report*, Chinkiang, 1892–1901, p. 446.

Since the mineral is found on the surface and can be concentrated without the use of elaborate machinery, the introduction of new technical methods was not an essential condition of the expansion of production. The industry, therefore, remained in Chinese hands.

CHAPTER X

THE FACTORY INDUSTRIES

THE Chinese governing classes were, for the most part, as incurious about Western industrial technology as they were about other features of European civilisation, and they allowed to pass unheeded for many years the new productive processes which had transformed manufacture in the West. Robert Bridges can hardly have been thinking of the nineteenth-century Chinese officials when he wrote of the Orientals whose

'. . . wiseacres have seen
the electric light i' the West and come to worship.'

The introduction of modern factory methods, therefore, had to wait for foreign initiative. It is true that exceptions can be found, but they are not numerous enough to disturb this broad generalisation and they can be briefly dismissed.

To the rulers of countries in a pre-industrial stage the chief attraction of modern technology usually lies in its contribution to military power and efficiency. It is not surprising, therefore, that the chief initiative shown by the Chinese Government in the industrial field during the nineteenth century was in connection with the production of armaments. China's military weakness had been amply demonstrated in her contacts with Western Powers, and it was with the hope of remedying this condition that during the sixties the Government built several arms-making factories. The same motive was behind the attempt of Chang Chih-Tung, towards the end of the century, to establish a centre of heavy industry near Hankow, although in this case the wish to found a Chinese source of supply of rails was perhaps equally important. Chang's project bore a resemblance to those exercises in entrepreneurship which, under the purposeful hand of the Japanese Government, were in the same period beginning to show noteworthy results. His undertakings included iron and coal mines, blast furnaces, a steel plant, an arsenal, a technical college and a laboratory. A number of European technicians, mostly Belgians, were engaged, and at one time forty foreigners were working at the ironworks alone. The venture seemed to promise well, and the Hanyehping Coal and Iron Mining and Smelting Company, which operated these plants, supplied a considerable amount of the rails, wagons and other equipment required by the Peking–Hankow Railway. Later, however, this ambitious enterprise suffered from mismanagement. The iron mines eventually passed under Japanese control and the other establishments closed.[1] The decaying Imperial Government was in no shape to pursue a consistent economic policy or to carry through projects of this kind to a successful conclusion.

In the last quarter of the nineteenth century the growth in the imports of cotton goods and the obvious superiority of machine-made yarn encouraged a few Chinese to experiment with cotton spinning in power-driven mills. The earliest attempts, however, met with as little success as the first ventures in the metallurgical industries. In 1878 an 'expectant Taotai' named Peng enlisted the support of the superintendent of foreign trade in Shanghai and formed a cotton spinning firm.[2] It was in his mind to hire a foreign manager and foreign skilled workers, but the project failed through lack of capital and technical skill. A decade later a number of Chinese founded a company to gin cotton with foreign machinery. The first equipment, 'consisting of steam engine and boiler, with forty ginning machines of most approved pattern',[3] was made in Osaka, and Japanese engineers and mechanics were employed. The enterprise was successful. Fresh capital was subscribed and a large two-storey building erected. It was designed to house spinning machinery as well as a ginning plant. 'A new and powerful engine and boiler were imported from England and additional ginning and spinning machinery from Japan.'[4] The statesman, Li Hung-Chang, interested himself in this industry and in 1888 he sponsored the establishment of the Machine Weaving Mill in Shanghai. This concern, after a series of misfortunes, began operations with 65,000 spindles and 600 power looms. Meanwhile, in 1890, another cotton mill, the New Spinning and Weaving Mill, was opened in Shanghai,[5] and at about the same time Chang Chih-Tung organised spinning and weaving mills at Wuchang under official control.

These early attempts by Chinese to introduce modern industries were not very impressive, while foreign manufacturing enterprise up to 1895 was inhibited by legal obstacles. As we have seen, the foreigners had long found it necessary to set up establishments for processing various Chinese export commodities, and so the first manufacturing enterprises in the hands of foreigners were those that were derived immediately from their merchanting activities. Most of these establishments were very small at the outset, and they usually remained so, partly because of the nature of the processes conducted in them, and partly because of the ambiguous legal position. Nevertheless, before 1895, these formed by far the most important part of Western manufacturing enterprise,

[1] *Chinese Customs Decennial Report*, Hankow, 1892–1901, p. 304. *See also*, p. 161, *supra*.
[2] *British Consular Trade Report*, Shanghai, 1878, p. 29.
[3] *Chinese Customs Decennial Report*, Ningpo, 1882–91, p. 381.
[4] *ibid.*
[5] H. D. Fong, *Cotton Industry and Trade in China*, vol. I, pp. 3–4.

and they long retained this position. Opportunities for further industrial development were afforded by the terms of the Treaty of Shimonoseki. This treaty gave Japanese nationals the right to engage in manufacture in the Treaty Ports and Open Cities, and under the most-favoured-nation clause this right was conferred also on the other Treaty Powers. Factory industry in China entered upon a new phase with the granting of these new privileges. There were, however, certain industrial enterprises which derived their legality from other grants of privilege, such as the mining concessions, and yet others which arose independently of any such grants.

Apart from the processing establishments set up by merchants to deal with export commodities, factory industry in China may be conveniently considered under four heads. First, there were the factories ancillary to the transport or mining enterprises operated by foreigners. Secondly, there were the factories established by foreigners, and later by Chinese, to produce goods that replaced manufactured imports; and thirdly, there were the factories which used Chinese labour and materials and Western enterprise and capital to produce manufactures for export. Some of these factories can be regarded as part of the industrial hinterland of a foreign country in the sense that they were intended primarily to turn out producers' goods or intermediate products for use in the home country by the manufacturers who operated them. Finally, there were the factories which produced goods of a type hitherto made by traditional methods for both the foreign and the home markets. There were comparatively few of these, and thus foreign enterprise did little directly to disturb the ancient manufacturing industries of the country, although the introduction of new types of goods had important indirect effects. The various categories will now be considered in turn.

The most important and the earliest manufacturing industry in the first category was the ship-repairing and shipbuilding industry which grew up to meet the needs of shipping companies which operated in Chinese waters. The first ship-repairing yard was established in Shanghai by a foreigner in the 1850's, and several others were soon opened. The most important of these, S. Farnham and Company, was active throughout the rest of the nineteenth century.[1] Another Shanghai concern, Boyd and Company, employed in 1880 between 1,000 and 1,400 Chinese workers. At that time it had just completed a dock 450 feet long and capable of taking the largest ships that visited Shanghai.[2] These and other shipyards were mainly concerned with ship repairing, but some of them also built ships. In 1856 a 40-ton steamer was built by an American, Captain Baylies; he used Chinese

[1] J. Dautremer, *op. cit.*, p. 67.
[2] *British Consular Trade Report*, Shanghai, 1879, p. 203.

oak and camphor wood and employed Chinese carpenters from Ningpo.[1] In 1863 a Shanghai-built steamer fitted with American boilers and machinery was plying on the Yangtse under the British flag.[2] A few years later steamships were built in a yard at Shanghai controlled by Tseng Kuo-Feng; this later became the Kiangnan Dock and Engineering Works. Boyd and Company built three steamers for Jardine Matheson's Yangtse service during the later seventies and eighties. In the new century that company and Farnham's amalgamated to become, in 1906, the Shanghai Dock and Engineering Company,[3] while a new British concern known as Jui Yung entered the engineering and shipbuilding industry and in 1910 the Tung Hwa Shipbuilding Works was founded at Shanghai by Sino-Japanese interests. In 1929 there were thirteen shipbuilding concerns in Shanghai, mostly foreign owned.[4] The Kiangnan Dockyard continued to be the chief Chinese concern, and it undertook the building of many vessels for the C.M.S.N.C.[5] The Shanghai Dock and Engineering Co. amalgamated in 1937 with another British dockyard in Shanghai, the New Engineering Co., to form Shanghai Dockyards Ltd.[6]

In this industry Hongkong was even more important than Shanghai; indeed shipbuilding and ship repairing became the island's chief industry. The two largest dockyards were the Hongkong and Whampoa Dock Company Limited, established in 1901, and the Taikoo Dockyard and Engineering Company, which Butterfield and Swire founded a few years later. These dockyards dealt primarily with repairs, but they also undertook a substantial amount of new building. Most of the vessels built by them were coasters, but some ocean-going ships were constructed. In fact, just before the Second World War larger ships were built in Hongkong than anywhere else in the British Empire outside the United Kingdom. At that time the two main dockyards together employed about 16,000 Chinese and a European staff of 280; the proportion of Europeans to Chinese had been falling for several decades as an increasing part of the skilled work was taken over by Chinese.[7]

Just as the shipyards were founded primarily to service the foreign

[1] G. Lanning and S. Couling, *The History of Shanghai*, p. 384.
[2] *British Consular Trade Report*, Kiukiang, 1863, p. 73.
[3] *British Diplomatic and Consular Reports on Trade*, No. 2731, Shanghai, 1900, p. 13; and E. M. Gull, *op. cit.*, p. 60.
[4] D. K. Lieu, *Growth and Industrialisation of Shanghai*, p. 46.
[5] *North China Herald*, 27 January 1931.
[6] *ibid.*, 17 March 1937.
[7] The Taikoo Dockyard at one time had its own technical training school, but in the 1930's this was superseded by the Technical College established by the Government of Hongkong. The Dockyard then organised evening classes for its engineering apprentices preparatory to their entering the Technical College. The Dockyard also maintained a school for the children of its employees, providing general education up to the age of sixteen; the teaching staff was paid by the Government.

shipping in Chinese waters, so the establishment of a number of engineering works followed on the building of the railways. Other small machine shops appeared in the largest centres to provide for the maintenance and repair of imported mechanical equipment. In China Proper, however, these concerns remained of quite minor importance, at any rate until the later thirties. The great foreign mining enterprises also gave rise to a number of manufacturing activities which were usually conducted by the parent concerns. Some of these factories were required to service the mining plants or transport equipment. Others were by-product plants or undertakings that hinged upon the production of fuel. Coking plants and brick, tile and glass works fall into this category. With the growth of modern constructional and civil engineering work a substantial demand for cement arose, and it was the Chinese forerunner of the Kailan Mining Administration that in 1876 built the first cement factory in China. About the turn of the century other cement works were built by British firms at Hongkong, Kowloon and Macao, and later the Japanese introduced the industry into North China and Manchuria. Their first factory was built at Dairen in 1909, and this was followed by others at Tsingtao in 1918 and at Kirin in 1933. During the thirties several works, equipped with German machinery, were built by the Chinese, whose Government had interests in some of them. Nevertheless, foreigners remained predominant in this field, especially in Manchuria, where after 1933 the industry underwent a great expansion at the hands of the Japanese.

A striking example of the second group of industries (namely those that produced goods to replace manufactured imports) was the cigarette industry. In 1890 the American Tobacco Company's agent, Mustard and Company, began to import cigarettes into China from Great Britain, and before the end of the century several of the leading British merchants had entered the trade. It was soon realised that economies in labour-cost and transport would be possible if the cigarettes required for this market could be made in China itself from imported leaf. In 1902 the newly formed British-American Tobacco Company took over the China business of the Imperial Tobacco Company and the American Tobacco Company, and then proceeded to establish cigarette manufacturing plants in various towns under the management of its subsidiary, the British Cigarette Company. By 1906 its factory at Pootung, Shanghai, was turning out cigarettes at the rate of 8 million a day. It was equipped with British and American machinery, and it employed about 2,500 Chinese and some 30 foreigners, as well as numerous agents who travelled the interior. At this time the Company had just completed a factory at Hankow with a capacity similar to that of its Shanghai plant and it subsequently built others at Tsingtao, Tientsin, Mukden and Harbin. The Chinese, inspired by foreign example, also

169

started manufacturing cigarettes, but most of their factories were small.[1]

The home-grown tobacco proved to be unsuitable for cigarettes, and at first the factories were supplied with leaf imported from America. By 1908 the British Cigarette Company had begun to experiment in the use of a mixture of Chinese and American tobacco, and large premises were built at Mukden for curing Manchurian leaf in the foreign manner.[2] The market was rapidly enlarged. In a report on the B.A.T. factory at Hankow in 1911, it was stated that the output was 10 million cigarettes a day, and that its products were ousting competing brands largely because of the success of its advertising and of the lowness of its price 'which yielded a profit of only three places of decimals on each packet'. This factory was apparently using mainly Chinese-grown leaf. 'Its foreign employees went far afield to . . . distribute American seed and teach the farmers improved methods of culture and preparation.'[3]

During the period of the First World War these efforts to substitute Chinese leaf of the American type for imported leaf were pressed further. After investigations in a number of provinces the B.A.T. found that Shantung possessed the most favourable conditions for tobacco growing and this became the main centre of the culture. Virginia tobacco was also introduced into Hupeh, Anhwei and Honan, and the region of the Mukden–Hailung Railway. The introduction of the new crop called not merely for much patient experimental work but also for tactful propaganda in overcoming the initial suspicions of the peasantry. In the initial stages compensation was promised to any farmer whose other crops were damaged by a change-over to tobacco growing. In Hupeh the farmers were at first reluctant to participate in the Company's experiments, but they were persuaded to lend a hand by the Company's promise to 'hand over free of charge barns used during the experiments'.[4] Again, when the Company's agents first brought American seed, with instructions for growing and treating it, to the Shantung farmers, they found little enthusiasm, and their offer of contracts was coolly received. But as soon as the farmers saw 'that the results far exceeded their expectations, they . . . inundated the Company with applications for contracts, and after a few years nearly all the wheatfields in the vicinity of Fangtze had been converted into American tobacco plantations'.[5]

[1] *British Diplomatic and Consular Reports on Trade*, No. 3943, Trade of China, 1906, p. 46.
[2] *ibid.*, No. 4366, Trade of Shanghai, 1908, p. 7.
[3] *Chinese Customs Decennial Report*, Hankow, 1902–11, p. 358. Virginian tobacco is of better flavour than the tobacco ordinarily grown in China; this latter had been introduced from America by way of the Philippines in the seventeenth century.
[4] *British Diplomatic and Consular Reports on Trade*, No. 5399, Hankow, 1913, p. 6.
[5] *Economic Development of Shantung, 1912–21*, U.S. Department of Commerce, Trade Information Bulletin, No. 70, p. 8.

The organisation of the business became very elaborate. The Company built numerous curing factories in the tobacco-growing districts. Around each of these it had a network of collecting points where the peasants could sell their leaf. The staff of these establishments included foreigners, many of whom were leaf experts with experience of tobacco production in the United States. Each establishment had a compradore who supervised the Chinese staff and acted as a link between the Company and the growers. Usually the land on which the curing factories and collecting stations were built was held in the compradore's name, as foreign firms were still not permitted to own land outside the Treaty Ports.[1] In addition to the fixed equipment operated by the foreign Company, it was necessary to provide the farmers with working capital, especially as the growing and treatment of American tobacco required the application of more labour and capital per acre than did Chinese-style tobacco. During the experimental period the Company often gave the peasants seed and fertiliser gratis and lent to them apparatus for the preliminary curing processes. Later the compradores provided seed, bean cake as fertiliser, and coal for curing, on credit. These loans were usually made through the intermediary of the local gentry who indeed sometimes furnished them on their own account. With the development of modern banks and co-operative credit societies, other sources of credit became available for the peasants. For example, during the early thirties an Association of Tobacco Growing Peasants was organised in Fengyang by the local gentry concerned in the tobacco growing business, and this raised funds from the Bank of China and from the Shanghai Commercial and Savings Bank for loan to individual peasants. These and other Chinese banks furnished the credit required by peasants in other areas also, usually through the medium of local merchants or gentry. Local officials were often active in fostering this trade, and a Chinese writer on the subject goes so far as to speak of the 'entente cordiale' that existed among the foreign firms, the Chinese compradores, the high officials of the Government, and the local gentry in the organisation and conduct of the leaf tobacco industry.

As the domestic cigarette manufacturing industry expanded, imports dwindled, in spite of the enormous growth in the size of the market.[2] They had been interrupted during the First World War, and during the twenties they declined steeply; by the early thirties they had become insignificant. Imports of leaf continued to rise until 1931, but after then they fell off rapidly, for home-produced leaf was by that time able to satisfy most of the demand. By 1934, it is estimated, there were about

[1] Chen Han-Seng, *Industrial Capital and Chinese Peasants*, pp. 25–6.
[2] Cigarette consumption in China is estimated to have been 300 million in 1900, 7,500 million in 1910, 22,500 million in 1920 and 88,500 million in 1933.

300,000 families engaged in growing American tobacco. In the three main centres, namely East Shantung, North Anhwei and Central Honan, three-fifths of the peasants participated in this trade, and tobacco had become the chief cash crop of these regions.

The industry remained largely in the hands of foreigners. In the middle thirties B.A.T. had seven cigarette factories in China Proper, three in Shanghai, two in Hankow, one in Tientsin, one in Tsingtao, besides others in Manchuria. These together employed about 25,000 Chinese workers. Further, B.A.T. gave much employment in its curing and collecting establishments, apart from that afforded to the tobacco-growing peasantry.

The supremacy of B.A.T. was challenged from several quarters. A number of Chinese companies in the first decade of the century had followed the lead given by B.A.T. The chief of these was the Nanyang Brothers Cigarette Company, established by Overseas Chinese. This concern had arrangements similar to those of the B.A.T. for distributing seed and collecting leaf in Shantung and elsewhere; but most of the other Chinese firms were small and made no attempt to participate in the leaf-growing business. Competition from the Chinese did not prevent an enormous expansion in the sales of B.A.T. products, and in the later twenties and thirties there was an absolute fall in the sales of Chinese-made cigarettes and some of their producers went out of business. This was in spite of boycotts inspired by nationalistic feelings from which the Company suffered at that time. The embarrassment caused by these boycotts was nevertheless sufficient for the B.A.T. in 1934 to undertake a reorganisation. The name B.A.T. ceased to be used in China; the concern was divided into several companies; and some of the companies which took over the former sales departments were placed under Chinese management. But the chief threat to the B.A.T. supremacy came from another quarter. Even before 1931 the Japanese had cigarette factories at Mukden where the To-A Company used a blend of local and imported tobacco. Subsequently they greatly extended their production in Manchuria. They also organised leaf-growing and later started manufacture at Peking, Tsingtao and elsewhere. By the time of the outbreak of the Sino-Japanese War it would appear that Japanese competition in this industry had been even more damaging to the Chinese concerns, which on the whole produced low-grade cigarettes, than to the Western producers. Indeed, the B.A.T., in spite of its difficulties under the Manchukuo régime, seems to have accommodated itself successfully to the new situation. In 1936 it set up two manufacturing companies under Manchukuo law to take over its properties in that country. These companies ran cigarette factories at Mukden, Liaoyang and Harbin, and in 1939 a new factory in New-chwang was opened in place of the one at Liaoyang. These factories, on the eve of the Pacific War, turned out nearly 10,000 million cigarettes a year.

Foreign entrepreneurs were responsible for starting several other manufacturing industries which produced Western-style goods for sale in the China market in competition with imports. None of these industries attained very large dimensions, and they will be only briefly discussed. The manufacture of electric lamps was started in Shanghai by the Japanese soon after the Revolution of 1911.[1] Then in 1918 General Edison Company set up a small factory and soon found that the consequent savings in labour cost and freight made it cheaper for them to manufacture lamps in China than to import them.[2] A few years later the International General Electric Company opened a large factory at Shanghai and by 1926 had succeeded in capturing much of the market.[3] This firm was linked with the American-owned Shanghai Power Company which, by the terms of some of its subscription services, supplied lamps to consumers free, and it thus had a large guaranteed market.[4] The pioneer Japanese concern was driven out of business, and attempts by its former Chinese employees to organise a new company failed. Other Chinese concerns, including one originally established by German interests, were more successful. During the thirties several Chinese lamp manufacturing concerns were operating, although the bulk of the demand was still supplied by the I.G.E.C. factory.[5]

The first attempts to supplant imports of wire nails by those of home manufacture was made by Chinese. This venture failed, and it was left for a British firm to introduce the industry by opening a large plant in which Western technicians were employed. Later, Overseas Chinese furnished capital for other plants; most of these were very small.[6] In the production of enamel ware in everyday use the Germans and Japanese took the lead; but by the thirties the industry in Central China had largely passed into Chinese hands. The manufacture of gramophones and of vacuum flasks had a similar history. In the manufacture of matches the Japanese, after 1895, were active, especially in Manchuria, and they set up a number of match factories, some of them in co-operation with Chinese interests. After 1918 the Swedish Match Corporation acquired many of the Japanese plants, and regained most of the market in Northern and Central China. It shared the South China market with Chinese producers. After the establishment of Manchukuo the Japanese took over production in that country, and in 1937 a government match monopoly was set up there.

[1] H. D. Fong, *Industrial Capital in China*, p. 29.
[2] C. Lewis, *America's Stake in International Investments*, p. 308.
[3] *Chinese Customs Trade Report*, Foreign Trade of China, 1926, p. 30.
[4] H. D. Fong, *Industrial Capital in China*, p. 29.
[5] *ibid.*, p. 30.
[6] *ibid.*, p. 28.

A few of the modern industries made a direct impact on old-fashioned Chinese manufactures. Flour-milling is perhaps the outstanding instance. In 1886 some German merchants opened the Chen Yu Flour Mill in Shanghai, and ten years later a British-owned mill was built there. Chinese enterprise in this industry followed after a considerable interval; the first Chinese-owned mill was set up in Shanghai in 1898.[1] Other modern mills were operated in Manchuria and North China during the first decade of the present century by Germans, Russians, French and Japanese. Some concerns were jointly capitalised with Chinese; for example, a Sino-British mill was opened at Hankow in 1905. The history of milling in Tientsin shows how an old trade responded to the new technique. Originally wheat was milled in that town by retail flour merchants. When the Japanese built a modern mill there in 1915, the Chinese merchants subscribed to its capital and, ceasing to mill wheat themselves, turned their primitive equipment to the milling of maize. This concern suffered from an anti-Japanese boycott immediately after the First World War, and in 1925 it was reorganised as a purely Chinese concern.[2] The sugar industry also falls into this category. Sugar had long been extensively grown in South China, but the refining methods were primitive. Then Jardine Matheson and Butterfield and Swire set up modern refineries at Swatow and Hongkong. In Manchuria, where beet sugar was produced, the Russians and the Japanese were responsible for the first factories.

The textile industries, which outstripped in importance all other modern factory industries, cannot be confined within any single group in our classification, for the new plants served a variety of markets. Some were intended to replace imports of Western semi-products or finished manufactures, and some to turn out such goods for sale abroad. Among those mainly concerned with export, certain plants (e.g. silk filatures) undertook by machinery what had hitherto been done by traditional processes, while others (e.g. carpet factories) formed virtually a new industry. Among all these trades the cotton-spinning industry is of special significance, not only because it was by far the largest of the modern factory industries of China, but also because a part of it was developed by foreigners to serve the needs of their cotton manufacturing industries overseas. The history of this trade, therefore, must be recounted in some detail.

The early attempts of the Chinese themselves to introduce modern technique into their spinning industry have already been described. Foreign enterprise in this industry originated after the Treaty of Shimonoseki had given legal sanction to foreign industrial undertakings and so made investment in factories in the Treaty Ports more secure

[1] D. K. Lieu, *Growth and Industrialisation of Shanghai*, p. 41.
[2] D. K. Lieu, *China's Industries and Finance*, p. 16.

174

than formerly. The British were in the van. In the year of the treaty Jardine Matheson opened the Ewo Cotton Spinning and Weaving Mill, and in 1896 another British concern, the Lao Kung Cotton Mill Company, whose mill was equipped with 35,000 ring spindles, began operations under the management of Ilbert and Company. About the same time the International Cotton Manufacturing Company's mill, managed by the American Trading Company, was established with 40,000 rings, and another mill was opened by German interests. By September 1896, 155,000 spindles were installed in these mills, while mills owned by Chinese had about 125,000 spindles.[1] Although foreigners had been quick to seize upon the fresh opportunities made available to them in this industry, they chose in most cases to associate Chinese investors and business men with their new enterprises, and in this respect the cotton industry became characteristic of large-scale manufacturing and mining industry in China during the new century. Thus, from the beginning, a substantial proportion of the shares in the Ewo mill were held by Chinese, and the company's board included both Chinese and British directors. The same was true of the Lao Kung Cotton Mill Company whose board of directors consisted of three foreigners and two Chinese, and also of the International Cotton Manufacturing Company with two foreign and two Chinese directors. These concerns are clearly to be regarded as Sino-foreign rather than as purely foreign, and it is to be noted that in the conditions of insecurity that existed in China, the privileges granted to foreign factory enterprise in the ports benefited Chinese capital interests no less than the foreigners.

By 1900 the number of spindles in China had risen to 565,000. During the first five years of the new century, the growth of the trade was arrested by the Boxer troubles and the uncertainties caused by the Russo-Japanese War. After 1905 the expansion was resumed, and by 1913 the number of spindles had reached 1,210,000. Both Chinese and foreigners contributed to this growth; although in the years just before the First World War the foreigners who were most active in the industry's development were no longer Westerners but Japanese. Indeed in subsequent years the history of foreign enterprise in cotton spinning in China became in essence the story of Japanese enterprise.

During the First World War the supply of cotton goods from the West was greatly reduced, and this stimulated the growth of home production. Most of the new mills set up during the war years were Chinese-owned, but after the revision in 1919 of the Chinese tariff, which raised duties on the type of yarn hitherto imported from Japan, the Japanese established many new undertakings. Between 1914 and 1925, 87 new mills in all were built, 53 by the Chinese, 33 by the

---

[1] *Rapports Commerciaux* of the Mission Lyonnaise d'Exploration Commerciale, 1895–7, p. 366.

Japanese and 1 by the British.[1] By the latter year the total number of spindles had risen to over 3½ million, and China had ceased to be a net importer of yarn, although her imports of cloth still remained large.

After 1925 many of the Chinese mills ran into difficulties. Some of them had been founded by men who had obtained their experience in foreign mills but whose own capital resources were inadequate. When they needed accommodation from the banks, they had to pay rates of interest which were never less than 10 per cent per annum and were often much higher. These rates reflected the high risks that had to be accepted by those who lent money to concerns seldom distinguished by sound financial policies. During prosperous years many Chinese mills were accustomed to distribute profits up to the hilt and they often made no proper allowance for depreciation. A Chinese economist in 1931 gave as an instance of this financial policy a large cotton mill which was unaccustomed to make any provision at all for depreciation.[2] Furthermore, the Chinese companies, unlike the foreign or Sino-foreign companies, suffered from arbitrary official levies. For all these reasons, during the difficult years that followed 1925, many Chinese mills had to close. The foreign concerns, on the other hand, were part of large commercial or industrial undertakings with ample resources, both of capital and managerial experience. This was true not merely of the British concerns already mentioned. The Japanese mills in China were owned by great cotton spinning or merchant firms in Japan Proper, while two Indian mills were operated by the Tata concern. The foreigners, therefore, easily held their own in this industry, and during the depression of the early thirties a large number of bankrupt Chinese mills, especially in North China, passed under Japanese ownership. In Shanghai an important new British mill was established during this period. The Calico Printers' Association, in the hope of regaining some of its lost China trade, bought and modernised a small print works that had originally belonged to some French missionaries. It added spinning and weaving plants, and these began production in 1935.

In 1937, when the number of spindles in China amounted to nearly 5 million, about half of them were in foreign mills. Less than one-tenth of these foreign-owned spindles were in Western mills; in other words, by this time foreign enterprise in cotton spinning meant Japanese enterprise.[3] The typical foreign mill was larger and better equipped than its Chinese competitors; the average spindleage of the Chinese mills was only 30,000 compared with 45,000 for the Japanese and 60,000 for the

[1] H. D. Fong, *Cotton Industry and Trade in China*, vol. I, p. 6.
[2] F. L. Ho, 'Problems of Future Industrial Development in China', in *Problems of the Pacific*, 1931, p. 143. He might have found other instances in Lancashire at that time!
[3] *Report of the U.K. Trade Mission to China*, 1946, p. 122.

British mills.[1] To a large extent these mills catered for different markets. Thus, in the thirties, the bulk of the yarns produced by the Chinese mills was in counts of less than 19, whereas the foreign mills turned out mainly medium and fine yarns, of which a considerable proportion was exported.[2] We have seen that after 1925 China ceased to be a net importer of yarn. During the early and middle thirties she came to be an exporter on a large scale. Many of the exports came from the Japanese mills, the function of which was, in part, to serve the needs of weaving sheds in Japan. Thus, structurally a section of the foreign spinning industry in China could be regarded as part of the cotton industry of Japan. The rest of the exports went to India and to the countries of South-east Asia.

As elsewhere, the mechanisation of the weaving side of the industry lagged behind that of spinning. Before the First World War power loom weaving could hardly be found in China, except in sheds attached to the spinning mills. After 1920 this section of the industry expanded and by the outbreak of the Sino-Japanese War there were about 60,000 power looms. A large proportion of them were in Japanese mills and many were automatic.[3] Even then this section of the industry was still in an early stage of development, and although imports of cotton cloth were reduced during the thirties, China remained, on balance, a net importer of cotton manufactures. The bulk of her own needs was still supplied by handlooms which turned out about four-fifths of the total cotton cloth production of the country.[4]

The cotton industry, like other large-scale industries, was highly concentrated in a few of the ports. It is true that in the inland districts there were a number of Chinese-owned mills which supplied local weavers with yarn. But these accounted for a very small proportion of the country's spindleage. In 1937 about half the total spindles were in Shanghai, and most of the remainder were in Tsingtao and Tientsin.[5] For this geographical concentration of equipment the legal status of the Treaty Ports and Concessions on the one hand and the lack of security in the rest of China on the other were responsible. It may be argued that the local privileges enjoyed by the foreigners distorted the location of this and other Chinese industries. Yet it may also be claimed that in the absence of these privileges large-scale industrial enterprise would have failed to develop at all.

The cotton industry was not confined to China Proper, as the above account may seem to imply, for Manchuria also had a share of it.

[1] *Chinese Economic Journal*, December 1933. Article by B. Lee, 'Rehabilitation of China's Cotton Industry', p. 605.
[2] *ibid.*
[3] *Report of the U.K. Trade Mission to China*, 1946, p. 124.
[4] G. E. Hubbard, *Eastern Industrialization and its Effect on the West*, p. 201.
[5] *ibid.*, p. 123.

Before 1931 this was very small. The Japanese had built a few mills, but their total spindleage amounted to only about 125,000.[1] After 1932 the industry shared in the general industrial expansion of Manchuria, and by 1939 there were eleven large cotton mills with a spindleage of about half a million and a loomage of 10,000. These mills were, of course, all Japanese owned, and were in effect branches of the large cotton concerns in Japan Proper.

Foreign enterprise played an important part in the creation of other modern textile industries. Between the two world wars wool-spinning mills were built at Tientsin and Shanghai by British, American, Japanese and Chinese interests. At Tientsin the Americans took the lead—their first mill started in 1924—and the yarn produced was used mainly in the manufacture of carpets. These plants were equipped with foreign machinery for spinning, weaving, dyeing and finishing. Most of the carpets were exported to the United States. This enterprise was built upon a long-existing carpet manufacture conducted in small establishments and based upon hand-spun yarn. It was prosperous during the twenties, but the export demand was reduced as a result of the heavy duties imposed by the Hawley-Smoot Tariff and the carpet industry then tended to revert to the craft stage which much of it had never left. The most important British undertaking in the wool industry was Paton and Baldwin's knitting wool factory which was built in 1932 when the firm found its market in China threatened by new import duties. This was a large integrated mill which undertook the whole process from top-making to the manufacture of finished dyed knitting-yarn. The firm maintained its own distributive organisation throughout the country and it held stocks in depots in the chief cities. Its success attracted competitors; among them were two British importers of engineering products who set up mills (one of them in co-operation with Chinese) for the manufacture of knitting wool and worsted fabrics.

A hosiery industry grew up at Shanghai and Tientsin during the First World War. In this trade, however, the foreigners' part was limited to the provision of machinery on credit to the small Chinese producers, and there was no foreign investment in large knitting plant. In lace-making their functions were more extensive. During the first decade of the century American missionaries in Swatow taught the local girls to make lace and by the 1930's there was a substantial industry. Most of the production at Swatow took place in the home to the orders of American merchants who exported the goods to the United States. The industry was not confined to this port, and at Wenchow small factories were built by foreigners which used linen yarn imported from Great Britain. These minor industries differed from one another in the markets they served. Thus, the carpet industry and the lace industry

[1] *Japan-Manchukuo Year Book*, 1934, pp. 604–5.

were developed by foreigners primarily to serve the needs of export markets, whereas the knitting wool and hosiery industries, though innovations in China, sold their products mainly in the home market.

In sum, these industrial developments, when judged by the standards of Western countries or of Japan, came to very little. In China Proper the textile industries, which in effect mean cotton spinning and weaving and silk reeling, constituted the only modern factory trades that were really substantial in size. Statistics are hard to come by. In the nine most highly industrialised provinces (but excluding Tientsin) the number of 'factory' workers was estimated in 1937 to be only 1,200,000, and even this total includes persons employed in small workshops. Textile factories accounted for 47 per cent of the total, and cotton alone for about 26 per cent. Even tobacco manufacture, which was the next most important single industry, had under 5 per cent of all the factory employees.[1] After forty years of industrial development factory production was still exceptional in China.

It is not difficult to explain why this should have been so. The Chinese business community lacked the technical and commercial experience necessary for the introduction of modern industry, and in any case the lack of order and security in the inland areas inhibited their enterprise. Until the thirties the Chinese Central Government, when it was not indifferent, was incapable of maintaining a sustained initiative in industrial affairs even in trades which touched upon national security. It looked upon any industrial enterprise as a ready source of public revenue rather than as a means of raising the real income of the people. As for the foreigners from whom innovations in other spheres normally proceeded, they lacked until 1895 any secure legal sanction for manufacturing enterprise, and without it the risks attending investments in large plants were excessive. Even after 1895 the foreigners' new privileges applied only to the Treaty Ports and Concessions, and this limited the area in which their enterprise could operate. It may be suggested, however, that there were, in addition, fundamental economic reasons for this technical backwardness. China possessed huge supplies of cheap labour. She lacked technicians, industrial managers and capital, and the supply price of Western personnel and Western capital was high. It was to be expected, therefore, that entrepreneurs, Western or Chinese, should choose labour-intensive methods of production rather than capital-intensive methods, except where the latter had some overwhelming technical advantage, and this preference favoured the domestic system of manufacture centred upon merchant employers. Moreover, so far as production for the internal market was concerned, the handicap imposed by China's inferior system of communications was very formidable. Large-scale manufacture for a widespread market cannot develop

[1] G. E. Hubbard, *op. cit.*, pp. 217–18.

without cheap and efficient transport. This particular obstacle might have been more successfully surmounted, to the encouragement of factory enterprise, if railway development had not been interrupted for two decades after the Revolution by civil war and disorder.

Some light is thrown upon this question by a comparison of the course of industrial development in China Proper with that in Manchuria. Up to 1931 the underlying economic conditions and the tempo of industrial growth were not very different in the two parts of the country. In the subsequent decade, there was a rapid expansion of large-scale industry in Manchuria on the initiative of the Japanese. The growth in the heavy industries—coal and ore mining, iron and steel production, chemical manufacture and electricity generation—was particularly remarkable. Engineering, including motor vehicle and aircraft production, made their appearance after the beginning of the Sino-Japanese War, and even the consumption goods industries, including textiles, were much enlarged. These developments were brought about by an export from Japan not merely of capital but of personnel, for large numbers of administrators, managers and technicians were recruited—almost exclusively from Japan. Manchurian industry became closely integrated with industry in Japan Proper, and a large proportion of the mineral and metal products were exported to Japan for use in her finishing factories. Most Western enterprises withdrew from Manchuria in the period between 1931 and 1937.

The motives behind this industrialisation were almost exclusively strategic, and it may well be that much of it could not be justified on strictly economic grounds. This conclusion is borne out both by the financial results of many of the ventures and also by the nature of the agents used by the Kwantung Army, which was in control of economic policy, in industrialising the country. Thus, before 1937 few of the S.M.R. manufacturing enterprises were profitable, and the S.M.R. and the *Shinko-Zaibatsu*[1] together exercised a virtual monopoly over Manchurian industry. Nevertheless, Japan's achievements in Manchuria cannot be lightly written off. She was responsible for one of the major economic developments of the period. For example, the technical improvements made in the use of low-grade ores (so it is claimed) had by the early forties given the Manchurian steel industry 'a strong competitive position in relation to other iron and steel producing centres'.[2] Even if some enterprises had a slender economic foundation, there had certainly been created in Manchuria 'an industrial potential ... far ahead of anything which existed elsewhere in East Asia, exclusive of Japan herself and of the Soviet Far East'.[3]

[1] The *Shinko-Zaibatsu* were the new business groups favoured by the military during the thirties to the exclusion of the older business groups.
[2] H. Foster Bain, 'Manchuria, a Key Area', in *Foreign Affairs*, October 1946, p. 116; and F. C. Jones, *Manchuria since 1931*, p. 160. [3] F. C. Jones, *ibid.*, p. 164.

These achievements were possible largely because Manchuria had passed under the control of a Government capable of maintaining order and intent upon fostering industrial growth. This does not justify imperialist aggression. The establishment of the new régime in Manchuria had the effect of weakening the Central Government of China and of destroying the possibilities of sustained economic advance there. But the experience of Manchuria, as well as the close association in China Proper between economic development and the privileges of foreign Powers, demonstrate how largely the slow rate of progress in China's economy as a whole, and especially her extreme backwardness in modern manufacturing enterprise, were attributable to the absence of ordered government and of competent economic administration at the centre. This is not to say that in more favourable political circumstances the pace of development in large-scale industry would have stood comparison with that of Western countries, for small-scale enterprise had many economic advantages in China; but that the pace of industrialisation would then have been much faster than it was can hardly be doubted.

PART II
JAPAN

CHAPTER XI

THE MODERNISATION OF
THE ECONOMY

A CASUAL observer in the middle of the nineteenth century might well
have considered that the attitudes of the Japanese and the Chinese
towards the intrusion of the Westerners conformed to the same pattern.
Both peoples opened their doors with reluctance. In both countries the
governments were compelled to yield by the pressure of superior force.
Even though a sharp divergence in policy soon showed itself, and while
the ultimate reaction of Japan was entirely different from that of China,
the initial phase had, it seemed, many features in common. Yet this
similarity was superficial. In nearly all respects, and at the beginning no
less than in later years, the contrasts were more striking than the
resemblances.

Even the causes which had originally led to the adoption of a
'seclusion' policy differed fundamentally in the two countries, and this
difference itself accounts for many of the subsequent contrasts in
behaviour. China, as the Emperor had informed George III's embassy
in 1793, possessed everything that man could desire and had no need
for foreign goods. Its Government was prepared to allow its merchants
to deal with the importunate foreigners who naturally wanted to share
in the benefits of a superior civilisation; but it saw no reason to encourage
foreign trade and, in placing restrictions upon foreign intercourse, it was
moved chiefly by a desire to preserve its national customs from contami-
nation by the barbarians. The exclusion policy thus sprang from
conservatism fortified by a consciousness of an immense superiority.
With the Japanese the motives were quite other. Before the Tokugawa
Shogun had established his authority at the beginning of the seventeenth
century, the Japanese had been an outward-looking people.[1] They had
welcomed foreigners and had shown an intense curiosity about foreign
ways. What led the Government in the middle of the seventeenth
century to exclude foreigners from Japan (except for the few Dutch
merchants who were allowed to trade at Deshima) and to forbid
Japanese to leave the country, was fear—fear of foreign aggression
and of the danger that foreign intercourse presented to the political
régime.

[1] The Shogun, or military governor, controlled the central government during the
period in which the Emperor held aloof from the administration of the country. The
House of Tokugawa governed the country as Shogun from 1603 to 1868. The
government of the Shogun was known as the *Bakufu*.

185

In the second place, the motives which prompted the foreigners to break down the barriers had little in common as they affected the two countries. Trade with China seemed to offer abundant opportunities of gain. At the beginning of the nineteenth century, China was the chief source of supply for certain commodities in increasing demand among Western consumers; while to the rising manufacturing industries of Europe there was a promise of vast markets in that populous and opulent land. As we have seen, even the disappointments and bitter experiences of the later years did not altogether dispel the errors of optimism of which the European traders were persistently guilty. Japan, on the other hand, was a small island with little to offer to Western consumers, and the prospect of finding markets for manufactures there excited little enthusiasm.[1] When the country was opened, there was no expectation of finding there the counterparts of the million Chinese women who were believed to be eagerly awaiting the opportunity of learning to play the piano.[2] Foreign governments were chiefly anxious to enter into relations with Japan because it lay across the Pacific sailing routes on which their ships, especially their whalers, needed facilities for obtaining supplies and for refitting. So it came about that the people who forced open the gates were not Europeans but Americans who had pushed to the Pacific coast and were now viewing their new horizons across the ocean. The Americans were not, however, the first in modern times to hammer on the gates. The Russians, who had moved across Asia and were now looking eastwards from Kamchatka, had appeared on the scene long before Perry's arrival. But the Russians, like the Americans, seem to have thought of Japan as a convenient port of call and a source of provisions rather than as an object of trade or conquest.

Finally, political and social developments in Japan itself during the eighteenth and early nineteenth centuries had disturbed the foundations on which the exclusion policy rested in a way that found no parallel in China. It has been frequently demonstrated by historians, both Japanese and foreigners, that the whole fabric of Tokugawa rule was disintegrating long before the incursion of the Westerners provided the occasion for its destruction.[3] The circumstances that attended this political upheaval have been described elsewhere, and it is sufficient here to call attention to those features of the Restoration which have a close bearing on our subject, and to point the contrast between China and Japan in their political reactions to the Western impact.

The governing class of China consisted of a bureaucracy selected by public examination and trained in a conventional interpretation of

[1] cf. G. B. Sansom, *op. cit.*, pp. 264, 290–1.
[2] *See* p. 18, *supra.*
[3] *See,* for example, E. Honjo, *The Social and Economic History of Japan*; W. E. Griffis, *The Mikado's Empire*, vol. I.

Confucian philosophy. It was no doubt admirably fitted for maintaining a traditional culture and for diffusing that culture over a vast land area. But the minds of these bureaucrats were 'closed to all idea of progress' and 'almost incapable of grasping the possibility, still less the need, for change'.[1] The ruling dynasty found its interests bound up with the preservation of the *status quo* and was incapable of providing the leadership needed in a period of change. Japanese society, on the other hand, was hierarchical in character. It had evolved from an earlier feudal structure, and although the Tokugawas had imposed a centralised administration, it still retained many characteristics of its former condition. The regional administration was in the hands of lords (*daimyo*), who enjoyed a considerable measure of independence of the central authority. Each *daimyo* claimed the allegiance of numerous retainers (*samurai*), a class military in origin from which those who exercised the main functions of administration in the several clans were drawn. Other classes in the community, the merchants, artisans and peasants, were in theory wholly subservient to these privileged groups and had no share in government.

By the middle of the nineteenth century this system had long been breaking up. Economic changes had destroyed the foundations of the older society and called in question many political institutions, and financial troubles threatened the stability of the Central Government. Apart from the few who held important administrative positions, the *samurai* had become impoverished, while some members of other, and in theory inferior, classes, notably the merchants, had become wealthy through profits gained in their capacity as financial agents of the *daimyo*.[2] The Tokugawa Shoguns had been regarded with jealousy by many *daimyo* ever since the time when they first established their ascendancy, and as their power weakened, they could be challenged on the ground that they had usurped the prerogatives of the Emperor. Thus, at the time when the foreigners demanded entry, political revolution was imminent in Japan, and there existed an important section of the theoretically privileged class which had everything to gain by change and little to lose by it. It happened, moreover, that this class of young and impoverished *samurai* threw up, about the middle of the century, a group of men of exceptional quality. These men played the major part in the overthrow of the old régime and then constituted themselves the leaders of new Japan in both civil and military spheres. It is true that resistance to change was at first by no means limited to the supporters of the Tokugawas, for at the outset the distinction between yielding to Western encroachments upon Japan's sovereignty and

[1] C. P. Fitzgerald, *China: A Short Cultural History*, p. 543.
[2] cf. E. Honjo, *op. cit.*, pp. 194–229; and S. Okuma, *Fifty Years of New Japan*, vol. I, p. 359.

opposition to the process of Westernisation was not clearly understood. Once the Shogun had been overthrown, however, there was little delay in recognising that the objective expressed in the injunction *Fukoku Kyohei* (Rich Country and Strong Army) required the whole-hearted acceptance of Western models.

The ease with which the transition was accomplished owes much not only to vigorous and imaginative leadership, but also to the fact that the political revolution represented merely a redistribution of power within the governing class rather than an upheaval destructive of the old society. Consequently Japan carried into the new era traditional senti-ments and loyalties which permitted her to undergo immense material changes without the loss of social cohesion. If it is true, as Knight says, that the most vital problems are not problems of economy but of maintaining social unity in the face of economic interests,[1] then it may be claimed that Japan largely succeeded in solving those problems in a period of far-reaching economic change. Even high officials of the Shogunate did not usually feel themselves precluded, on the overthrow of the old order, from serving under the new Imperial régime, which was thus able to recruit many able bureaucrats trained in the business of government.[2]

The contrast with China is very striking. Whereas in that country the sentiment among the ruling classes when confronted by the Western intruders was almost wholly conservative, in Japan the arrival of the 'black ships' provided the occasion for a change of policy which was to lead to a complete transformation of her material fabric. Furthermore, Japan's Imperial dynasty far from being wedded to the preservation of the existing arrangements was, through its relations with the Shogun brought into the camp of those who wanted change. 'Revere the Emperor' became the watchword of the new Japan, and this brought together in a common cause persons of diverse outlook and interests. The most ancient of Japan's institutions was thus called upon to sanctify her journey into a new world.

Contrary to what was once believed in the West, Japan was not ill-prepared for the adoption of Western forms of organisation. All the efforts of a stern Government had not succeeded in restraining the Athenian curiosity of the Japanese about new things which Xavier had noted in the sixteenth century. Through the medium of the Dutch language, knowledge of Western scientific advances had become fairly widely diffused, especially among the *samurai* of the western clans, and so the educated Japanese of the first half of the nineteenth century were not ignorant either of the material progress of the West or of its pre-eminence in the applied sciences. In the second quarter of the

[1] F. H. Knight, *Risk, Uncertainty and Profit* (1933 edition), p. xxx.
[2] G. B. Sansom, *op. cit.*, p. 331.

188

nineteenth century, young *samurai*, including some who afterwards played a leading part in the creation of new Japan, went abroad secretly for the purpose of studying Western civilisation. Several of the *daimyo*, notably the Lord of Satsuma in Kyushu, had long connived at illicit trading on the part of Chinese and European merchants and, usually in an attempt to arrest the deterioration in their finances, they had established various mining, manufacturing and trading enterprises. These, though often financed with the help of the merchants, were managed by the *daimyo*'s retainers as monopolistic undertakings. When Western pressure on Japan increased, plants for the manufacture of metals, ships and armaments were set up, and foreign instructors were engaged by the clan governments to teach the native craftsmen.[1] Even the Shogun himself had taken steps to introduce the manufacture of Western-type warships and guns, and had engaged foreign technical experts. Sir George Sansom has summed up the achievements as follows: '... before Commodore Perry's arrival in 1853 Japan had already gone through the preliminary stages of transition from an agrarian to a mercantile economy, and even manufacturing industry was fairly well developed in certain lines. There were no power-driven machines beyond a few hydraulic flour mills of ingenious construction, but there were complicated handlooms for weaving silk and cotton in elaborate patterns, and a few processes in mining and metallurgy were tolerably well understood. Many handicrafts, using small mechanical devices, had long reached a high state of perfection. Shipbuilding and the manufacture of iron and steel had made fair progress under foreign guidance before the Restoration. Japan was, therefore, already prepared to develop machine industries and to learn the necessary technical lessons from more advanced countries in the West.'[2]

Internal commerce also was fairly well developed. Some of the merchant firms who financed the *daimyo* and looked after the disposal of their rice revenues operated on a large scale. They had branches in different parts of the country, and arrangements for the transmission of funds and the transport of commodities by sea were systematically organised. There were markets in which dealings in futures took place, and credit instruments not unlike those used in the West were familiar to the business world of Tokugawa.[3] Although experience in the conduct of foreign trade was lacking, it was not difficult for the Japanese, on the opening of the country, to remould their existing commercial institutions and practices so as to accommodate them to the needs of a modern economy. Yet this degree of prior accomplishment in the technical and commercial arts cannot be regarded as crucial

[1] E. H. Norman, *Japan's Emergence as a Modern State*, pp. 119 *et seq.*
[2] G. B. Sansom, *op. cit.*, p. 527.
[3] cf. N. Skene Smith (ed.), *Tokugawa Japan*, esp. chaps. 4 and 5.

to the subsequent successful modernisation of Japan, for China could claim to have attained to an equivalent level of achievement. The main cause of the contrast between the two countries in their reaction to the West lay in the willingness of one and the reluctance of the other to accept change, and the key to Japan's success is to be found in the quality of the innovators whom she threw up.

We are not here concerned with recounting in detail the events that led to the opening of the country or the diplomatic negotiations that attended it. It is sufficient to state that by 1858 commercial treaties had been signed between Japan and the leading Western Powers. These provided for consular jurisdiction over foreign nationals, threw open certain ports to foreign ships, gave foreign nationals the right to reside at those ports and also at Tokyo and Osaka (though their right to trade in the interior was limited) and fixed rates of import duties.[1] In 1866 a revised tariff convention had the effect of imposing duties at an average of 5 per cent *ad valorem* on all imports and exports. These 'unequal treaties', as they came to be called, shocked public opinion and had a powerful influence on Japan's subsequent economic policy as well as on her diplomatic relations with foreign Powers. A determination to secure the revision of these treaties lay at the heart of policy. The Japanese 'made up their minds to take over foreign ways of life not so much because they recognised the absolute merits of Western culture . . . as because the sooner they could display to the world a colourable imitation of Western society, the sooner would the unequal treaties be revised'.[2]

In the decade that followed the opening of Japan, the Shogunate as well as the *daimyo* pressed further with schemes for introducing Western industrial methods—'not for their own sake but rather to establish those industries which we might conveniently call strategic, as the *sine qua non* of a modern army and navy'.[3] Smelting furnaces, iron foundries, shipyards and plants for arms manufacture were established by several of the clans and by the Central Government. For instance, in 1856 the Lord of Mito made a shipyard at Ishikawajima in Tokyo Bay; between 1854 and 1859 the Shogun founded a shipyard and a navigation school at Akuura, where twenty-two Dutch experts were employed as instructors, and between 1865 and 1871 an iron foundry and shipyard were constructed at Yokosuka under the supervision of French experts. Nor were these innovations confined to the heavy industries. In 1857 the

---

[1] Shimoda and Hakodate had been opened to American ships in 1854 and limited concessions were also given in respect to trade. After the treaties of 1858 Yokohama, Nagasaki, Kobe, Hakodate, Niigata and Osaka were the 'open ports'. After 1899 many other ports were opened and ultimately the total number in Japan Proper was forty-one.
[2] G. B. Sansom, *op. cit.*, p. 402.
[3] E. H. Norman, *op. cit.*, p. 118.

enterprising chief of the Satsuma clan laid down the first electric telegraph line at Kagoshima. In 1859 he ordered cotton-spinning machines from Platt Brothers of Oldham and engaged an English manager and six English assistants to see to their installation at Kagoshima and to supervise their operation.[1] These early experiments could certainly be regarded as tentative steps towards the modernisation of the country, but the tottering Shogunate could not command an advance at the pace required. With the establishment of the Imperial Government in 1868 the policy of Westernisation was at once pursued with new vigour, and it was then that Japan can be said to have entered upon her career as a modern State. The new Government brushed aside all opponents to change and set out to create without delay the institutions, services and industries considered necessary for political security and economic efficiency. It took over the factories, shipyards and mines hitherto operated by the Shogunate and the *daimyo*, and it proceeded rapidly to improve their equipment and organisation. Additional foreign instructors were engaged for the Yokosuka shipyard and for the Sekiguchi arsenal. In 1873 the Government interested itself in an iron smelting works at Kamaishi which had been erected at the command of a *daimyo* from Dutch drawings. With the help of British engineers two modern furnaces were built and a railway constructed to connect the ironworks with the harbour.[2] In the previous year German experts had been appointed to design and to erect a Western-style brewery; German machinery was imported, and the experts remained for ten years to supervise the brewery operations.[3] About the same time American and Austrian experts were called in to set going a modern-style paper mill.[4] Modern silk reeling mills equipped with Western machines were erected by the Government at Maibashi and Tomioka between 1870 and 1872, and French and Italian supervisers and skilled workmen were engaged to construct and staff them. These foreigners included not merely experts in silk reeling but also mechanics and building artisans who taught the Japanese to make the bricks needed for the erection of the factory.[5] Ten years later several modern cotton spinning mills were built to the orders of the Government at Hiroshima and in the Aichi Prefecture; these were equipped with the latest English machines. The Government had inherited various mining undertakings from the Bakufu, and Western mining engineers were brought to Japan to introduce the latest mining methods. Thus, English engineers were engaged to modernise operations at the Government's silver mine on the Isle of Sado, and others helped to sink new

[1] These examples of industrial enterprise are taken from J. E. Orchard, *Japan's Economic Position*, pp. 85–6, 89 *et seq.*; E. H. Norman, *op. cit.*, pp. 119 *et seq.*; and E. Honjo, *op. cit.*, pp. 301–4.
[2] J. E. Orchard, *op. cit.*, p. 105.
[3] *ibid.*, pp. 108–9.   [4] *ibid.*, p. 109.   [5] *ibid.*, pp. 100–1.

coal-mines. At one period during the early seventies the Government employed eighty foreign mining experts in its coal and metalliferous mines.[1] There were, indeed, few modern industries in which the early Meiji governments did not participate.[2] In the words of Professor Orchard: 'At one time or another the Government has built and operated porcelain works, silk spinning mills, cotton spinning mills, wool spinning and weaving mills, a linen factory, cement and brick plants, plants for soap-making, type-founding and paint-making, food factories, iron and steel plants. There are few modern industries in Japan today that do not owe their existence to Government initiative.'[3]

The State also assisted private firms, by loans or subsidies, to introduce new manufacturing methods, and in some industries it adopted the practice of buying foreign machinery and lending it to the firms. All these new enterprises were staffed with foreign teachers and managers as they were required, and large numbers of young Japanese were sent abroad to study Western technique. Transport and communications also received early official attention. Tokyo and Yokohama were connected by telegraph in 1869 and a modern postal system was introduced in 1871. In 1869 the construction of the first railway—between Tokyo and Yokohama—was begun on the proceeds of a Government loan raised in London. The work was carried out under the supervision of British engineers and with materials and equipment imported from England. The growth of a modern mercantile marine also owed much to official encouragement.[4] Foreign instructors were employed to train the seamen and for many years a considerable number of the ships were staffed with foreign captains, engineers and pursers. Meanwhile the modernisation of the banking, legal and educational systems proceeded rapidly, and in all the new schools, including the technical schools, foreign instructors played an indispensable part.

This is not intended to be a detailed history of the Westernisation of Japan, and the outline given above of the Meiji governments' crowding activities in the economic field is intended merely to provide the setting for a discussion of the rôle of foreign enterprise in the general process. Yet even a brief account of what was attempted and achieved brings out clearly the contrast between the attitude of the Japanese and the Chinese Governments towards the adoption of Western economic forms. The Japanese, though by no means willing to concede moral or cultural superiority to the Westerners, seldom allowed prejudice or conservatism to deflect them from their study and emulation of Western technique

[1] J. E. Orchard, *op. cit.*, p. 104.
[2] The Meiji era, i.e. the reign of the Emperor Meiji, extended from 1868 to 1912. The establishment of the Imperial Government after the overthrow of the Shogunate is known as the Restoration.
[3] J. E. Orchard, *op. cit.*, p. 90. For further information, *see* Appendix F *infra*.
[4] *See* pp. 218–20 *infra*.

and applied science. They drew on the supplies of foreign expertise wherever it could be found. They compared the achievements of the several Western nations in various spheres of activity and, wherever superiority was found, it was from there that they took their models. British, American, French, German, Dutch, Swiss, Italian and Russian experts and teachers were all employed in the modernising of Japan, not merely in the sphere of technical education but in general education also.

The use of Western models and Western teachers did not end with the first period of enthusiasm. Whenever in later times it was decided to introduce a new industry into Japan, foreign instructors were brought in to assist. It is, of course, a common practice everywhere to make use of foreign experts whenever a firm or a Government introduces equipment or manufacturing processes which have their origin abroad and are unfamiliar to persons in the country of their introduction. What is exceptional in Japan's case is not so much the scale on which these foreign experts were employed as the fact that their use was, of set purpose, an integral part of official policy, and remained so throughout Japan's modern economic history. When the Government set up its great iron and steel works at Yawata in the closing years of the nineteenth century, it bought most of the plant from Germany and had it erected under German supervision.[1] Just after the First World War, when it was decided to create an aircraft industry, the staff of a British firm was engaged and remained for four or five years until the Japanese personnel were fully competent in design and operation. Normally the foreign experts were employed only for the period necessary to install the equipment and to train the Japanese in the technique. Thus the turnover of the foreign experts was high, for the Japanese had every confidence in their own aptitude as pupils. In some instances, however, the employment of foreign experts remained a permanent feature of an enterprise. This applies to certain breweries, engineering works and several other plants. In the mercantile marine the employment of foreign officers continued for a long period. Their numbers indeed grew, with the expansion of Japanese shipping, until 1895, when there were 210 foreign captains, engineers and pursers in the employment of the N.Y.K., compared with 540 Japanese. It was not until after the First World War that the line became entirely staffed by native officers.[2]

Not all the experts were wisely chosen, and in some cases the early undertakings came to grief either through the incompetence of the experts or through failures on the Japanese side. These troubles were probably due, as a general rule, to deficiencies in management and

[1] *British Consular Reports*, Annual Series, 1900, quoted in Y. Hattori, *The Foreign Commerce of Japan Since the Restoration*, p. 63 n. It is stated that twelve Germans were employed in this project.
[2] Nippon Yusen Kaisha, *Golden Jubilee History*, pp. 163–6.

organisation rather than to technical incompetence. It has been re-marked by a Japanese commentator that in those days the importance of the managerial problem was insufficiently appreciated by the Government.[1] This may be so, for all new-comers to industrialism find it easier to import technical knowledge than to naturalise the art of management.

During the early years of Meiji most of the foreign experts and instructors were employed directly by the Central Government itself. This was chiefly because the majority of the new Western-style under-takings were then owned by the State. During the last two decades of the nineteenth century, however, the Government followed the policy of transferring the majority of its industrial and mining properties to private hands, and most of them passed into the possession of a few great family businesses in which the control of most of the modern sector of Japan's economy was concentrated. When this happened, the foreign experts became employees of the private firms; but until very recent times a considerable number of foreigners were still employed in national undertakings and in the Government's technical schools and colleges.

So far we have been concerned to show that while foreign models and foreign instructors were indispensable for Japan's modernisation, the initiative in that process was primarily a native initiative. In early Meiji the chief entrepreneurial function was exercised by the State, and in later years by the State and the *Zaibatsu* together.[2] Thus, it would seem that in the translation of Western scientific civilisation into Japanese, foreigners were employed merely to elucidate obscurities in the text. But this view of Japan's modern economic history, though substantially true, cannot be accepted without some important qualifications. These qualifications do not extend to fundamental policy, at any rate not after the first years of Meiji; but so far as the mechanics of modernisation are concerned, they are nevertheless important. In other words, although foreign enterprise never had a dominant rôle in the creation of a modern Japanese economy, its contribution was indispensable in the Meiji era and was far from negligible down to very recent times. This can be attributed in part to the superiorities that the foreigners long retained not merely in technical accomplishments but in experience of modern business practices and methods. At the beginning the Westerners derived great advantages from their connections with the financial, mercantile and industrial interests of their own and other countries. These advantages diminished in the course of time, but they did not entirely disappear. Moreover, as the West continued to be responsible

---

[1] T. Yamanaka, 'Japanese Small Industries during the Industrial Revolution', in *Annals of the Hitotsubashi Academy*, October 1951, pp. 30 *et seq.*

[2] *Zaibatsu* means 'money-groups' or 'plutocracy'. This is a term commonly used to describe the great business houses, notably Mitsui, Mitsubishi, Sumitomo and Yasuda; these were broken up during the Occupation.

for all major innovations in industrial technique, its entrepreneurs still found opportunities in Japan in the introduction of the latest devices and processes.

These advantages, which arose mainly from the greater maturity of the Western economies and the superiority of Western applied science, were reinforced in the earlier years by the provisions of the 'unequal treaties' which limited the sovereignty of Japan and conferred privileges on the nationals of foreign Powers. In the period immediately after the opening of the country, these privileges were no doubt necessary to attract foreign residents, and had they been denied, the growth of trade and the inward flow of expertise would have been delayed. But in Japan, where order was firmly maintained and where the Government was intent upon modernising the country's institutions, the privileged status of the foreigners did not remain an essential condition of foreign enterprise, as for many years it did in China. Indeed, by 1899, when these privileges were surrendered, they had probably become a handicap to foreign enterprise inasmuch as they tended to embitter relations between the Japanese and foreigners. An equally important restriction on Japan's sovereignty was, of course, the 'unequal treaty' provisions that governed the rate of customs duties. Until freedom in this respect had been gained, the Government was not wholly at liberty to mould her economy as she wished. This stage can be said to have been passed in 1899, even though the Tariff Conventions signed in that year still prevented Japan for another decade from embarking upon a strongly protectionist policy.

CHAPTER XII

THE WESTERN MERCHANT
IN JAPAN

THE discussion of Japan's response to the Western impact has shown that, while the Westerners had a more narrowly restricted rôle in that country's economic development than in China's, it would be wrong to infer that they were deprived of opportunities for displaying their entrepreneurial skill. It is true that some of the foreigners who came to Japan, both in the early years of Meiji and in later times, were merely salaried employees of the Government or of large Japanese concerns. Yet there were others who could justly claim to have been responsible for introducing many new forms of economic activity. The foreign merchants had a particularly well-founded right to this claim. It was through them that Japan was exposed to the vitalising effects of international trade, consumers given access to foreign sources of supply, and producers brought into contact with foreign markets. If the development of the strategic industries and basic services was the outcome of a well-executed official design, the inception of other new industries and the expansion of many old ones occurred largely as a response to the opportunities of which the Japanese first became aware through foreign mercantile enterprise. There was thus an extensive area in which foreign merchants rather than the Government were the chief instruments of modernisation, and their imprint was clearly stamped on the Japanese economy of the last half of the nineteenth century.

At the end of the Tokugawa era Japan had a fairly substantial internal trade, organised with considerable elaboration, and there were a few business houses skilled in the conduct of domestic finance and commerce. Yet experience in the technique of foreign trade and acquaintance with foreign markets and sources of supply were almost wholly lacking. It was natural, therefore, that at the outset foreign firms should monopolise the import and export trades. Techniques and commercial information, however, can easily be acquired, and it might have been expected that this foreign dominance would have been short-lived. In fact, it lasted until the end of the century, and even as late as the 1930's foreign merchant houses were still important, although they had long lost their lead. The explanation is that success in commerce depends not merely upon technical competence but also upon the power to win and hold the confidence of suppliers and customers—a power that a new-comer only gradually acquires. Foreign merchants, many of

196

whom had connections with well-established firms abroad or ran branches of old commercial houses, enjoyed for a long period a goodwill not shared by their Japanese competitors. They had other advantages also. When towards the end of the nineteenth century the Tokyo Chamber of Commerce, at the suggestion of the Department of Agriculture and Commerce, inquired into the prospects of direct import and export trade by Japanese merchants, its report listed the impediments to such enterprise. Apart from the 'ignorance of the Japanese merchants . . . of the conditions of commerce abroad', these impediments were considered to be the 'imperfection of the credit system . . . the high rate of interest in Japan', and the 'want of uniformity in the quality of Japanese manufactures and the frequent deterioration of Japanese manufacturing processes'.[1] This last-mentioned trouble has been noted in the case of China also; it is indeed likely to be found whenever small-scale, manual trades in a pre-industrial society are suddenly called upon greatly to expand their output. The implication of the report is that the foreign merchants whose demands had provoked the expansion were likely to be able to cope more effectively with the problems that arose than were native merchants unacquainted with the standards that foreign customers insisted upon.

For all these reasons nearly the whole of the import and export trade was in the hands of foreign merchants from the time of the opening of the country until the later years of the nineteenth century. The foreigners and their spokesmen had no doubt that they were indispensable to the growth of this trade. Speaking of conditions in the early years of Meiji, a British consul declared: 'For the progress which [she] made at that time, Japan is entirely indebted to the resident European merchants, among whom those of British nationality were far predominant.'[2] In 1880 the *Japan Gazette*, intent upon refuting a charge made by the President of the Nobles' Club that foreign trade (and by implication the foreign merchants who handled it) was responsible for the export of specie and the embarrassed state of the Government's finances, stated: 'Every advance in the arts of modern civilisation . . . is due entirely to foreign commerce. Deprived of her foreign trade which statesmen, merchants and Chambers of Commerce seem to agree to denounce as injurious upon grounds devoid alike of truth and justice, Japan would sink back into her former insignificance and disappear from the list of nations.'[3] A British consular report of 1897 put the point more temperately: 'The trade of Japan would never have reached

[1] Y. Hattori, *op. cit.*, p. 29 n.
[2] J. H. Longford, *The Evolution of New Japan*, p. 90. He added that the 'honesty, capacity and enterprise' of these foreign merchants 'remedied *vis-à-vis* buyers and consumers in Europe, the deficiencies that were universally characteristic of the native traders'.
[3] *Japan Gazette*, 14 August 1880.

its present proportions had it not been for the foreign resident merchants; and what is true of the past will remain true for a considerable time to come, until the Japanese obtain the knowledge and foresight in business transactions which can only be acquired by experience, and succeed in inspiring the commercial world with confidence. Their credit is not at present sufficiently high for success in direct dealings with foreign countries, and the difficulties of financing their transactions more than counterbalance the gain they make by saving the commission they would otherwise pay to the foreign merchants. No foreign bank would buy a bill drawn on a Japanese firm unless the firm had previously opened credit, and before it could do so it would have to be guaranteed by a Japanese bank of good standing. No firm in Europe or America would at present rely on a Japanese merchant's faithfully executing a contract for articles of Japanese manufacture, or would authorise the Japanese merchant to draw a bill on shipment of the goods.'[1]

The merchants who settled in Japan upon the opening of the ports included several well known for their dealings in other Eastern countries. For example, William Keswick of Jardine Matheson was sent to Japan in 1858 and set up an office at Yokohama. The firm soon opened additional branches at Kobe, Nagasaki and other ports, and it was not long before its ships were running on a regular service between Yokohama, Kobe and China.[2] By 1866 there were more than forty foreign merchant firms in Yokohama where most of the trade was then conducted. Later their numbers increased both there and at Kobe and other ports. Several firms that were still doing business in Japan during the 1930's could trace their origins to the pre-Restoration period or to the first years of Meiji.

In the initial stages both the foreigners and the Japanese who dealt with them were in the dark about the commodities likely to be in reciprocal demand. A former Shogunate official has left a description of the trading methods then followed at Yokohama: 'In those early days . . . the two thoroughfares of Honcho and Bentendori were lined with shops displaying, in a haphazard manner, lacquer, porcelain, copper-ware, fancy goods, piece-goods and what not, in the fashion of a bazaar today. . . . Foreign merchants fared no better. They had a foreign bazaar where woollen and worsted fabrics, woollen and cotton mixed goods, and haberdashery were all on view, so that they could get a line on the Japanese taste in merchandise.'[3] During the first few years there was an export surplus in the commodity trade, and this continued until the eve of the Meiji Restoration when the Government began to enlarge its purchases of ships and munitions.[4] The way in

[1] *British Consular Reports*, Miscellaneous Series, No. 440, 1897.
[2] '*Jardines' and the Ewo Interests*, p. 16.
[3] Oriental Economist, *op. cit.*, pp. 14–15.
[4] *ibid.*, p. 17.

which this favourable balance came about reveals the curious circumstances in which Japan's international trade began. Many of the foreign merchants 'did not bring with them any commodities with which to open trade, but brought, instead of goods, shiploads of silver dollars. . . . It was a common thing for a foreign merchant of standing to hold at least 200,000 dollars (Mex.) in imported specie for trade purposes.'[1] This practice was no doubt attributable in some measure to the fact that, apart from the strategic materials sold to the central and local governments, the foreigners found it difficult to judge which Western products would command a sale in Japan. But the main cause must be sought in other directions. The initial operations cannot be properly understood without some acquaintance both with Japan's monetary system at that time and also with the type of exchange operations that were called into being by the commercial dealings with Western merchants. These must be briefly described.

In the middle of the nineteenth century, Japan's currency was in a confused condition. Besides the various gold, silver, copper and iron coins issued by the Central Government, there were also coins and notes issued illegally by the *daimyo* for circulation within their several domains, and 'wrapped money' issued by private exchange houses.[2] During the previous century the coinage had suffered from successive debasements to which the Tokugawas had resorted in an effort to meet their increasing financial difficulties. When the foreign merchants came to Japan during the fifties they brought, as we have seen, supplies of Mexican dollars, the usual medium of exchange in the Far East. The circulation of these dollars, however, was confined to the open ports, for the Japanese Government prohibited their use in the interior. It was necessary, therefore, to make arrangements for exchange transactions between dollars and Japanese coins. By agreements signed with the foreign Powers in 1859 the Mexican dollar was to be exchanged weight for weight for Japanese silver coins known as *ichi-bu-gin*. Now the *ichi-bu-gin* was in effect a token coin, for the Tokugawa Government, having a monopoly of silver-mining, had found advantage in over-valuing silver in terms of gold (and copper). The gold-silver ratio was, in fact, fixed at about 1 : 5 compared with a ratio of about 1 : 16 in the outside world. The agreement of 1859 at once opened prospects of extremely profitable exchange transactions to the foreigners, and they were quick to seize their opportunities. They imported Mexican dollars, exchanged them weight for weight with the *ichi-bu-gin*, turned the latter into gold coins (*koban*) at a ratio of 5 : 1, shipped the gold to Shanghai

[1] *Japan Gazette*, 26 February 1881.
[2] M. Takizawa, *The Penetration of Money Economy in Japan, passim*. 'Wrapped money' consisted of gold or silver coins wrapped in paper and sealed by the exchange houses that issued it; the value was marked on the paper wrapper. See Mitsui Bank, *A Brief History*, p. 5.

and there bought silver at 16:1.[1] It is scarcely an exaggeration to say that the foreign merchants of 1859, like the Dutch before them, were attracted to Japan as much by the opportunities of these profitable exchange dealings as by those afforded by commodity trade. Indeed, it appears that 'the largest and most lucrative part of the business done [in Japan] by foreigners [during 1859] was in the purchase of gold coin; and probably more than one million dollars' worth of those coins was exported during that year'.[2]

The effect of this over-valuation of silver was not, of course, limited to such transactions as these. Japanese silk, tea and copper wares could also be purchased by the foreigner at artificially low prices, and this was a powerful inducement to the merchants to acquire them for export. The conditions could not, of course, persist for long, and after 1860 the ratio of gold and silver became equivalent to that in the outside world. Before this parity had been reached Japan certainly suffered a loss which her finances could ill afford, but it may well be that this was in part offset by a more rapid development of trading intercourse with the West than would otherwise have occurred. The English commentator who affirmed that 'foreign commerce could not have begun in this country without the aid of the blunder by which foreign silver was admitted at the over-valuation . . . which it enjoyed in 1859' was no doubt exaggerating;[3] but he is in respectable company in arguing that a profit inflation brought about by the behaviour of the monetary system is a sharp spur to enterprise, especially in the initiation of novel and massive developments.[4]

During the early sixties the imports consisted mainly of textile yarns and piece-goods, metal goods, ships, munitions and pharmaceutical chemicals, while the exports consisted of the products either of Japan's agriculture or of her traditional handicrafts, such as lacquer and copper wares.[5] The two chief export commodities then and for many years afterwards were tea and raw silk. In the tea trade the foreign merchants had to concern themselves not merely with commercial transactions, but also with the organisation of the industry. The Shizuoka Prefecture had long been one of the chief tea-producing regions, and as its port, Shimoda, the first in the eastern part of the country to be opened to foreign trade, was conveniently located for handling the product, the merchants looked to that prefecture to furnish the supplies they required. They had to ensure that the tea was exported in a form suitable for foreign, chiefly American, markets, and so they interested

[1] D. H. Leavens, *The Gold-Silver Ratio in the Early Foreign Relations of the Far East*; and U.S. Department of Commerce, *The Currency System of Japan*, pp. 5–6.
[2] *Japan Gazette*, 12 March 1881.
[3] *ibid.*
[4] cf. J. M. Keynes, *A Treatise on Money*, vol. II, p. 149.
[5] *Oriental Economist, op. cit.*, p. 16.

themselves in the various preparatory processes. As time went on, they set up factories in Shizuoka, where the leaves were treated after they had been purchased from the Japanese dealers.[1] A vast expansion in the output of tea in this prefecture followed. Exports rose from an annual average of about 90,000 piculs in 1868–9 to an annual average of about 270,000 piculs in 1879–80. The trade continued to grow until the early nineties when it entered upon a slow decline. Even in the 1930's, however, there was still a substantial export (over 200,000 piculs a year),[2] and nearly all the trade remained in the hands of foreign merchants, chiefly Americans.

The creation of a foreign market for Japanese silk was assisted by fortuitous events in Europe. The opening of the country coincided with the outbreak of silkworm disease in Europe, and Japan was called upon to meet an urgent demand for silkworm eggs as well as for raw silk. In the first year of Meiji, silkworm eggs made up nearly a quarter of the value of the export trade, and silkworm eggs and raw silk together over two-thirds of it. (Tea accounted for much of the remainder.) During the seventies the egg trade declined, as by then the French had reconstructed their industry; but exports of raw silk itself grew substantially and Japanese competition in European markets was strengthened by the opening of the Suez Canal. When the French and Italian crops failed in 1876, Japanese exports rose very steeply, and after 1880 when the United States began to take large quantities a great secular expansion began. Up to this time almost the whole of the trade was in foreign hands. The Western export houses supplied most of the resources needed to finance the Japanese dealers from whom they bought their supplies at the ports, and through them they indirectly financed the reelers and silk-raisers in the country districts.

The country was as responsive to the enterprise of the Western merchants as to the industrial activities of the Government. Although for several decades the volume of foreign trade remained very small, it was sufficient greatly to disturb an economy held rigid by years of seclusion and to compel a widespread redistribution of economic resources. The producers of cotton textiles suffered through the import of cheap Manchester goods, while farmers, silk-raisers and reelers flourished through the new foreign demand for their products. At first the Japanese had no choice but to acquiesce in the foreign merchants' monopoly of the trade; but they soon coveted a share in it. The foreigners perceived a challenge to their supremacy when, during the seventies, the Government itself undertook a number of export transactions. On several occasions it bought stocks of tea and rice and sold them abroad. This action, however, did not spring from any intention to develop State trading; the ventures were simply a means of obtaining

[1] J. E. Orchard, *op. cit.*, p. 107. [2] Picul = 133⅓ lbs.

foreign exchange urgently needed for the purchase of Western equipment. The really serious threat came from other quarters. From the early years of Meiji, Marquis Okuma was insistent upon the necessity that his countrymen should participate in international trade, and he used his political influence to encourage Japanese merchants to engage in foreign ventures. The Mitsuis, who for 150 years had agents at Nagasaki for purchasing goods imported by the Dutch, were among the first to enter this field. They set up a branch at Yokohama immediately upon the opening of that port, and in 1876 they joined this enterprise with a trading company organised by Marquis Inouye, and so founded the famous Mitsui Bussan Kaisha.[1] This soon began to secure a share of the raw silk exports. Other Japanese business houses followed this lead. Japanese merchants exhibited goods at an international exhibition at Philadelphia in 1876, and soon afterwards eight of them established shops in New York for the sale of their products. For the reasons already given, however, the dominance of the foreign merchants was not easily disturbed. Thus, only one of the New York businesses succeeded, namely that founded by Baron Morimura; the others failed for lack of experience.[2] It was estimated that in 1887 nearly nine-tenths of Japanese foreign trade was still handled by foreign merchants.[3] Up to that time it was only in the trade with China that the Japanese merchants seemed to be making much headway.

During the next decade their efforts had more success. By this time the Japanese were no longer strangers to modern business transactions; they had created banking and commercial institutions needed for servicing foreign trading ventures; after fifteen years of monetary disorder they had achieved financial stability; and large-scale manufacturing industry, especially cotton spinning, was making its appearance. Moreover, the leading business houses were now extending their interests and had ample resources for foreign trade. M.B.K., which had helped to found one of the first large modern spinning companies, the Kanegafuchi, gained a large share in the import of Indian cotton for the growing textile industry, and it opened an office in Bombay to supervise the business. The same concern was active also in the raw silk trade, where it organised production and improved the methods of the silk raisers, operated reeling mills, and took part in export. In 1898 it began a trade in sugar-importing from Java.[4] Even when new export trades were worked up by foreign merchants, it was not long before Japanese firms obtained a share. For example, from the early eighties an export in silk fabrics had grown up, and this at first was entirely conducted by foreign

[1] Mitsui Gomei Kaisha, *The House of Mitsui*, pp. 12 and 33.
[2] *Japan Year Book, 1933*, p. 390.
[3] *ibid.*, p. 391; *see also*, Y. Hattori, *op. cit.*, pp. 28–9.
[4] *op. cit.*, pp. 33 and 37.

merchants. In 1894, however, a Japanese firm, Horikoshi, began to export silk fabrics to the United States, and it was soon joined by others.[1] The result was that the proportion of the total foreign trade in the hands of foreigners fell, so it is estimated, from about four-fifths in 1890 to just over three-fifths in 1900.[2] This relative decline did not mean that the absolute amount of trade in foreign hands had diminished, for the volume of imports and exports more than doubled during that decade.[3] But it was the Japanese rather than the foreign entrepreneur who was responsible for the larger part of the increase.

Meanwhile, alterations in the structure of Japan's trade had occurred. Among the exports, raw silk, tea and rice were responsible for nearly two-thirds of the total during the early eighties; by 1894 raw silk had increased its share of the larger total, while that of tea and rice had declined. These three commodities, however, still made up three-fifths of the total exports. By 1900 the effects of industrialisation were making themselves felt; cotton yarn and piece-goods and silk fabrics then accounted for about 22 per cent of the total, and the share of the older exports had consequently diminished. Japanese firms had secured a large proportion of the export of these new goods, while they had also come to participate to a much greater extent in raw silk exports which still remained by far the largest of the trades. On the import side the biggest increases occurred in raw materials, especially raw cotton, and here again Japanese firms took a very large share.

The relative importance of the various nationalities among the foreign merchants also underwent a change. Great Britain had taken the lead in the development of Japan's trade during the early years of Meiji, and up to the middle eighties most of Japan's imports were from that country. With the shift in Japan's sources of supply from countries selling manufactured goods to those selling raw materials, and with the growth of the American market for raw silk and the Chinese market for cotton goods, the British share in the trade fell and with it, though to a less degree, the relative importance of the British merchant. German and American merchants now became more prominent, although the British were still in the lead. Chinese merchants handled a fair proportion of the trade with the China Coast.

In the new century these trends continued. The volume of Japan's international trade more than doubled between 1900 and 1913, and it doubled again between 1913 and 1929. With the rapid progress of manufacturing industry and, in particular, with the expansion of the textile industries the changes in the structure of her foreign trade were carried much further. During the twenties raw materials accounted for over half the total imports, and the proportion of finished manufactures

[1] *Japan Year Book, 1933*, pp. 390.   [2] *ibid.*, p. 391.
[3] Oriental Economist, *op. cit.*, pp. 31–6.

fell to only 15 per cent. Among the exports, while raw silk still continued to be the chief item, cotton manufactures steadily increased their share; in 1928–9 textile manufactures and raw silk together accounted for two-thirds of the total exports.

Most of this great expansion was attributable to the enterprise of the Japanese themselves. In the early years of the new century, the foreign merchants definitely lost their predominance, and the share in Japanese hands steadily increased until by the twenties it far exceeded that for which foreigners were responsible. This applied particularly to the imports. By the 1920's the foreigners' activities in that section of the trade had become of minor importance, except in the supply of machinery where foreign agents or branches of Western engineering firms were prominent, and in chemicals where Brunner Mond did a large business. The import of raw materials was handled mainly by a few great Japanese business houses, especially M.B.K., Mitsubishi Shoji and Okura. The major export commodities also had passed into Japanese hands. Cotton goods exports, for instance, were concentrated very largely in a few merchant firms which also undertook the import of raw cotton, and by the middle twenties only about 16 per cent of the raw silk exports were left with foreign houses.[1] In Asia, especially in China which had become the chief market for Japanese manufactured goods, the Japanese merchant had gained most of the trade. By this time a substantial commerce had been built up between Japan and her colonies, Korea and Formosa, and this trade was handled almost entirely by the Japanese. Nevertheless, the foreigners still retained their predominance in the tea exports to the United States, and they were also responsible for a considerable quantity of silk piece-goods and of miscellaneous manufactured exports to Western countries. In these classes of goods, and in those markets, their Western connections, their knowledge of Western tastes, and the goodwill which they enjoyed among purchasers overseas, still gave them an advantage over their Japanese competitors.

The success of the Japanese in wresting control over their foreign trade from Westerners was in some degree associated with the highly integrated character of their country's economic organisation as it developed in the later years of the Meiji era. Whereas in China native mercantile enterprise was handicapped by the inferiority of the Chinese financial organisation and of the 'service' industries ancillary to merchanting, by the fact that much large-scale manufacturing industry was in foreign hands, and by the indifference or incapacity of the Government in economic affairs, Japan's mercantile activity rested on a secure institutional basis and an industrial hinterland that had been developed mainly by native initiative. Furthermore, the spearhead of the country's

[1] *Japan-Manchukuo Year Book*, 1936, p. 376.

economic advance was provided by a small number of very great firms which in some respects acted as agents of the Government's economic policy. Each of these firms had a very wide range of activities which extended to industry and finance as well as to trade. For instance, Mitsui owned banks and insurance companies, shipping lines, stevedoring and warehousing companies, shipyards, factories and mines. Mitsubishi had a similar range of interests, and both firms had numerous branches and properties overseas. It is true that a particular Mitsui or Mitsubishi undertaking would not necessarily draw its supplies or place its contracts with another branch of the same house if a competitor offered more favourable terms; but, *ceteris paribus*, its orders were likely to go to members of the same group, and each house was able to provide all the ancillary services that were required. Thus M.B.K., in its activities as a silk exporter, drew much of its supplies from reeling mills under its own control, obtained its financial accommodation from the Mitsui Bank and had available Mitsui warehouses, stevedoring companies and shipping lines, as well as agencies overseas. In the cotton industry Mitsui owned one of the chief spinning-weaving companies and also one of the three largest merchant firms engaged in exporting cotton piece-goods and importing raw cotton.[1] It had unrivalled resources for breaking into new markets as well as for encroaching upon established trades. In these circumstances it is not surprising that the part of the foreign merchants, especially after the First World War, became increasingly confined to dealings in specialities and that most of the bulk-goods trade was wrested from them.

Yet if their share of the trade steadily diminished, the foreigners continued to benefit from, and to contribute to, the great expansion that took place in the quantity of Japan's international trade. Moreover, although it was in the export of miscellaneous goods and the import of specialities that the foreign merchant found his greatest opportunities, he was by no means completely ousted from other lines. In the middle twenties, as we have seen, he still handled a considerable volume, though a declining proportion, of the raw silk exports and the chemical imports. In the rapidly growing import trade in mineral oil, foreign concerns remained pre-eminent. Although Japan from the later years of the nineteenth century had produced a small quantity of mineral oil, the bulk of her needs from that time were supplied from abroad. In the first decade of the twentieth century the two chief foreign concerns, the Rising Sun Petroleum Company (a Shell subsidiary) and the Standard Oil Company, besides importing refined oils, set up refineries

---

[1] Another of these firms, namely Goshi, before the First World War had been cotton brokers who bought cotton from Ralli Bros. on behalf of Japanese mills. From this Goshi went on to handle the importing itself, and ultimately built up a huge business.

for dealing with imports of crude oil, and after the First World War·the volume of trade handled by them grew very fast. Japanese companies, e.g. Ogura, M.B.K. and Mitsubishi, participated in the trade, but the bulk of it remained with the foreigners. These foreign companies not merely handled the import and the refining of the product, but they also built up a distributive chain, both in Japan Proper and in the Japanese Overseas Empire.[1]

We have seen that in China during the period that followed the First World War the dichotomy between native and foreign enterprise tended to disappear in some branches of trade. This was true of Japan also. Japanese concerns obtained interests in foreign companies, both at home and abroad; while some foreign concerns became linked with Japanese houses. Thus, in the raw silk trade one of the largest Japanese exporting concerns had affiliations with an important American firm of importers, E. Gerli and Company of New York. These connections, however, were most numerous in manufacturing industry, and they will be considered in Chapter XIV.

During the 1930's the position of the foreign merchant was affected profoundly by the political and economic changes that occurred in Japan. The development after 1932 of what came to be called a 'quasi-war-time economy' (*Junsenji Keizai*) was accompanied by increased governmental intervention in economic affairs, and this complicated the problems of the Western trader. For example, the Government considered that the country's dependence upon imports for over 90 per cent of its mineral oil was a source of strategic weakness, and it imposed differential duties on crude and refined oil so as to encourage the establishment of refining capacity in Japan. The result was that during the thirties the bulk of the oil imports came to consist of crude. But the Government was not satisfied. The foreign companies still handled most of the import and shared largely in its internal distribution. For example, in 1935 Standard Oil and Rising Sun Petroleum were responsible for about 45 per cent of the total sales of petrol in the country. The Government, therefore, subjected the production, refining, importing and distribution of oil to a licensing system and compelled the firms concerned to store a quantity of oil equivalent to sales during a six-monthly period. At first the new regulation did not affect the foreign companies; but by 1936 they were brought under control.[2]

Another type of intervention which affected all classes of foreign traders resulted from the establishment of export guilds (*Yushutsu Kumiai*). For many years the Government had tried to improve the reputation of Japanese exports, especially those handled by small firms,

[1] S. Uyehara, *The Industry and Trade of Japan*, p. 208.
[2] E. B. Schumpeter (ed.), *op. cit.*, pp. 433, 774–6.

through introducing machinery for the inspection of goods destined for foreign markets. In 1925 these efforts were carried further by a law which encouraged the formation of export guilds among merchants who dealt in certain commodities. During the depression of the early thirties the Government gave financial inducements to merchants to establish these guilds with the object of promoting foreign trade. At that time inspection remained one of their chief functions. Later on, when foreign countries began to discriminate against Japanese goods, there was a change of purpose, and the guilds became concerned mainly with distributing export quotas among their members and with promoting agreements about prices and quantities so as to forestall foreign restrictions. The Government took powers to compel the formation of guilds and to secure the adherence of traders to their regulations. Foreign merchants had to join the guilds or submit to their directions, and some of them claimed that the operations of these bodies were detrimental to their trade inasmuch as they themselves had no control over the administration of the rules. Whether this was so or not, the foreigners' freedom of action was obviously limited by a form of regulation which brought a substantial part of Japan's export trade, directly or indirectly, under official supervision.[1]

To this extent the position of the foreign merchant became weaker during the thirties, and in many of the older trades the decline in the foreigners' share persisted. Thus, by the middle thirties the foreign merchants' proportion of the raw silk exports had fallen to 4 per cent —from 16 per cent in the middle twenties—and this meant an absolute as well as a relative decline over that period.[2] By 1935 three great Japanese firms, Nippon Silk (Mitsubishi), M.B.K. and Asahi Silk were responsible for 70 per cent of the total silk exports. At the same time the rise in Japan's own production of certain goods previously imported, a rise that was in part associated with the fall of the yen in 1931, damaged the business of other foreign merchant houses. For instance, the import of certain chemicals (such as ammonium sulphate, caustic soda and soda ash), which had once been largely in the hands of a British and a German firm, became very small after 1931 because of the rise in home production.

In spite of these set-backs, the foreign merchants during the period between 1931 and 1937 were, in the main, prosperous and they certainly increased the absolute amount of their turnover. This can be explained in part by reference to the buoyancy of Japan's trade as a whole in the period that followed the fall in the exchange value of the yen. During the twenties and especially during the first two years of the world

[1] *ibid.*, pp. 751–60; and Yokohama and Tokyo Foreign Board of Trade, *Annual Report*, 1935–6, p. 15.
[2] *Japan-Manchukuo Year Book*, 1936, p. 376.

depression, Japan's currency had probably been considerably over-valued on the exchanges. When, towards the end of 1931, the gold standard was abandoned and the yen allowed to depreciate, this handicap on the export trade was removed. At the same time the agricultural depression and the collapse of the silk trade provided abundant and cheap labour for manufacturing industries, including the small-scale industries engaged in the production of miscellaneous consumption goods. Japan thus became a cheap producer. Foreign merchants played an important part in cultivating these new opportunities, and a considerable number of new merchant businesses were set up after 1931 to take advantage of the favourable conditions. Among these new-comers German and Indian firms were particularly noticeable. Some of the overseas buyers themselves tried to get into close touch with Japanese suppliers. They either established buying branches in Japan or sent their representatives periodically to the country to arrange for consignments of goods. Immediately after the fall of the yen large numbers of buyers from European and American importing houses and chain stores came to Japan with samples which they induced the local manufacturers to copy, and the rise in the exports of miscellaneous manufactured goods in subsequent years owed much to their efforts as well as to those of the foreign agents and export houses in Yokohama and Kobe. The goods were normally purchased from Japanese middlemen who financed the small producers. As this was a period of extremely keen competition for orders, the exporters had little difficulty in getting the supplies they wanted at very low prices.[1]

Some examples of what was done at this time may throw further light on this trade. Before 1931 there were a number of factories in Japan which produced canvas shoes with rubber soles for sale at home and in China. The Chinese boycott, however, destroyed the chief market, and the producers were left with surplus capacity. At this moment a large American chain store sent its buyers to Japan and, in co-operation with foreign merchant firms at Kobe, it selected suitable lasts, bought canvas and rubber, and contracted with a few shoe factories for a large supply of canvas shoes which were retailed in the United States at 20 cents a pair. Other American stores followed this lead, and a very large export to the United States was built up, only to be killed by a rise in the American tariff in 1933. An entirely new export trade in cheap cotton gloves was created after 1934 by the enterprise of a New York firm in collaboration with an Osaka manufacturer. About the same time the representatives of American chain stores brought samples of Czech glass atomisers and table ware to Japan and placed large orders for cheap copies with local producers. Before 1933 woollen hoods for hat-making

---

[1] The information in this and subsequent paragraphs is based on personal inquiries made in Japan during 1936.

had been manufactured in Japan but the export trade was then very small. In that year the representative of an American importer spent several months in one of the factories where he helped to organise the production of a hood suitable for the American market, and by 1935 a large export had been worked up. When Italian goods were being boycotted in the United States during the Abyssinian crisis, an Italian merchant in Kobe obtained from Italy samples of straw hats of a type formerly sold in the American market. These he had copied for export, and a British merchant in Yokohama followed his example.

Many of the export goods produced during this time were of a type or quality not hitherto made by the Japanese. Thus, the Shimada glass factory in Osaka, which was the largest glass table-ware establishment in Japan, had been unaccustomed to sell its regular products abroad, and the goods which it supplied for export after 1931 were all produced to samples furnished by American merchants. A lamp-shade manufacturer in Yokohama who had previously found his customers mainly among the departmental stores of the Japanese cities was persuaded by the representatives of a Chicago chain store to undertake orders for large quantities of very cheap shades. The same methods were employed in building up an export of lead-pencils, hosiery, rugs, rayon kimono, rubber goods, metal small-wares and neckties. Samples of Western bicycles, gramophones and toys found their way into Japanese workshops and small factories, and these became very active in fulfilling the orders of the foreign merchants who supplied them.

It was not only in the miscellaneous trades that the foreigners were prominent. For instance, several British firms in Kobe, which had formerly been concerned with the import of Yorkshire fabrics, did much business after 1932 in the export of Japanese worsteds. Several Indian firms set up in Kobe during the same period and gained a share in the export of cotton textiles and other commodities to India and South-east Asia. Even in the import of raw cotton foreign merchants, especially Indians, were able to extend their business. The three large Japanese firms which previously handled the bulk of the raw cotton imports and the piece-goods exports had their own purchasing establishments in India and other cotton-growing regions. The fall of the yen, however, made it cheaper for the import business to be conducted from Japan. Consequently, foreign merchants, as well as a number of the smaller Japanese merchants, captured an increased share of the trade, and between 1931 and 1936 the proportion of the imports for which the 'big three' were responsible fell from 70 to 45 per cent.[1] Foreign merchants also did much to stimulate the export of Japanese raw products during the thirties. For example, British firms helped to develop the trade in canned fish and crab, black tea, Hokkaido butter,

[1] Personal inquiries.

and oak. This was a period in which Japan was increasing the mechanisation of her plants and enlarging her capital equipment. Western engineering firms, therefore, set up branches in Japan to take advantage of the new demand for machine tools and other types of machinery, and these branches handled a good deal of the import trade in that class of products.

Some of these foreign merchant firms had long operated in Korea, Formosa and Manchuria as well as in Japan Proper. They participated in the tea export trade of Formosa and the soya bean export of Manchuria, and in the chemical, machinery and rubber goods import trade of all those countries. The foreign oil companies, as we have seen, had distributive organisations in Korea and Formosa and, up to 1935, in Manchuria. Most of the foreign firms who took part in this colonial trade were branches of merchant houses with headquarters either in Japan Proper or in Shanghai. Their business was mainly in products exported to or imported from countries outside the Japanese Empire, and it tended to contract during the thirties as the proportion of the colonies' trade with Japan increased. Some of the firms withdrew from these countries because the imperialistic economic policy of the time reduced the opportunities of foreign merchant houses. For example, Jardine Matheson closed their offices in Manchuria in 1932, and the foreign oil companies withdrew from that country in 1935 when the sale of most oil products became a Government monopoly.

CHAPTER XIII

BANKING AND COMMUNICATIONS

1. Banking

At the time of the opening of the country to the West, Japan's financial institutions were broadly in the same stage of development as those of China in the days of the Cohong. The largely self-sufficient life of the various feudal territories into which Japan was divided, the fact that most payments were still made in kind, and the virtual absence of overseas trade, were conditions unfavourable for the development of a banking system of a modern type. Nevertheless, the merchant houses which acted as the financial agents of the *daimyo* conducted banking operations of a kind. They collected the dues and taxes, which were paid in rice, sold part of these in the chief commercial centres, such as Osaka, and transferred the receipts to the feudal treasuries. They accepted deposits, gave loans to officials and local governments, and issued notes against their reserves. The system of the *Sankin-Kotai*, moreover, stimulated the growth of banking business by making it necessary to provide for the frequent transmission of funds from the provinces to the capital.[1] Various types of credit instruments were in use, and the chief houses had a network of branches all over the country. This financial organisation, however, was designed primarily to serve the needs of governments, both local and central. Although some of the concerns, such as Mitsui and Konoike, were later to become leading participants in the modern banking system, they had to re-organise completely their business in the early years of Meiji by reference to foreign models. The currency system, which has already been described, was likewise in urgent need of reform before it could be regarded as adequate to a modern economy.

In China the task of creating a modern monetary and banking system was hardly begun before the end of the nineteenth century, and until the 1930's native banking institutions were scarcely competent to deal with the financial requirements of the developing commerce. Consequently, it was left to foreign institutions to provide not merely for the finance of foreign trade and other international transactions, but also, in some measure, for the actual means of payment within China itself. In Japan, on the other hand, the Government immediately after the Restoration assumed without hesitation the responsibility of modernising the country's monetary institutions, and before the end of the

---

[1] *Sankin-Kotai* may be translated 'alternate attendance'. It refers to the obligation of *daimyo* to reside for part of each year in Yedo (Tokyo).

211

century it had succeeded in establishing a sound currency and a carefully contrived banking system.[1] This is no place in which to trace in detail the stages in the execution of this policy, and a brief outline of what was done must suffice.

Immediately after the Restoration the Government found itself in grave budgetary difficulties which it met partly by borrowing from Mitsui and other merchants, including foreigners, and partly by the issue of paper money. Many of the old 'exchange houses' had failed during the early sixties, and the Government sought to replace them by encouraging the foundation of new 'exchange houses' with the right of note issue. With one exception, however, these too met with difficulties and ultimately failed. In the meantime, the Government paper had depreciated steeply in terms of specie. Nevertheless, by 1871 the new Government had consolidated its position and felt ready to attempt far-reaching financial reforms. In that year legislation was passed which defined the content of the gold yen and made it the standard coin; while at the Treaty Ports the silver yen, equivalent in content to the Mexican dollar, was declared to be legal tender. A mint was opened at Osaka equipped with foreign machinery and staffed by an English master of the mint and several foreign experts.

The Government raised new financial problems for itself when in 1871 it abolished the *han* (the feudal territories of the *daimyo*). By this step it assumed responsibility for the administration of the local territories and for compensating the displaced *daimyo* and *samurai*; but it encountered difficulties in collecting the local revenues. Further issues of inconvertible notes were therefore made with the result that in the early seventies the gold yen commanded a high premium in terms of paper. Further issues of notes were necessary for meeting the Government expenditure incurred in suppressing the Satsuma Rebellion of 1877.

Meanwhile, a banking system of a Western type had been inaugurated, and, on the advice of Prince Ito, it was the American system of national banking that had been chosen as a model. According to regulations issued in 1872, a national bank was given the right of issuing notes to the extent of 60 per cent of its capital, provided that it deposited Government paper money to the same amount with the Treasury in return for interest-bearing Government bonds and held a gold reserve equivalent to 40 per cent of the note issue. This experiment was not very successful, and only three national banks were formed. In 1876, however, the regulations were revised and the national banks were now

---

[1] For data concerning the early history and development of Japan's modern banking and monetary system, *see* M. Matsukata, *Report on the Adoption of the Gold Standard in Japan* (1899); United States National Monetary Commission, *Reports*, vol. xviii (1910); S. Okuma, *A General View of Financial Policy during Thirteen Years, 1868–1880* (1880); G. C. Allen, *Japan's Banking System* (Japan Chronicle, 1924), and *A Short Economic History of Modern Japan, 1867–1937*, for a bibliography (1946).

permitted to issue notes against a deposit with the Treasury of Government bonds equal to 80 per cent of their capital, and in place of a specie reserve the banks were now required to keep only a reserve of Government paper money. The change had been introduced in part as a consequence of the commutation for Government bonds of the hereditary pensions of the *samurai*.[1] It was hoped that the new banking regulations would not merely stimulate banking activities, but would also create a market for the bonds. This was a political necessity; for if the bonds depreciated, unrest among the *samurai* would follow and the régime be endangered. About 150 new national banks were, in fact, established after 1876, and to the Government's issues of paper money there was now added a large issue of inconvertible bank-notes. The silver yen, which became legal tender throughout Japan in 1878 when a bi-metallic standard was officially adopted, rose steeply in terms of paper money, and all the symptoms of a violent inflation showed themselves. The Government, however, soon had control over the situation. The taxation system had been reorganised in the middle seventies, and the Government increased taxes as a disinflationary device. Further, it was quick to realise the disadvantages of the banks, and so in the early eighties a new financial policy was formulated which aimed at the establishment of a central banking system. The Bank of Japan was founded in 1882 as the country's central bank; the inconvertible Government paper and the national bank-notes were rapidly retired; and by 1886 the Bank of Japan was able to begin specie payments against its own notes. Eleven years later Japan carried through the transference from a silver to a gold standard.

Meanwhile, the great finance minister, Prince Matsukata, had begun to apply a principle which he enunciated in a memorandum of 1882. It was that a sound banking system depended upon the existence of banks with specialised functions. These functions included the provision of long-term loans for industry and agriculture, the conduct of foreign exchange transactions, the handling of domestic commercial business, and the collection of savings from the poorer classes. During the next eighteen years this policy was carried out. The most important of these special banks, the Yokohama Specie Bank, was founded in 1880, and a few years later it began its career as the chief foreign exchange bank of the country. The Japanese Government saw no reason why foreign banks should handle all Japan's international financial transactions, and it realised that an exchange bank under its control would be a valuable instrument for guiding the country's commercial development as well as for giving the Government itself authority over the disposal of foreign exchange funds. The State provided one-third of

[1] The Central Government had assumed the obligation of paying these pensions on the abolition of the feudal system in 1871.

the capital of the Specie Bank, and the Minister of Finance was given power to appoint the President and Vice-President. From the beginning the Specie Bank had a privileged position in the foreign exchange market. The Bank of Japan was required to advance to it a permanent loan at a low rate cf interest and to discount its foreign bills at a specially low rate. Ultimately the Yokohama Specie Bank became responsible for financing the bulk of Japan's foreign trade.

During the nineties other parts of Matsukata's financial programme were carried out. The Hypothec Bank of Japan was founded in 1895 for making long-term loans to agriculture and the fishing industry, and in the next few years agricultural and industrial banks with the same functions were established in each Prefecture. In 1900 the Industrial Bank of Japan was set up to furnish long-term loans to industrial concerns; during the decade before the First World War an important part of its business consisted of the introduction of foreign capital into Japan. Colonial expansion led to the formation of other official banks. Among these was the Bank of Taiwan, founded in 1899 as a central bank for Formosa. It also undertook foreign exchange business, especially in connection with Japan's trade with Formosa and the South Seas. In 1900 the Hokkaido Colonial Bank was established to assist in the development of Japan's northern island, and in 1909 the Bank of Chosen was founded as the central bank of Korea. The Chosen Industrial Bank, which was formed in 1918 by the amalgamation of local official banks originally set up in 1906, and the Oriental Development Company, established in 1908, were concerned mainly with financing the industrial development of Korea and Manchuria. All these banks were capitalised in part by the Government and were subject to official supervision. With the modernisation and expansion of Japan's economy other types of banks came into existence. Among these were Savings Banks, the operations of which were regulated by a law of 1891, and numerous commercial banks. Some of the latter developed out of the 'exchange houses' of pre-Restoration times; others had begun life as national banks during the seventies. Most of them were small and their business local; but a few notably, the Mitsui, Mitsubishi, Sumitomo and Yasuda Banks, had become by the first decade of the present century large institutions with many branches and great resources. Thus in the half-century after the opening of the country, there had been created in Japan an elaborate and highly organised financial system. In the inception and development of this system the Government had played a decisive part.

In the face of these successful efforts by the Japanese themselves, the foreign banks naturally fulfilled a more modest and a more highly specialised rôle in Japan than in China. Nevertheless, for two decades after the opening of the country they were indispensable to the conduct of Japan's foreign trade, and even in the 1930's they financed a considerable proportion of it. At the outset, the Western merchant firms which handled Japan's exiguous foreign trade were branches of substantial houses already established in other parts of the Far East, especially the China coast. As they had large resources themselves, the demands for specialist banking facilities were few. By the beginning of 1866, however, five foreign banks had opened in Yokohama, viz. the Oriental Bank Corporation, the Chartered Mercantile, the Central, the Commercial and the Hindustan. The Oriental and the Mercantile were by far the most important, and their supremacy was confirmed when the other three closed after the Overend and Gurney crisis. Both the Hongkong and Shanghai Banking Corporation and the Comptoir d'Escompte de Paris were represented in Yokohama by mercantile agents until the latter opened its own office in 1867.[1] In Kobe there were no foreign banks in business at the time of the Restoration, although the Hongkong Bank and the Oriental were represented by mercantile agents. They both established their own offices there in 1870.[2] The chief business of these foreign banks was the buying and selling of bills on England, Shanghai and Hongkong, and the volume of their transactions then and for many years to come depended largely on the condition of the silk trade. Until 1871 they kept their accounts in Mexican dollars because the official rate of exchange fixed for *ichi-bu* was considered to be unfavourable; but neither then nor subsequently did they ever issue notes in Japan, for the Japanese Government's own currency policy precluded this. By 1879, when the Chartered Mercantile had closed, the Hongkong and the Oriental were the only foreign banks that remained in business, and in them the vast majority of the foreign exchange transactions were concentrated.[3]

These banks provoked a controversy among foreign traders both in Japan and Hongkong by agreeing in September 1879 to accept the silver yen at par with the Mexican dollar, in spite of the fact that the former had previously been exchanged at a discount with the latter on the China coast. The Japanese Government had taken the initiative in bringing about this official parity, because it saw advantage in establishing the silver yen as a normal medium of exchange in the China trade; but the foreign community feared that they would incur losses through being obliged to accept payments in a coin which did not circulate at par with the Mexican dollar in the outside world. The

[1] This information is from the report of an inspector sent to Japan by the Chartered Bank in February 1866. It has been given to us by Mr. Leighton-Boyce of that Bank.

[2] *Japan Chronicle, Jubilee Number*, 1918, p. 34; and U.S. Department of Commerce, *Japanese Banking*, pp. 266–72.

[3] *The Currency of Japan* (a collection of reprints of articles, letters and official reports, 1882), p. 296. The Comptoir d'Escompte may also have been doing business.

episode is significant for the light which it throws on the lack of confidence felt by foreigners in the intentions or capacity of the Japanese Government. In weight and fineness the silver yen was the equivalent of the Mexican dollar; but at a time when the Government was in financial difficulties, the outside world doubted whether this standard would be maintained, even though the Osaka mint was managed by a foreigner.[1]

Before the Yokohama Specie Bank began its operations, the Western banks and merchants conducted most of the foreign exchange transactions of the country. But the Japanese were ill-content to leave this function in foreign hands, and with the financial reorganisation of the early eighties and the start of the Specie Bank's exchange business in 1887, the relative importance of the foreign houses diminished. During the nineties the Specie Bank was joined by the Bank of Taiwan and, during the first decade of the new century, by the Bank of Chosen, in the financing of foreign and colonial trade. A few of the commercial banks also opened foreign exchange departments, and by 1914 seven of them, including the Mitsui, Mitsubishi and Sumitomo Banks, were conducting this business. At that time, however, 'their operations in this field were either confined, in the main, to financing the business of the trading firms with which they were associated, or were on a relatively small scale'.[2] In the inter-war period the commercial banks increased substantially their foreign exchange transactions, and by the thirties the three banks mentioned above had branches in all the leading financial centres abroad. The Yokohama Specie Bank retained its predominance, although it could no longer claim to be the only Japanese foreign exchange bank of importance.

The establishment of these Japanese banks for a time left ample scope for the foreign banks. Indeed, as long as the greater part of Japan's imports and exports were handled by foreign merchants, the foreign banks remained pre-eminent in the foreign exchange business. Even when, after the turn of the century, the foreigners ceased to conduct the major share of the trade, the absolute amount of business done by the foreign banks continued to grow; for in the rapidly developing economy there was room for both native and foreign banking enterprise. The British banks derived advantage from the fact that Japan made extensive use of the London money market. A substantial part of her currency reserve was held in sterling; while before the First World War some 80 to 90 per cent of her foreign bills were payable in London and practically all her export bills were sent to London for discount.[3]

[1] *The Currency of Japan*, pp. 297 et seq.
[2] J. Inouye, *Problems of the Japanese Exchange, 1914–1926*, p. x.
[3] *ibid.*, pp. 4–5.

Throughout this period the Hongkong Bank remained the leading foreign institution. It had been joined early in the Meiji era by the Chartered Bank of India, Australia and China, which established an agency in Yokohama in 1880 and one in Kobe in 1895.[1] On the other hand, the Oriental Bank Corporation met with difficulties during the eighties and went into liquidation in 1893. The rise of the Japanese banks did not deter other Western banks from seeking business in Japan, and in the early years of the new century several of them opened branches there. An American bank, the International Banking Corporation, began business at Yokohama in 1902; the Deutsch-Asiatische Bank set up a branch in 1905; and in 1912 the Banque Franco-Japonaise was established as a joint enterprise by French and Japanese interests. Just after the First World War two Dutch banks, the Nederlandsche Handel-Maatschappij and the Nederlandsch Indische Handelsbank, opened offices; a Russian bank, the Dalbank, began operations in 1925; and the National City Bank of New York came into the field when it took over the agencies of the International Banking Corporation.[2] A few other banking concerns started business in Japan during the present century; but these proved to be short-lived. By the time of the outbreak of the Sino-Japanese War in 1937, there were seven foreign banks with offices in Japan: the Hongkong Bank, the Chartered Bank, the National City Bank, the Banque Franco-Japonaise, the two Dutch banks and the Bank of China.[3] Some of these banks had several offices in Japan and a few did business in Manchuria also. Their transactions with the Japanese colonies were normally conducted through agencies held by the Japanese banks.

The activities of the foreign banks, which shrank considerably during the thirties, were confined largely to the financing of foreign trade. The two leading banks, the Hongkong and the Chartered Banks, had a diversity of exchange business and financed trade between Japan and many different countries; but most of the others were specialised. For example, the Dutch banks were concerned chiefly with trade between Japan and the Dutch East Indies; the Dalbank handled Russo-Japanese trade; and the National City Bank's business was centred on the financing of raw cotton imports and raw silk exports.[4] The two British banks and the National City Bank also helped in the floatation of Japanese loans on the London and New York markets; but none of them at any time appear to have invested heavily in Japanese securities

[1] Among the Eastern banks a 'branch' was commonly distinguished from an 'agency' in that the former had the right of note-issue and the latter had not. No foreign banks issued notes in Japan, and so, strictly speaking, it is incorrect to refer to their branches by that term.
[2] U.S. Department of Commerce, *Japanese Banking*, pp. 269–72.
[3] Department of Finance, *Financial and Economic Annual of Japan* (various years).
[4] U.S. Department of Commerce, *Japanese Banking*, pp. 269–70.

or to have taken part in industrial financing. To sum up, the foreign banks were essential to the growth of Japan's international trade during the early Meiji period; but their scope became restricted once the Japanese Government had carried through the banking policy formulated by Prince Matsukata. Even in the financing of foreign trade, where the connections of these banks with foreign money markets were of advantage to them, their original dominance was before long undermined by the activities of the privileged official bank, the Yokohama Specie Bank.

2. Shipping

In shipping, as in trade and finance, the foreigners' rôles were similar in Japan and China during the years immediately after the opening of those countries; but in this branch of economic activity as in others a contrast soon appeared. At the outset the foreign merchants and shipping firms brought their vessels to Japan to seize the new opportunities presented to the carrying trade, and for some years not merely the foreign-going ships but also most of those engaged in the coastal trade were owned and controlled by Westerners. Count Okuma testified that 'from the time preceding the Restoration until 1875 the coasting trade was entirely in the hands of foreigners, and Japanese had to travel by foreign mail steamers'.[1] Jardine Matheson were early in the field and introduced a regular service between Yokohama, Kobe and China;[2] while in the sixties the P. and O. ran a special steamer from Europe to Japan for the benefit of the foreign purchasers of Japanese silkworm egg cards.[3] As was to be expected, the Americans took a considerable share of the new carrying trade with Japan. The Pacific Mail Steamship Company, which in 1867 had started to run ships between San Francisco and Shanghai, instituted three years later a service between Yokohama and Shanghai via Kobe and Nagasaki, and so obtained a large proportion of the passenger and goods transport between those centres.[4] In 1867 the P. and O. introduced a service between Yokohama, Shanghai and Hongkong and this had the effect of linking Japan with South-east Asia and beyond.[5]

For at least twenty years after the opening of the country Japan relied almost exclusively on foreign ships for carrying her imports and exports, and until the end of the century the bulk of her commerce was carried in foreign bottoms. The Meiji Government, however, regarded the creation of a mercantile marine as one of its most urgent tasks. It began

---

[1] S. Okuma, *A General View of Financial Policy during Thirteen Years, 1868–80.*
[2] *'Jardines' and the Ewo Interests*, p. 23.
[3] J. E. Orchard, *op. cit.*, p. 98.
[4] Nippon Yusen Kaisha, *op. cit.*, pp. 2–3.
[5] *ibid.*, p. 5.

with very slender resources, for its inheritance from the Tokugawa and clan governments consisted of only a very few modern steamers, and these were classified as warships. A year after the Restoration the Government issued shipping regulations designed to encourage the development of native enterprise, and in 1870 it formed a shipping company (Kaiso Kaisha) which acquired vessels formerly owned by a clan government. At first this venture did not prosper; but a subsidised service between Tokyo and Osaka was started in 1872. Meanwhile Yataro Iwasaki (a *samurai*) obtained three steamers from the head of his clan and ran them between Tokyo, Osaka and Kochi. In 1873 his concern assumed the name of Mitsubishi Shokai and, with assistance from the Government, it made rapid progress. It absorbed the Kaiso Kaisha in 1875, obtained in that year a virtual monopoly of the coastal trade and started a weekly service between Yokohama and Shanghai. About the same time it bought the ships which the American Pacific Mail Steamship Company had employed on the Yokohama–Shanghai run, together with that company's wharves and sheds in Far Eastern ports. In 1879 Mitsubishi ships introduced a service to Hongkong, and in 1881 to Vladivostock. These developments owed much to official help and encouragement. In return for this assistance Mitsubishi placed its ships at the disposal of the Government during the Satsuma Rebellion of 1877 and, at the request of the Government, it founded a school for training marine officers.[1]

Other concerns were formed with Government aid during the late seventies, and some of these came together with Mitsubishi in 1885 to found the Nippon Yusen Kaisha. At that time the new company had 58 ships and a gross steamer tonnage of 65,000.[2] The Government guaranteed dividends of 8 per cent on the company's capital for fifteen years and in return exercised supervision over its routes. Just before the foundation of the N.Y.K. a number of small ship-owners engaged in the coastal trade amalgamated to form the Osaka Shosen Kaisha, and this became Japan's second largest shipping company.[3]

During the eighties Japan's shipping services did not extend beyond the China coast; but in the next decade her ships began to go farther afield. Services to Manila were started in 1890, and in 1893 the N.Y.K., by opening a line to Bombay, won the greater part of the carrying trade in Indian cotton from the Western companies.[4] In 1896 shipping was given further encouragement by the Navigation Subsidy Act. This soon had the desired results, for the Japanese shipping companies bought larger ships and began to extend their operations to distant parts of the

---

[1] *ibid.*, pp. 2–5.   [2] *ibid.*, p. 11.
[3] *ibid.*, p. 3.   [4] *ibid.*, pp. 18–19.

world. By the end of the century the N.Y.K. was running services to Europe, Australia and North America, and early in the new century this and other companies opened up new routes. In its successful competition with foreign shipping the Japanese mercantile marine was assisted not only by official subsidies, but also by the fact that the leading shipping companies were part of the great business houses whose interests embraced also trade, industry and finance. It is doubtful, however, whether either the nationalistic economic policy or the integrated organisation of the Japanese economy was the chief contributor to the rise of the Japanese mercantile marine. Japan possessed natural advantages for developing efficient shipping services and she showed enterprise in cultivating them.

Foreign shipping companies during the Meiji era gained far more by the great extension of Japanese overseas trade than they lost by the development of the Japanese mercantile marine. Thus the tonnage of foreign steamships entering Japanese ports rose from 440,000 in 1873 to 12 million tons in 1913 and to over 18 million tons in 1929. It was, moreover, many years before their predominance in the carrying trade was wrested from them. In 1885 foreign vessels carried over 90 per cent of Japan's overseas trade and represented about 83 per cent of the steamer tonnage entering Japanese ports. Even in 1900 their shares were about 70 per cent and 65 per cent respectively. In spite of the rapid growth of Japan's own shipping during the new century, in 1913 foreign ships still carried over half her trade.[1] Thus it was not until the First World War that the foreigners lost their leading position. From then onwards, however, the Japanese rapidly went ahead, and by the early thirties the foreigners' share of the cargo carried had fallen to about 30 per cent. By this time the Japanese mercantile marine was not merely handling the bulk of the trade between Japan and foreign countries, but it was also heavily engaged in carrying goods between foreign ports. Indeed, this industry had become one of Japan's chief sources of foreign earnings; in 1936 net receipts from shipping services amounted to 194 million yen, nearly half the value of the raw silk exports.[2]

The position of the various Western countries in this business changed considerably. Up to 1875 American ships predominated and the British were a poor second. By 1880, however, the British had gained the lead which they continued to hold down to the outbreak of the Second World War. German ships began to play an important part during the eighties, and by 1913 the tonnage of German ships entering Japanese ports was second only to the British. After the First World

---

[1] Oriental Economist, *op. cit.*, pp. 440–9.
[2] Foreign Relations Council, Japan Economic Federation, *The Shipping Industry of Japan*, pp. 28, 31.

War the Americans gained second place, although in the early thirties their tonnage was well under half that of the British.[1]

3. Other Means of Communication

In other forms of communication the Japanese, from the first, were determined to keep control in their own hands. In the building of the first railways the Government took the initiative. As early as 1869 it planned to construct a line to link Tokyo with Kyoto and Kobe, and as a first step it proposed to build a section from Tokyo to Yokohama. Financial resources were inadequate and the Government therefore accepted the offer made by an Englishman to float a loan of £1 million in London for this purpose. A body of British engineers was engaged to carry out the project and materials and equipment were brought from England. The first section of the line was completed in 1872 and a section between Osaka and Kobe in 1874. From then on the construction of the railway system proceeded steadily, at first entirely under Government initiative, and then for some years after 1882 under private enterprise.[2] The significant fact is that although in these early days Japan relied upon foreign capital, foreign expertise and foreign equipment, she retained the control and ownership of the railway system in her own hands. There were no 'concession' lines as in China. The same was true of the urban transport services. It was, however, an American who in 1913 began the first taxi service in Tokyo.

In the early days of foreign intercourse, the various governments set up their own post offices in Yokohama, Kobe, Nagasaki and other open ports to handle foreign mails. This system did not survive for long. Japan introduced a modern postal system in 1871, and in 1873 the Americans withdrew their postal agencies and in 1879, when Japan entered the International Postal Union, the British and French did the same. The control over the foreign mail thus passed entirely into Japanese hands.[3]

When the foreign cable companies were planning to extend their system to the Far East they encountered some difficulties in obtaining permission to land their cables in China; but the Japanese Government was quick to realise the value of this form of communication, and in 1870 it readily agreed to the request of a Danish telegraph company to land its cables at Nagasaki. By 1871 Japan was linked to Europe and China by cables laid between Nagasaki and Vladivostock and Nagasaki and Shanghai, and the Government set about the construction of land lines to connect the main centres of Japan with the cable terminus. In 1883 the Danish company laid cables between Korea and Japan, but

[1] Oriental Economist, *op. cit.*, pp. 440 *et seq.*
[2] World Engineering Congress, Tokyo (1929), *Industrial Japan*, pp. 140 *et seq.*
[3] Y. Kinosita, *The Past and Present of Japanese Commerce*, p. 101.

221

eight years later these were purchased by the Japanese Government. After this time, although the lines from Nagasaki continued to be owned by the Danish company, the terminals were managed by the Government.[1] Thus Japan welcomed foreign enterprise in this field, but intervened to ensure that it operated in a way that served her national interests.

[1] Y. Kinosita, *op. cit.*, p. 105.

CHAPTER XIV

MANUFACTURING INDUSTRY AND CAPITAL INVESTMENT

1. Manufacturing Industry

In merchanting, shipping and the financing of foreign trade the Westerners performed functions essential to the growth of the Japanese economy. Until the end of the nineteenth century they retained pre-eminence in those spheres, and it was not until after the First World War that their rôle became a subordinate one. In manufacturing industry, however, the history of Western enterprise was quite different. Although in the decades that immediately followed the opening of the country, Western advisers and experts had an important influence on the country's industrial evolution, and although the commercial inter-course which the foreign merchants made possible had profound indirect effects on industrial production, instances of Western industrial enter-prise as such were very few. Indeed, direct participation by Western firms in Japan's industrial expansion, though always limited to a small number of industries, was considerably more important in the twentieth century, especially after the First World War, than at any time during the nineteenth century. It might have been thought that Western industrial entrepreneurship would have found ample scope in a country where the Government was deliberately fostering industrialisation, but where the business classes had at first but small acquaintance with modern methods of organisation. That this was not so needs explanation.

The legal restrictions on the foreigners' rights of acquiring land and of residing in the interior cannot be regarded as a major cause of their failure to set up manufacturing industry during the later decades of the nineteenth century; for they had extra-territorial privileges and special rights in the 'open ports', and they could in any case have operated through Japanese agents. The chief reasons are probably to be found in the attitude of the Japanese Government towards the economic activities of foreigners and in the economic prospects of Japan as these were viewed by the early Western residents. The Japanese were fearful lest their country should be reduced to a colonial status, and for this reason, while they were intent upon introducing modern industrialism, they were equally determined that the control of such undertakings should rest in Japanese hands. The Government, therefore, as already shown, took the lead in founding new manufactures and later gave ample financial support to those Japanese business houses that were judged to be capable of carrying out the programme of industrial modernisation. The scope for Western-owned enterprise was thereby narrowed. Far from being in a privileged position for developing new industries as they were in China, the Westerners were presented with a situation in which any undertakings of their own were likely to have to compete either with official concerns or with companies subsidised and otherwise supported by the State.

The Japanese Government's attitude towards foreign enterprise is well illustrated by its reluctance to borrow from abroad. It might have been expected that a country desirous of rapid industrialisation but short of capital would have looked to foreign investors to provide the resources it required. But had investment been successfully encouraged —either direct investment by Western firms in industrial undertakings or Government loans raised in foreign capital markets—then there was a danger that the foreigners would obtain an influence over the country's economic policy which would mean the realisation of the patriot's worst fears. Consequently, apart from two small foreign loans raised in the first years of Meiji, the Government eschewed foreign borrowing until after the turn of the century when the 'unequal treaties' had been revised and the country's strategic position immensely fortified. One of the two foreign loans mentioned was for the construction of the first railway; but, as we have already explained, although this railway was built with foreign capital and by foreign engineers, its ownership and control were vested in the Japanese Government. In contrast to what happened in China, neither in communications nor in mining were foreign concessions granted.[1] Western expertise was hired, but the Western industrial entrepreneur was in the early days kept at arm's length. This policy may have retarded the pace of industrialisation, for it compelled a reliance upon domestic savings in the process of capital formation and it meant that resources had to be diverted into the exporting industries in order to furnish the means for obtaining imports of capital goods.[2] These exporting industries were, of course, the traditional

[1] This applies to Japan Proper. In Korea, Western firms had participated in mining undertakings and, indeed, had been pioneers in the gold-mining industry before Japan's annexation of the country. One of the largest concerns was the Oriental Consolidated Mining Company. This was an American company, of which part of the capital was held in the United Kingdom, and its mining properties were at Unzan, in North-west Korea. Under the terms of its concession it had the right to import mining machinery and supplies free of duty, and these it obtained from the United Kingdom. There were other foreign-owned gold-mines, including one belonging to the Chosen Mining Corporation, a company registered in the United Kingdom. These concerns, which had operated with increasing difficulties during the nineteen-thirties through the restrictions imposed by the Japanese, were finally sold to Japanese interests just before the outbreak of the Pacific War.

[2] cf. T. Yamanaka, 'Japanese Small Industries During the Industrial Revolution', in *Annals of the Hitotsubashi Academy*, October 1951, pp. 33–5.

Japanese trades concerned with the production of such goods as tea and silk.

Finally, what may well have been the chief reason for the absence of foreign industrial enterprise in the first few decades of Japan's modern era was the misgivings of the foreigners themselves about the country's financial stability and economic prospects. These misgivings were well expressed in a passage in the *Japan Herald* of 9 April 1881: 'Whilst by no means of opinion that the natural resources of Japan, whether mineral or agricultural, are particularly or noticeably great, or that its population is especially hardworking or prudent, nevertheless it has the promise of a moderate future before it. Without expecting too much from its Government—for a government is seldom found to differ widely from the people whose affairs it administers—a condition of moderate affluence and tolerable content is before it. Wealthy we do not at all think it will ever become: the advantages conferred by nature, with the exception of climate, and the love of indolence and pleasure of the people themselves, forbid it. The Japanese are a happy race, and being content with little, are not likely to achieve much.' The foreigners saw Japan as a supplier for export of certain products of small-scale agriculture and as a market for textiles and other manufactured goods imported from the highly industrialised West. They hardly conceived of her as having advantages as an industrial producer, and those types of modern enterprise in which foreigners normally participate in the early days of a country's modernisation, namely communications, mining, and public utilities, were in fact if not in law closed to them by official policy,

After the later nineties, when the process of rapid industrial expansion began in Japan, the economic environment had become unfavourable to foreign enterprise, with a few exceptions, for other reasons. By then Japanese entrepreneurs could match the foreigners in skill and experience in many branches of industry, and leadership had become concentrated in the formidable *Zaibatsu* with their immense range of interests. The foreigner was not able, as he was in China, to operate within a legal and institutional framework of his own, and as compared with his Japanese competitors he had few technical and managerial advantages to offset the difficulties presented by an environment that was strange to him. He found, it is true, some niches where he was able to build up substantial undertakings, and he was able in a number of the newer industries to collaborate effectively with Japanese firms; but the structure of Japanese industry had been created by native hands.

In the discussion of Western industrial enterprise in China it was shown that many of the early manufacturing establishments in that country were set up by Western merchants for the purpose of preparing or processing natural products required for export. Frequently the merchants were compelled to undertake operations of this sort in order to maintain a satisfactory standard of quality. It might have been expected that in the period when the bulk of Japan's exports consisted of natural products or semi-products (e.g. tea and raw silk), the Western merchants in that country would have found it expedient to follow the example of their compatriots in China. Furthermore, it would have been reasonable to suppose that Japan's abundance of cheap labour would have made certain types of manufacturing enterprise attractive to the Western entrepreneurs. Now important undertakings were indeed established for these reasons; but, as compared with China, the instances were few.

The best known and earliest example was referred to in Chapter XII. When the export of tea began the foreign merchants and the wholesalers found that the curing of the tea, which took place in farm-houses or in small factories located in the fields, failed to yield a product grateful to the taste of American consumers. They were therefore obliged to set up establishments of their own where the leaves could be re-fired, cleaned and sorted. This practice continued until recent times. 'The raw tea', as Professor Orchard stated in 1930, 'continues to be produced in small establishments . . . but the leaves are still re-fired and packed for export in the larger factories of the wholesalers or exporters. . . . Most of the wholesalers are Japanese, but with one exception the exporters are all foreigners, chiefly Americans, who have their headquarters in their home country and who go to Japan only for the tea season.'[1] Another early example of a foreign manufacturing enterprise based upon local supplies of materials and cheap labour was the manufacture of rice-straw rugs. These were first made in Japan in a factory capitalised by foreigners who sent the output to a New York rug dealer. Similarly, one of the first factories for the production of toothbrushes in Osaka was owned and managed by Americans, and the entire output was shipped to the United States.[2]

Yet foreign manufacturing enterprise of this type was far less common in Japan than in China. The foreign exporters were normally content to obtain their supplies from Japanese wholesalers, and, although they sometimes obtained financial interests in their suppliers, they seldom went so far as to acquire complete ownership and control of the establishments from which they drew the goods. For this contrast with China there are several explanations. Some of these have already been offered; but two causes may be emphasised in accounting for the foreigners' meagre participation in this sector of Japanese industry. First Japan, from the beginning of the modern era, never lacked native centres of industrial initiative. These were found not so frequently

[1] J. E. Orchard, *op. cit.*, p. 107.   [2] Personal inquiries.

among the older commercial families (although they too furnished some entrepreneurs of distinction) as among the *samurai* of lower grade. In the shadow of the more successful of their undertakings a host of small producers flourished, and, as time went on, the enterprise of the great *Zaibatsu* pervaded the workshops of even the distant provinces.[1] Secondly, the Government, apart from its activities as an industrial innovator, was expeditious in devising regulative machinery to promote the efficient conduct of those small-scale trades in which it did not directly participate.

The best example of this regulation is to be found in the raw silk trade. The development and maintenance of a large silk export were dependent upon the capacity of the industry to provide filament of a uniform quality. Yet the technical unit of production in the silk industry was necessarily small in all its various branches. The cocoons were produced by peasant households, and even the modern filatures, which by the time of the First World War reeled the bulk of the silk, were scattered about the silk-raising districts and were comparatively small. In these circumstances uniformity of product could only be secured by the imposition of control or supervision at certain key points. This control became possible in part through the appearance of a few large silk-reeling concerns which owned numerous filatures and had close contacts with organised groups of cocoon-raising peasants. These large concerns provided the peasants with standardised eggs and gave them technical help and expert advice.[2] In this way they secured large supplies of standardised cocoons. One of the greatest of these concerns, Katakura, started as a small family business in 1878 and steadily expanded until in the early thirties it controlled nine egg-producing establishments and fifty-four filatures. It operated raw silk testing laboratories at Yohokama as well as a number of research institutes in the country districts. After the First World War Katakura opened a New York office and subsequently it sold a large proportion of its output direct to the American manufacturers. In the middle thirties this firm employed about 34,000 persons.[3] Yet great firms such as this were not typical of the raw silk industry, and the Government also had to take a hand in the task of improving quality and maintaining uniformity in the product. By an Act passed in 1885 a Silk Conditioning House was set up at Yokohama and through this all silk for export had to pass. After various experiments in supervision the Government in 1911 subjected egg production to a licensing system which ensured that the cocoon raisers were supplied with high-grade uniform eggs. Official research

[1] cf. G. C. Allen, 'The Concentration of Economic Control in Japan', in the *Economic Journal*, June 1937.
[2] *The Japan Silk Year Book, 1935–36, passim;* E. B. Schumpeter (ed.), *op. cit.*, pp. 511–20.
[3] Pamphlet issued by Katakura and Company Ltd. (1934).

stations also were built and their results communicated to the producers in the several branches of the industry. The Government gave much encouragement to associations of sericulturists. These associations included among their functions the co-operative purchase of eggs and fertilisers and the sale of cocoons on joint account for their members.[1] The small technical units were thus able to share in the commercial and financial advantages of large scale organisation. It was largely through this skilful combination of private initiative and official regulation that by the time of the First World War Japan was able to overcome Chinese competition and to gain a pre-eminent position as a raw silk producer and exporter. Although for many years the foreigner, as already shown, participated in the commercial and financial operations of the silk export trade, he was left with few functions to perform on the productive side of the industry.

In China a number of foreign factories, especially in the engineering industry, originated through the need for providing facilities for the repair of equipment used in the foreign-owned mines and transport undertakings. In Japan a foreign firm was responsible in the early days for starting a small engineering works to carry out repairs to foreign ships; but since mines and transport systems were developed under native initiative and as the establishment of shipyards was actively encouraged by the Government, foreign enterprise was not drawn into this sector of the economy. In the same way, the public utilities in Japan were from the beginning in native hands. Indeed, the only part of Japan's manufacturing industry in which foreign firms became largely engaged were industries that were closely dependent upon advanced Western technology. To the rise of manufactures of that kind after the turn of the century—and still more after the First World War— foreigners made important contributions, sometimes in close partnership with Japanese firms and sometimes alone. It is significant, however, that some of the firms in which foreigners participated had been founded by Japanese, and that the foreigners came in at a later stage when additional capital and technical experience were found necessary for further development. In such case the rôle of the foreigner was scarcely that of a pioneer. In many ways it closely resembled that of the foreign experts brought to Japan during the early years of Meiji. Whereas in those days the industrial technique could usually be learned merely by engaging foreign experts, in later times access to the results of advanced technological research and development could be obtained only by admitting foreigners to a partnership with the native firms.The licensing of patents, which were important in many of these new industries, and the sharing of 'know-how',

---

[1] T. Mori, 'Silk Control in Japan', in *Commodity Control in the Pacific Area* (ed. W. L. Holland), pp. 200–22.

required in Japan as elsewhere a financial association among the firms concerned.

The decade preceding the First World War saw the establishment of a number of joint concerns in the heavy industries. For example, in 1908 Babcock and Wilcox, in association with Mitsui, formed a company, Toyo Babcock, for the manufacture of water-tube boilers.[1] In this concern, which continued in operation until the outbreak of the Second World War, the English partner had the majority holding. In 1907 the Japan Steel Works, which produced steel castings, forgings, ordnance and industrial machinery, was founded by Mitsui and a great English steel and engineering company.[2] After the First World War the practice of establishing joint enterprises became common, especially in the field of electrical engineering. One of the best known instances was the Shibaura Engineering Company. In origin this was a purely Japanese firm founded during the last quarter of the nineteenth century by H. Tanaka. After various vicissitudes it passed into the Mitsui empire, and in 1919 became a joint undertaking of Mitsui and the International General Electrical Company of America. During the inter-war years the Shibaura Engineering Company was the leading producer in Japan of electrical apparatus and equipment which it turned out at two large factories, one at Shibaura in Tokyo and the other at Tsurumi between Tokyo and Yokohama.[3]

In the years immediately after the First World War several other foreign companies became associated with large Japanese electrical engineering concerns. For example, the Japan Electric Company, established in 1889 for the manufacture of telephone and telegraph apparatus, became linked with the Western Electric Company of America and manufactured under licence from that firm.[4] Siemens Schuckert of Germany joined with Furukawa in setting up factories for the production of electrical equipment of many kinds, and the Mitsubishi Electrical Engineering Company, which turned out a wide range of electrical machinery, made an alliance with the Westinghouse Electrical Manufacturing Company and manufactured many products under licence from that firm.[5] Other links which involved close technical association and patent licensing arrangements existed between the Toyo Electrical Engineering Company and Dick Kerr and Company of England, and between the Sumitomo Electrical Wire and Cable Company and several American, British and Italian cable-making companies.[6] Associations

---

[1] Personal inquiries.
[2] *The House of Mitsui*, pp. 20–1.
[3] ibid., p. 20; World Engineering Congress, *Industrial Japan*, p. 249.
[4] World Engineering Congress, *op. cit.*, p. 251.
[5] ibid., pp. 250–1; Mitsubishi Goshi Kaisha, *An Outline of Mitsubishi Enterprises*, 1935, pp. 58, 61.
[6] *Industrial Japan*, p. 251; and Pamphlet, issued by Sumitomo, 1936, pp. 26–7.

of this sort were not confined to electrical engineering, but extended to other branches of the engineering and metal industries. For example, in the inter-war years Mitsubishi produced turbines under licence from Eschen, Wyss and Ljungstron, and the Hidachi Engineering Works made boilers under licence from Yarrow.[1] Mitsui also entered into arrangements with a number of foreign engineering firms for the manufacture of patented products, and in some instances this resulted in the creation of a joint Japanese-foreign company.[2]

It was in the engineering field also that the chief instances of purely Western industrial enterprises are to be found. One of the earliest was concerned with the manufacture of electric lamps. Before the end of the nineteenth century the bulk of Japan's demand was met by imports from Germany, although a small Tokyo lamp-making company had been in existence since 1890. In 1905 the General Electric Company of America absorbed this concern and formed a new company, the Tokyo Electric Company. In 1906 another Japanese lamp-making firm in Osaka was acquired. When the First World War cut off German imports, the Tokyo Electric Company enlarged its plants and after the War it absorbed other producers. By 1936 the company had a capital of about 40 million yen and it was the outstanding lamp producer in Japan. By that time Japanese concerns, including Mitsui, had acquired interests in it.[3]

In the manufacture of motor-cars, vans and lorries two foreign companies, Ford and General Motors, were not merely pioneers, but down to the outbreak of the Second World War they produced the vast majority of the motor vehicles used in Japan. The Ford Company began production at Yokohama in 1925 and General Motors a year later at Osaka. Both plants were essentially assembly plants, for the engines, chassis and many other components were imported from the United States.[4] This left, however, many parts and materials to be obtained in Japan itself, and so the growth of these firms created a large demand among Japanese producers of tyres, batteries and upholstery. A production of motor vehicles by Japanese firms, chiefly for military use, began with the assistance of subsidies in the early twenties, but it was not until the middle thirties that this production became significant, and

---

[1] Personal inquiries.
[2] According to the Report of the Federation of British Industries' Mission to the Far East, 1934, British manufacturers 'lagged behind their American competitors' in the establishment of joint ventures with the Japanese. The Report mentioned, among others, the following American concerns which had put up factories in co-operation with the Japanese: Otis Lifts, Harley-Davidson Motor Cycles, Corn Products Company, Associated Oil Company of California. See *Report of Mission to the Far East*, p. 38.
[3] T. Uyeda, *The Small Industries of Japan*, pp. 266–8; and personal inquiries.
[4] E. B. Schumpeter (ed), *op. cit.*, pp. 804–5; *Japan-Manchukuo Year Book*, 1936, pp. 448–51.

even in 1936 the two foreign manufacturers were responsible for about three-quarters of Japan's output of motor vehicles. The share in Japanese hands would have been still smaller if the Government had not taken steps to handicap the foreigner in this industry in order to provide greater opportunities for its own nationals. For example, a law of 1935 placed the assembly of motor-cars under a licensing system, and it was then laid down that as long as more than half the shares in the foreign companies were held by foreigners, no expansion in the capacity of their plants was to be permitted.[1]

In the manufacture of motor and cycle tyres and of other rubber goods, such as golf and tennis balls, a foreign firm was the pioneer and retained a predominant share in the trade. This was the Dunlop Company. A few Japanese firms had started rubber manufacture towards the end of the nineteenth century; but most of the country's requirements were then satisfied by imports. The raising of the Japanese tariff on rubber goods after the treaty revisions of 1899 induced the Dunlop Company, which had a market in Japan, to start manufacturing there.[2] In 1909 it built a large factory near Kobe and for the next three decades it supplied the bulk of the motor tyres used in Japan as well as large quantities of cycle tyres and other goods. Foreigners also had interests in the Yokohama Rubber Company, the second most important producer in this trade. This company owed its existence to the co-operation of the Goodrich Company and Furukawa. In the inter-war years numerous Japanese producers of rubber goods sprang up; but the industry remained dependent for technical development on these foreign firms.[3]

There were a few other concerns which began manufacturing in Japan when their market was threatened, during the 1920's, by the raising of import duties. Examples are provided by the Victor and Columbia firms which manufactured gramophones, although by the middle thirties their plants had been sold to Japanese producers.[4] Besides these, a number of foreign firms well-known in the production of specialities set up manufacturing establishments. In 1932 an English firm built a factory in Kobe for the production of cotton card-clothing. Mitsui's held a minority interest in this and then bought it outright in 1940. Other foreign firms were engaged in the production of sewing thread, carbon brushes, automatic sprinkler equipment, paper bags and protective paints. There were also foreign interests in the Japanese rayon industry.[5] Yet, except in certain branches of engineering and in the

[1] *Japan-Manchukuo Year Book*, 1936, pp. 450–1.
[2] T. Uyeda, *op. cit.*, pp. 182–4.
[3] *Japan-Manchukuo Year Book*, 1936, pp. 451–2; *Industrial Japan*, pp. 505–10.
[4] United Kingdom Department of Overseas Trade, *Report on Economic and Commercial Conditions in Japan*, June 1936, pp. 70–1.
[5] This information was obtained from personal inquiries.

rubber industry, it would appear that Japanese enterprise itself had been mainly responsible for the inception and growth of all the important branches of manufacture.

2. Capital Investment

The part of the foreign investor in Japan stands contrasted with that which he played in other Far Eastern countries where foreign enterprise was prominent. Japan had, from the outset, taken control over her own destinies, and she had been determined not to incur financial obligations to foreigners which might at some stage invite political interference for their enforcement. The foreigners, for their part, at first lacked confidence in the financial capacity of the Japanese Government and in the prospects of an economy that was clearly intended to be built according to a native plan. Consequently, they were reluctant to put large resources at risk. In other words, during the critical period that followed the opening of the country, the fears of the Japanese prevented any considerable resort to foreign capital markets, while the misgivings of the foreigners inhibited any large direct investment. Japan's economic development thus owed no major debt to the Western investor, although there were two short periods, 1899 to 1913 and 1924 to 1930, of which this conclusion is true only with qualifications. During the first of these periods, however, the motives which led her to borrow abroad were not solely, nor even predominantly, for the purpose of financing industrial expansion; for the chief loans were intended to cover expenditure on war or war-preparation. Even in the second period a substantial part of the capital raised abroad was required for reconstruction after the Great Earthquake.

These generalisations apply to long-term investment, and this was, of course, not the only type of foreign capital of which Japan made use. The Western merchants were important channels through which Japan's economy, especially in the early days, was supplied with working capital needed for the conduct of foreign trade and often for financing the manufacture of and dealings in many kinds of export commodities. Through the foreign banks, moreover, Japan obtained access, before the development of her own exchange banks, to the resources of Western money markets. There were wide fluctuations in the size of the balances maintained by foreigners in Japan, and at times these were much affected by speculative operations in the Japanese currency. On the whole, however, while supplies of short-term capital were qualitatively important at certain periods in the country's modern economic history, the amount of financial resources placed by foreigners at the disposal of the Japanese economy through these means can never have been very large in proportion to its total requirements.

In the early years of Western intercourse the public authorities frequently resorted to the foreign merchants and banks for temporary accommodation. Even before the Restoration the foreigners at Nagasaki sometimes gave financial assistance to the local *daimyo*, and one of these transactions was to lay the foundations for a massive future development. This was when local foreigners lent money to the Lord of Tosa to enable him to found a trading company to deal in the products of his domain and to acquire ships from abroad to carry his cargoes.[1] It was from this venture that the great Mitsubishi enterprise afterwards sprang. The Shogun himself, during the period between the opening of the country and his downfall, borrowed small sums from abroad, and at one time he obtained a loan of $500,000 (Mex.) from the Oriental Bank Corporation to enable him to pay a debt due to the French.[2] Later, foreign merchants came to the help of the young Meiji Government to enable it to tide over some of its initial difficulties. In 1868, for example, the foreign merchants lent 890,000 yen, and in 1869 100,000 yen, to the Government. Both of these were short-term loans and were repaid by 1871.[3] The first long-term loan to be floated abroad was issued in 1870. This was for 9,760,000 yen (£1 million) and it was raised in London at 9 per cent interest and at an issue price of 98. The proceeds were applied mainly to cover the expenditure on the first railway line. In 1873—a time of great financial stress in Japan—a second foreign loan of 23,400,000 yen (£2,400,000) was raised in London; it carried 7 per cent interest and its issue price was 92½. These were the only occasions on which the Government resorted to foreign capital markets until the very end of the nineteenth century, and by then both of these loans had been redeemed, the first in 1882 and the second in 1897. No municipality or company had issued capital abroad up to that time.

By the end of the century Japan had long escaped from the tribulations of the early Meiji period. Her prestige had been raised through her success in the Sino-Japanese War of 1894–5 and her currency reserves strengthened through the payment by China in gold of an indemnity equivalent to 231·5 million taels (£38 million sterling).[4] In 1897 she had successfully carried through a transference from a silver to a gold standard and two years later she had freed herself from the shackles of the 'unequal treaties'. Her credit was so much improved that she was now in a position to raise capital abroad on favourable terms, while her Government was no longer haunted by the dread that foreign political domination might follow the foreign investor. It could, therefore,

[1] R. Iwai, *Mitsui Mitsubishi Monogatari* (The Story of Mitsui and Mitsubishi), pp. 239 *et seq.*
[2] *Japan Year Book*, 1936, p. 300.
[3] S. Okuma, *A General View of Financial Policy during Thirteen Years, 1868–80.*
[4] M. Matsukata, *op. cit.*, p. 173.

contemplate large-scale capital developments financed by foreign borrowing. Among the developments which the Government had in mind were the officially sponsored Iron and Steel Works at Yawata and an enlarged system of railway and telegraphic communications. At the same time rivalry with Russia in North-east Asia was compelling Japan to increase her armaments, and she looked abroad for the financial resources to enable her to do so. So, in 1899 a period of large-scale foreign borrowing began. In that year the Government issued a long-term sterling loan of 95,600,000 yen,[1] and between then and 1903 a quantity of domestic bonds issued by both central and local governments was sold abroad. By 1903 the total amount of foreign debt had been raised from an insignificant amount in the early nineties to 195 million yen.[2]

With the outbreak of War with Russia Japan resorted to the London capital market on an even greater scale. In 1904 two long-term loans to the amount of 215 million yen was issued, and in 1905, when Japan's victories had raised her credit, further loans to the total amount of 830 million yen were issued. In addition, the scrip of internal loans was sold abroad and a railway debenture issue made. By the end of 1905 the total outstanding foreign indebtedness of Japan was about 1,410 million yen.[3] The debt continued to rise up to the outbreak of the First World War. Japan had assumed responsibility for Korea, Southern Saghalien and the South Manchuria Railway Zone, and this compelled her to make substantial investments in the development of these regions. At the same time there were plans for further industrial development at home, and expenditure upon armaments remained heavy. These burdens could not be borne without resort to foreign borrowing; as it was, the policy of territorial and economic expansion ran down the gold reserves and caused anxieties in the Ministry of Finance. Nevertheless, Japan's credit during this period was high, and she was able to convert part of her outstanding foreign debts on favourable terms as well as to use some of the proceeds of her foreign loans to pay off internal debt raised at a high rate of interest.

Most of her capital imports took the form of Government issues on the London and Paris markets; but several Japanese municipalities made issues abroad to finance the construction of public utility undertakings, including waterworks, harbour works and electricity generating plants. Between 1905 and 1914 several issues of railway bonds and debentures were also made in London and Paris. During this period the Industrial Bank of Japan became an important channel of foreign

---

[1] The sterling value of the loan was £10 million. Its issue-price was 90 and it carried an interest rate of 4 per cent. For other details of this and other loans, see *Financial and Economic Annual of Japan* (various years); J. Inouye, *op. cit.*, pp. 230–1.

[2] J. Inouye, *op. cit.*, p. 229; and Oriental Economist, *op. cit.*, p. 696.

[3] J. Inouye, *op. cit.*, pp. 229, 230; for details of loans, including issue-prices, terms and interests rates, see *Financial and Economic Annual of Japan* (for appropriate years).

investment. Some of its capital was held by foreigners, and between 1900 and 1911 it raised 350 million yen abroad by the sale, either of its own debentures or of those of other public corporations, notably the South Manchuria Railway Company. The total amount of Japan's outstanding foreign indebtedness in 1914 was just under 2,000 million yen; three-quarters of this consisted of loans issued by the Central Government.[1]

During the First World War Japan earned net credits on international account to the extent of over 3,000 million yen. Most of this went to swell her gold holdings or her balances in New York and London, and only a small part of it was applied to the redemption of her long-term foreign obligations which in 1919 still stood at 1,720 million yen. During the next few years the indebtedness declined, and then in 1924 the second period of heavy foreign borrowing began. The Great Earthquake of 1923 provided the occasion. This disaster occurred at a time when the liquid reserves accumulated during the war had been run down through a series of unfavourable balances of payments, and it compelled heavy investment in the reconstruction of Tokyo and Yokohama. At the same time several foreign loans fell due for repayment. So the Government raised two loans in 1924—one in London and the other in New York—for converting the outstanding balances of earlier loans and for reconstruction purposes. Two others were raised in 1930. The outstanding feature of this period, however, was not the increase in the Government's foreign indebtedness, but rather the extent to which municipalities, public corporations and industrial concerns resorted to the foreign capital markets. A very large quantity of debentures was issued abroad in the later twenties, many of them in connection with electricity supply undertakings; and there was a considerable purchase by foreigners of existing domestic securities. In 1930 Japan's total indebtedness was estimated at about 2,470 million yen of which about three-fifths was Government debt. During the thirties no further loans were issued abroad and the redemption of existing obligations went on rapidly. An estimate made in 1932 put the total gross foreign indebtedness in Japan in that year (excluding short-term balances) at about 2,270 million yen (gold). This was made up of foreign issues amounting to 1,400 million yen of Government bonds, 235 million yen of municipal bonds and 470 million yen of corporation bonds, together with about 50 million yen of domestic government bonds held by foreigners and about 110 million yen of investments by foreigners in domestic issues of Japanese companies.[2]

[1] J. Inouye, *op. cit.*, p. 229, and *passim*; also, information supplied by Bank of Japan.
[2] *See* authorities cited above; also Mitsubishi Economic Research Bureau, *Japanese Trade and Industry*, pp. 9–10, 82–5; and E. B. Schumpeter (ed.), *op. cit.*, pp. 873 *et seq.*, and tables. The total does not include foreign holdings of Japanese shares nor the properties of foreign companies in Japan.

These figures do not cover direct investments by foreigners in Japan. They were, however, never very large; they were estimated to have been 40 million yen in 1904 and 70 million yen in 1913.[1] During the 1920's they rose considerably along with the development of joint enterprise by foreign and Japanese concerns, and by 1932 the total may have been of the order of 245 million yen.[2] The British and the Americans were responsible for most of this direct investment as they were also for the portfolio investments.

No estimate can be made of the short-term capital investments in Japan at various periods, and the figures given above do not of course provide any indication of Japan's net indebtedness. Even in 1913 Japan had already become a considerable investor abroad, particularly in Manchuria and China, and her long-term investments were then estimated at about 460 million yen.[3] Subsequently she exported large quantities of capital, mainly to other parts of Asia, including Malaya, the Philippines, the Dutch East Indies as well as to Northeast Asia. By 1932, before the 'Manchukuo' era had begun, the value of Japan's investments abroad was put at 1,650 million yen, of which the greater part consisted of properties in Manchuria and China. As at that time a proportion of the sterling and dollar bonds were owned by Japanese nationals (perhaps one-third), it is clear that the net indebtedness of the country was quite small.[4] During the thirties she passed into a creditor position through her enormous investments in Manchuria (over 3,000 million yen between 1932 and 1939), and through the purchase of foreign industrial properties in Japan itself.

In summary, it may be said that while capital formation in Japan came about mainly through the medium of domestic saving, foreign borrowing was of significance during a critical period. In the absence of the foreign loans raised during the first decade of this century, it is improbable that Japan would have been able either to accelerate the rate of industrial development as she did at that time, or to realise her plans of territorial expansion on the continent. In the same way the foreign investor came to the rescue in the twenties when he made possible the rapid reconstruction of the country after the Earthquake. He shared also during that decade in the provision of the capital needed for the large-scale development of electric power resources which was a

[1] E. B. Schumpeter (ed.), *op. cit.*, pp. 919–22.
[2] United Kingdom Department of Overseas Trade, *Economic Conditions in Japan to Dec. 31st 1932*, p. 21; and H. G. Moulton, *Japan: An Economic and Financial Appraisal*, pp. 524–5.
[3] E. B. Schumpeter (ed.), *op. cit.*, p. 922.
[4] United Kingdom Department of Overseas Trade, *op. cit.*(1932), pp. 21–2. The figure for Japanese investments does not include the loans made during the First World War to the Chinese and Russian Governments, since these had to be written off.

condition of the great industrial expansion of the thirties. Further, as we have already seen, his direct investment in the electrical engineering industry was qualitatively important, since it was associated with the creation of joint enterprises and the use of foreign patent specifications and 'know how'.

SUMMARY AND CONCLUSIONS

CHAPTER XV

SUMMARY AND CONCLUSIONS

THE present survey, though brief in relation to its theme and incomplete in many particulars, has, it is hoped, succeeded in pointing the contrast between the experience of China and Japan in their reaction to Western entrepreneurial activity. The Westerners came to both countries in search of trade, and trade remained their major pre-occupation. But even if they had wished to do so, they could not have limited themselves to that field. The economic activities of a people form an organic whole; an expanding commerce is dependent upon, and at the same time makes possible, the existence of novel types of financial institutions, means of communication and forms of industrial organisation. When, therefore, traders from advanced countries make their impact upon 'under-developed' societies, they cannot restrict themselves to a single type of economic activity, and since in the country of their new adventure there are seldom found native economic institutions and ancillary services adequate to sustain a large-scale foreign trade, they are impelled to import these also. Once these institutions and services have been introduced, they soon cease to be mere adjuncts of merchanting, for they come to exist, as it were, in their own right for ministering to the needs of the developing economy.

In China the best examples of this extension outward from merchanting are the early manufacturing establishments where the products acquired by the foreign merchants for export were graded and processed. The merchants dealt in goods produced by numerous small peasants, and there was usually no class of Chinese merchant capable of organising the flow of supplies. So foreign enterprise had to concern itself with production, for only in this way could regularity in deliveries and uniformity in quality be assured. When, as was often the case, the preliminary processing of the products could be more efficiently carried out by the use of Western technical devices, an additional reason was present for foreign participation in production. From this it was but a step to the establishment by the foreigners of industries designed to use the ample supplies of cheap Chinese labour in new manufacturing processes. Where this labour could be employed to operate Western machines in large factories—a development that was delayed and handicapped in China by insecurity and legal restrictions—foreign enterprise found fresh opportunities that were not directly dependent upon nor derived from purely mercantile interests. In the same way the foreign ships, introduced into Chinese waters to carry the foreign-going cargoes of the

Western merchants, soon showed their superiority to the native junks, and a demand grew up on the China coast and in the inland waters for ship-space among the Chinese themselves. The same course of development, *mutatis mutandis*, was followed by Western financial institutions. On the opening of the ports, China and Japan showed many similarities in all these respects; but their courses soon diverged. These divergencies are to be explained not primarily by contrasts in the material resources of the two countries, but rather by differences in their political and social constitution. And these local differences in the economic environment meant not merely that the forms assumed by foreign enterprise varied between China and Japan, but also that the limits to the extension and scope of that enterprise were determined by policies and conditions that had little in common in the two countries. Until very late in her modern career, China was as reluctant a host to Western material civilisation as to the Western entrepreneurs themselves. Her dynasty and her bureaucracy, with some notable exceptions, were resistant both to the importunities of the agents of Western civilisation and also to the forms of the civilisation itself. But since they could not eject these unwelcome intruders, they strove to hinder and frustrate. To the extent that they were successful, they retarded the modernisation of their country's economy no less than they restricted the extension of Western enterprise. Further, their policies reduced the efficiency with which that enterprise was conducted. Since they made no effort to accommodate China's institutions and laws to its needs, they forced such development as occurred to take place within an institutional environment of extra-territorial privileges and a geographical framework of foreign concessions and settlements. This distorted the location, organisation and growth of enterprise.

For the same reasons such undertakings as were concerned with foreign markets proved to be very vulnerable to outside competition. It has been shown how damaging and even fatal were the regulations which hedged about foreign undertakings in the large-scale manufacturing, mining and transport industries. Even industries that started with great advantages faltered or failed before this massive conservative opposition. Tea and silk provided illuminating examples. Traditional peasant industries of this type can be transformed into suppliers for international trade only if large-scale centralised organisation can be introduced into them at some point from a source exterior to the peasant economy itself and its traditional merchanting bodies. In the Japanese silk and tea trades this organisation was provided by the Government and by the great merchanting houses; in the Indian and Ceylon tea trades it was supplied by foreign plantation companies. But in China none of these agencies was available. The Government had no interest in promoting a revolution in organisation; there were no Chinese

242

merchants capable of effecting it; and the foreign merchants could not undertake the whole task because in those industries their rights did not extend to the point at which they could effectively impose regulations on the scattered multitudes of suppliers, modify the existing forms of land tenure, or re-fashion the traditional social and trading relationships.

In the absence of a native government interested in economic change and competent to promote it, the necessary reorganisation could only have come from a more extensive foreign political control than in fact existed. As it was, many trades languished in the face of competition from industries in other countries which had been able to adapt themselves to the needs of foreign markets, and China's economic development was thus seriously impeded. Foreign enterprise in China could build on what it found and could modify traditional arrangements in some degree; but it could not penetrate far enough to bring about a thorough-going transformation of the traditional economic structure. When China was at last ready to leave her exhausted past and to come to terms with the modern world, she was distracted for two decades by civil war and the modernisation of her institutions was further retarded.

In Japan the limits set to Western enterprise were of a different kind. Modernisation was early accepted as the condition of national survival by those who occupied the seats of authority, and the Government's major task was conceived to be that of hastening the introduction of Western economic and legal forms and Western technical devices. The more rapidly this aim could be achieved, the sooner could Japan free herself from the 'unequal treaties' and dispense with Western initiative in the promotion of her commerce and industry. Thus, from the time of the Restoration, the stimulation of economic development became a leading object of national policy. The Western entrepreneur in trade, finance and shipping was accepted as an essential agent of this process, but limits were placed upon his field of activity and he was relegated to a subordinate role as soon as native enterprise had achieved maturity.

In both countries the contributions of the Westerners may be grouped under three headings, namely, capital resources, expertise and entrepreneurship. But whereas in China, Western capital and expertise followed in the wake of Western enterprise, in Japan the relationship between these factors was more intricate. There the development of the initiative in large-scale manufacturing industry, inland transport and mining was early seized by the Government and later came to be shared between the Government and the great native business houses. Foreign expertise in these fields was necessary, but it entered as the servant not of Western but of Japanese enterprise. The important exceptions which we have noted do not disturb this general rule. Similarly, the flow of

243

capital into China followed upon other foreign activities and the Chinese Government was an almost passive recipient. Direct invest-ment by foreigners in the concessions was outside Chinese jurisdiction; while other types of investment were intimately linked either with foreign enterprise in the mines and railways or with loans raised to pay foreign indemnities. These loans led to the extension of foreign control over the Customs and the Salt Gabelle for the purpose of ensuring that revenue should be applied to their servicing. Thus, foreign investment took place in circumstances which brought about a derogation of China's sovereignty, and any display of financial initiative by the Chinese Government was thus made more difficult. In Japan, on the other hand, the amount of direct investment by foreigners was very small, and the Government resisted the temptation to resort on a large scale to foreign borrowing until it was in a position to raise capital on terms which presented no menace to its freedom of action or to the execution of its own economic policy. The wide difference between the functions performed by foreign enterprise in the two countries is seen most clearly in the financial sphere. The commanding position which the foreign banks maintained in China right down to the 1930's stands in striking contrast to the specialised role to which they were limited by the early rise of a modern native banking system in Japan.

The Western entrepreneurs' responsibility for Japan's economic development must not, however, be depreciated. We have seen that Western mercantile activities were for many decades essential to the growth of large sectors of Japan's economy and that they remained of importance even in recent times. But to recognise this is not to deny the fundamental difference in the Westerners' roles in the two countries. In China they were for long the only agents of modernisation and the limits to their activities were determined by what they could accomplish in the unfavourable environment of old-fashioned economic institutions, official hostility and political insecurity. In Japan the limits to the exercise of their entrepreneurial functions were set by national policy intent upon modernisation carried out so far as possible through the agency of native enterprise. It would not be an exaggeration to say that in China the foreign business community performed, of necessity, many duties which in Western countries at the same period were normally undertaken by the Government. The activities of the foreign banks in respect of the monetary system furnish a striking example of this. It was largely because the Japanese State hastened to assume extensive economic functions—and indeed in many respects to go beyond the limit of what was then generally regarded as the proper duty of govern-ment—that foreign enterprise was narrowly restricted in its scope in that country. Japan's policy was so successful that by the first decade of the present century she was able to join with the Westerners in the modernisation and development of Asia. From that time onwards she was primarily to be regarded not as a subject for Western enterprise but rather as a leading contributor to the flow of capital, technique and enterprise to the continent. It is true that territorial aggrandisement and political power were more prominent among Japan's ambitions in China than among those of Western European countries whose interests —at least in recent decades—were mainly commercial; but this did not make the impact of her enterprise on the Chinese economy any less resounding.

Both the internal organisation of foreign enterprise and the relations between Westerners and Orientals went through clearly marked changes during the period under investigation. The typical merchant firm in the middle of the century undertook a wide variety of functions and supplied itself with most of the ancillary services required for the conduct of its business. As time went on, the mercantile, banking, insurance, shipping and other functions became differentiated and there was a growth of specialist industries and services. These changes permitted the existence of smaller merchant and other firms than those of the earlier epoch, and the trend was assisted by the increased speed of communications which encouraged the growth of commission business. Nevertheless, there were many cross-currents. Vertical disintegration, as it was called, seems to have been the predominant tendency of the later years of the nineteenth century, but in the present century the rise of new types of trade, e.g. sales of engineering goods and branded products, was accompanied by the appearance of firms with very extensive activities, manufacturing, mercantile and financial. Moreover, while the mortality among Western firms was high, and while from time to time notable firms went out of business, there were a few large houses with wide interests that held their own from generation to generation.

With the change in the internal organisation of the foreign firms there occurred also an alteration in the relationship between them and the native business communities. At one time the foreign merchant seldom penetrated beyond the Treaty Ports and concessions, and he normally depended upon Chinese traders for access to supplies and markets. Later the foreigners themselves organised the supply of export commodities, even those furnished by remote provinces, and they became actively engaged in the cultivation of their up-country markets. As Chinese business practices became assimilated to those of Europeans and as linguistic barriers were lowered, the distinction between foreign and native enterprise became less clear-cut. Joint Sino-foreign enterprises, especially in manufacturing industry, appeared as important features of the economy and Chinese shareholders participated in foreign companies. The decline of the compradore was a symptom of this changing relationship. There were parallel movements in Japan

245

where, after the First World War, a number of important joint under-takings were set up in manufacturing industry.

A recital of the achievements of Western enterprise in particular spheres may easily lead to an exaggerated notion of its effects on the Chinese economy. To appraise fully those effects would require a much deeper examination of social and economic changes than has been possible in this study. But some comment is called for if merely to set in due proportion the instances of foreign enterprise described in the preceding chapters. In this connection the size of China's foreign trade during the century after the Treaty of Nanking is relevant, and the table in Appendix A brings out the fact that, in spite of the trade expansion during the present century, the volume remained very small. Forty years after the Treaty of Nanking imports were valued at about £21 million a year at the current rate of exchange, while exports were about 10 per cent less. By the time of the First World War China's imports had risen to about £76 million a year and exports to about £60 million; that is to say, her total trade was about one-tenth of the annual value of British overseas trade at that time. By the period immediately preceding the Manchurian Incident (i.e. in 1927–31) imports stood at about £144 million a year and exports at £113 million. For a country with a popula-tion estimated in 1931 at 450 million this was not an impressive total; foreign trade a head worked out at about 11*s*. a year. In 1929, a favourable year for such comparisons, China's share of world trade was 2·1 per cent compared with 2·9 per cent for Japan and 13·1 per cent for the United Kingdom.[1] China's national income in relation to the size of her population was very low—though at present any attempt to measure it would appear to be a futile exercise. Nevertheless, it is clear that even at the moment when her international trade was at its maximum, the ratio of that trade to the national product was very small.

This conclusion, if offered without qualification, would be misleading. Averages may obscure the truth when they are applied to such a huge country in which communications are poor. The distant provinces were \at no time much affected by foreign enterprise, but it was otherwise with the coastal areas and those served by the internal waterways and railways.[2] Great ports, with busy industrial hinterlands, had risen as a direct result of Western (and later Japanese) enterprise. Large-scale industries, especially textile industries, had grown up there, and the

[1] *Statistical Year Book of the League of Nations, 1931–32*, p. 201.
[2] It was estimated that in 1929 industry was largely confined to six provinces (Kiangsu, Liaoning, Hopei, Kwangtung, Shantung and Hupeh). These had only one-tenth of the area of China and well under two-fifths of the population, yet they had about nine-tenths of the cotton-spinning, silk-reeling, oil-pressing and electric power capacity and about two-thirds of the coal- and iron-mining capacity. *See* O. S. Lieu, 'Industrial Growth of China', *Problems of the Pacific*, 1931, p. 139.

economic life of certain other regions (such as those producing vegetable oils and oil seeds, tobacco and silk) had become partly dependent upon markets opened up by the foreigners, while multitudes of consumers had become accustomed to use imported products or goods manufactured by Western technical methods.[1] By 1913, over a great part of the country the people's clothing was made either of imported cloth or, more usually, of cloth woven from imported yarn, and native vegetable oil had been replaced by imported mineral oil for lighting. The activities of large numbers of peasants had become affected by foreign trade, and the kind of crops which they produced responded to the fluctuations in world markets. For instance, towards the end of the nineteenth century there was a decrease in the production of sugar-cane, flax and indigo, and the land formerly under those crops was used for growing cotton, opium, groundnuts and soya. During the period of the expansion of tea and silk exports, land under rice and other cereals was converted to tea and mulberries, and then when these exports declined it went under cereals again. We have noted how the great expansion of the cigarette industry in the present century brought about the conversion of wheat lands to tobacco.

The changes in the country as a whole were not on a sufficient scale to produce an agricultural revolution, but they had important marginal effects and in some areas the consequences were far-reaching. All these changes were made possible by the means of transport which the foreigners introduced and by their commercial and industrial enterprise. That these efforts failed to yield larger harvests in the present century was mainly due to the lack of ordered government and to the disturbances caused by the civil wars. It was the persistence of these conditions that confined such a large part of the new industrial enterprise to places under foreign political control, namely, the concessions and Manchuria. The developments that took place there suggest what might have been achieved had strong and ordered government been established after the Revolution, just as they indicate that, with political conditions as they were, economic progress would have been brought to a standstill if these foreign enclaves had not existed. It was otherwise with Japan. By the 1920's the effects of Westernisation had penetrated into every corner of the economy and the country's material welfare had become closely dependent upon her foreign and colonial trade. Her manufacturing industry, though for long specialised to textiles, gradually became more highly diversified. It drew the great bulk of its raw materials from overseas, while the colonies furnished about a fifth of the rice consumption of the homeland. Japan paid for these imports

[1] cf. R. Firth, 'The Peasantry of South-east Asia', in *International Affairs*, October 1950, p. 507: 'Conservative in his techniques of production, the peasant has shown himself enterprising in consumption. The result has been that at many points, without realising it, the peasant has become geared to the Western economic system.'

247

with exports of raw silk, manufactured goods and shipping services, and by the Taisho era she had become integrated with the world economy.[1] The presence of Western business men in China and the examples of their practices were not without their influence on the outlook of the Chinese business community. The foreigners not merely offered Chinese merchants new opportunities for trade but they also introduced them to Western business methods and technical devices. Gradually the Chinese merchants gained experience which enabled them to take over functions at one time monopolised by foreigners, and some of them escaped from the subordinate position which they had occupied in the old society and played, with the Westerners, a dynamic role. Some members of this new business class emerged from the more alert members of the bureaucracy and the gentry; others were drawn from Overseas Chinese; and yet others had their origins among the compradores who had learned foreign ways and had acquired capital in the service of Western firms.[2] By the early years of the present century these Chinese business men were beginning to establish modern manufacturing enterprises. Later, graduates educated in Western-style universities in China and abroad, as well as technicians trained by foreign industrial concerns, became more numerous and the supply of personnel competent to manage modern industrial undertakings was thus augmented. With the rise of Western factory industries in the concessions and in Hongkong, and with the spread of modern means of communication in China, there grew up a body of industrial workers available for employment in Chinese and Western enterprises alike.

Yet the environment in which the Chinese entrepreneurs operated was still discouraging. They were 'at the mercy of officialdom' and subject to the arbitrary exactions of central and local authorities. Even when enlightened officials invited their co-operation in some enterprise, they hesitated because they had little confidence in the consistency of Government policy. In the era of civil war the elementary condition of personal security was lacking. In these circumstances it was natural that Chinese, like foreign, enterprise became concentrated in the concessions where it could shelter under the protecting arm of Western power. It has been well said: 'The foreign settlements . . . furnished a stable setting for Chinese business expectations in certain respects. Most notably they provided banks in which funds were secure against the depredations of the most powerful Chinese officials, and they also provided a residential area in which Chinese business men were personally safe.'[3]

[1] The reign of the Emperor Taisho was from 1912 to 1926.
[2] M. J. Levy and Shih Kuo-Heng, *The Rise of the Modern Chinese Business Class, passim.*
[3] *ibid.*, p. 15. cf., also, R. Feetham, *op. cit.*, p. 317.

Throughout the greater part of the period under review the Westerners (joined by the Japanese after the close of the century) provided, as their contribution to the development of the modern Chinese economy, technical knowledge, capital and a legal and political framework for business dealings, while the Chinese for their part supplied labour, a subordinate commercial organisation and natural resources. This clear-cut separation of functions persisted for a very long period, but it could not survive the establishment of a strong national government intent upon modernisation. During the inter-war period, and especially after the consolidation of the Kuomintang Government, signs began to accumulate that the Westerners' position was changing. The increase in the number of joint Sino-foreign enterprises, though in some respects the result of Chinese attempts to shelter themselves from official depredations, was also an indication that the business relations between Westerners and Chinese were being modified. Chinese-owned industrial establishments became more numerous, and even Western firms began to employ a larger proportion of Chinese technicians and managers. As Chinese banks of a modern type appeared and as the Chinese Government put into force its new monetary policy, the Western banks lost many of the functions which they had formerly discharged. Western predominance in economic affairs was also challenged during the thirties by the rise of official trading corporations, and the Government, which had secured tariff autonomy in 1928, became sufficiently powerful to pursue an economic policy which showed no deference to the economic interests of foreigners.

These tendencies, which the Westerners accepted without much demur, though not without misgiving, provoked a violent response on the part of the Japanese who were not prepared to surrender their 'rights'. In the succession of cataclysmic changes that followed, Western enterprise and Western interests were marked down as victims by both sides. The Japanese first ousted Western enterprise from Manchuria, and then, after the outbreak of the Sino-Japanese War, seriously interfered with Western business in the parts of East and North China which they overran. When in 1941 that war was merged in the Pacific War, the Japanese confiscated Western properties in those regions, and subsequently many of the undertakings were seriously reduced in value by war-time damage, the removal of machinery and under-maintenance. Meanwhile, the Western Powers had surrendered their extraterritorial rights, and their concessions were handed back to China. In 1945, therefore, Western business found itself faced not merely with the task of reconstructing its capital assets and its organisation, but also with the problem of adjusting itself to a novel basis of relationships with the Chinese. Strong nationalistic sentiments led to discrimination against Western firms and even to the withdrawal of opportunities for trade

249

which the Chinese themselves were not yet ready to seize. The Westerners were treated unfavourably in such matters as the granting of import licences, and a ban was placed on the operations of foreign shipping in the inland waterways and coastal services. Moreover, whereas the retreat of the Westerners from their privileges during the thirties had been a concomitant of the Chinese Government's new-found administrative capacity, in the post-war period the Government sank to unexampled depths of corruption and incompetence. In these circumstances the restoration of Western business, now bereft of its former extraterritorial citadels, was a formidable task.

The Communist Revolution completed the discomfiture of the Westerners. They were subjected to various disabilities, including penal taxation and the obligation to subscribe to Victory Loans. No foreign firm was permitted to dismiss its workers without the agreement of the appropriate trade union, even when business flagged, nor could a business close without official permission.[1] All movements of foreigners both inside China and to and from the country were strictly controlled; no firm was allowed to withdraw its manager from China without substituting a man of equal standing. After the outbreak of war in Korea, the difficulties facing foreign business increased and in the summer of 1952 British firms came to a common decision to withdraw. The Americans had already gone. The only footholds now left to the West were Hongkong (together with the adjacent leased territory) and Macao, and such trade with the Western world as still remained had to be conducted from those centres or by circuitous routes. The remarkable chapter in the history of Western enterprise that opened with the Treaty of Nanking in 1842 and closed a century later was written in circumstances that are not likely to recur. For twenty years before the Communists established their hegemony it had been clear that commercial relations with the Chinese were entering upon a new phase, and Western enterprise had been under every inducement to display its traditional skill in adapting itself to a succession of novel situations. By 1952 little seemed to have survived the 'injuries of time and fortune', and, on a superficial view, Western intercourse with China appeared to have returned to the conditions of the Cohong days. It would be rash to assume, however, that no reasonable accommodation between Western enterprise and China will ever again be possible.

---

[1] A British firm was compelled to pay 20,000 workers for over two years although it had no work for them. In 1950 it was estimated that about £375,000 a month was being sent from the United Kingdom and Hongkong to finance British firms in Shanghai. These remittances were necessary to secure the safety of foreign staffs in China who were held personally responsible for their companies' compliance with regulations and the payment of levies. See G. E. Mitchell, 'China and Britain: Their Commercial and Industrial Relations', in *Journal of Royal Central Asian Society*, July–October, 1952, p. 251.

By one of the ironies of history the Pacific War, which contributed so largely to the contraction of the Westerners' part in China, had the effect of drawing Japan's economy more completely within the Western orbit. In the thirties Japan's autarkical policy reduced the opportunities for Western enterprise in her territories and increased the importance of her economic ties with the Asian continent. After the war, and especially after 1949, her victors were compelled to assist in the rehabilitation of her industry and trade. Apart from lavish American 'aid' necessary to supply her with foodstuffs and raw materials, there was a resumption of foreign investment in Japan, notably in the petroleum industry and in the electrical generating industry. Numerous contracts were signed between foreign and Japanese concerns for the provision of technical assistance. After the conclusion of the Peace Treaty, moreover, the Japanese showed themselves anxious to attract foreign capital and offered favourable conditions to foreign enterprise.[1] In the early fifties, therefore, it appeared that foreign enterprise and investment could look to a promising future in Japan.

While it is not difficult to estimate the immediate effects of Western enterprise on the economies of these countries, the deeper social consequences are more obscure, and we must pass most of them by with scarcely a glance. There is no doubt that in Japan the modernisation of the economy led to a steep rise in the national income and this, during the 1930's enabled a population more than twice as large as in the 1870's to enjoy a standard of life far higher than at that time—and far higher than that found in any other Asian country. China lagged a long way behind Japan in this respect, and much of the country was still in a pre-industrial stage. Yet even in China modernisation had a marked influence on the standard of life in those areas to which it had penetrated, and such improvements as had occurred could be attributed mainly to the enterprise of the Westerners. Examples have been given in the course of this book to show that the establishment of new foreign undertakings was usually accompanied by a rise in the earnings of Chinese workers in the localities affected. The increases in the areas in and around the foreign concessions were particularly noteworthy, even though the standard of life when judged by Western European criteria remained deplorably low. A comment made in 1897 about the conditions of the workers in the recently opened mills of Shanghai is apposite. 'What especially strikes the spectator is the well-fed and generally prosperous appearance of the numerous female Chinese employed in the filatures and cotton factories. The women and girls are now able to earn from 5 to 15 dollars (Mex.) a month. This is absolute wealth to people who, before, found it difficult to make two

[1] Foreign Capital Research Society (Bank of Japan), *Japanese Industry Today*, pp. 152–7.

dollars a month by toiling all day at a hand loom to produce native cloth . . .'[1]

The point need not be laboured. To the extent that Western enterprise flourished, it was naturally accompanied by a rise in the income of the communities affected by it. This influence was not limited to manual workers, for fresh economic opportunities were given for the remunerative employment of Chinese as technicians and administrators. The foreign industrial establishments and the areas under foreign jurisdiction also saw the beginnings of a modern system of industrial relations, an incipient trade unionism, and the first attempts to introduce improved working conditions.[2] Both China and Japan, however, were backward in these respects, according to European standards. To a large extent this was a reflection of the stage of industrialisation which they had reached. In Japan the development of a modern system of industrial relations was also hindered, partly by repression of trade unionism, and partly by the transference into modern industry of the paternal relationships that had distinguished the older society. In China, where the employers in the modern factories were mostly foreigners, traditional relationships were not carried over into the factory industries, and the cleavage between the older economic forms and the new were therefore much sharper than in Japan.

These consequences of Western intrusion, and these contrasts between the two countries, are easy to understand. What is more perplexing is that technical and economic innovation for which the West both in China and Japan was largely responsible appears to have exercised a more deeply corrosive influence on Chinese than on Japanese society, despite the fact that the extent of modernisation was far greater in Japan. This had been observed before the outbreak of the Pacific War by Dr. Hu Shih, then Chinese Ambassador in the United States.[3] He set out to explain how it was that, in spite of seven decades of modernisation, Japan still retained in substance the institutions and outlook of her feudal past, while China, far less Westernised in her economic life, had abandoned more completely her old civilisation. Twelve years later the antithesis seemed sharper than ever. In China all things traditional had been swept away by a successful Communist Revolution. In Japan even defeat in war and prolonged Occupation had left her social and political foundations apparently unimpaired. Although a complete explanation would require us to stray beyond the subject-matter of this book, the material presented here may contribute something towards the elucidation of the problem. It is well to remind ourselves, however, that recent

---

[1] *British Diplomatic and Consular Reports on Trade*, No. 2156, Trade of Shanghai, Soochow and Hangchow, 1897, p. 15.
[2] *See* E. M. Hinder, *Life and Labour in Shanghai, passim*.
[3] An address on *The Modernisation of China and Japan* at a meeting of the American Historical Association, 29 December 1939.

events cannot yet be seen in proper perspective. We can be certain that the confusions of the forties and fifties in the Far East will look very different when viewed from the comfortable distance of half a century, and that history will pass her customary ironical comment upon the judgments and interpretations of contemporaries.

APPENDICES

A   China's Foreign Trade.

B   Foreign Investments in China.

C   Foreign Investments in Japan.

D   Open Ports, Foreign Settlements and Concessions
    in China.

E   A Note on Telegraphic Communications.

F   A Note on Foreign Residents and Experts in Japan
    during the early period of Westernisation.

G   Bibliography (1) China.

            (2) Japan.

CHINA'S FOREIGN TRADE

1. AVERAGE ANNUAL VALUE OF THE FOREIGN TRADE OF CHINA, 1882–1931[1]

(in £ million)[2]

Period	Net Imports	Exports
1882–1886	21	19
1887–1891	28	23
1892–1896	29	22
1897–1901	35	25
1902–1906	54	32
1907–1911	60	45
1912–1916	76	60
1917–1921	181	146
1922–1926	171	133
1927–1931	144	113

[1] Adapted from T. R. Banister, *op. cit.*
[2] Figures converted from Haikwan Taels at average rate of exchange for each year.

2. AVERAGE ANNUAL VALUE OF THE FOREIGN TRADE OF CHINA, 1882–1931[1]

IMPORTS

(In hundred thousands of Haikwan Taels)

Period	Machines and Machinery	Electrical Equipment	Raw Cotton	Cotton Manufactures	Tobacco, Cigars and Cigarettes	Kerosene Oil	Opium	Others	Total Net Imports
1882–1886	—	—	—	255	—	—	261	283	799
1887–1891	5	—	—	432	—	—	295	466	1,198
1892–1896	14	—	—	565	—	69	301	697	1,646
1897–1901	17	—	—	870	—	139	317	970	2,313
1902–1906	101	5	15	1,429	47	176	367	1,547	3,687
1907–1911	169	15	22	1,283	80	254	410	2,094	4,327
1912–1916	160	24	53	1,593	179	290	320	2,548	5,167
1917–1921	393	65	146	1,951	338	441	—	3,506	6,840
1922–1926	431	83	617	1,963	446	604	—	5,774	9,918
1927–1931	552	140	1,125	1,604	528	561	—	7,926	12,436

[1] Adapted from T. R. Banister, op. cit.

3. AVERAGE ANNUAL VALUE OF THE FOREIGN TRADE OF CHINA, 1882–1931[1]

EXPORTS

(In hundred thousands of Haikwan Taels)

Period	Bean Cake and Beans	Egg Products and Eggs	Skins and Furs	Vegetable Oils	Tea[2]	Silk[a]	Others	Total Exports
1882–1886	—	—	12	1	321	238	122	694
1887–1891	—	—	14	3	293	335	282	927
1892–1896	22	—	29	9	302	424	457	1,243
1897–1901	74	—	72	24	267	598	659	1,694
1902–1906	103	19	126	39	263	747	968	2,265
1907–1911	369	33	162	86	345	908	1,373	3,276
1912–1916	508	76	224	159	407	980	1,707	4,061
1917–1921	839	193	237	341	174	1,213	1,707	5,445
1922–1926	1,396	325	253	443	219	1,743	2,448	7,640
1927–1931	2,032	436	407	525	339	1,631	3,261	9,460

[1] Adapted from T. R. Banister, op. cit.
[2] Detailed figures are given in the following table.

259

4. AVERAGE ANNUAL EXPORTS OF TEA AND SILK FROM CHINA, 1882–1931[1]

| | TEA | | | | SILK | | | | | |
| | Black | Green | Brick and miscellaneous | Total Value | Raw, all kinds | Steam filature[3] | Cocoons | Waste, all kinds | Manufactures | All Silk |
Period	(In hundred thousand piculs)[2]			(In hundred thousand Haikwan Taels)	(In thousand piculs)[2]				(Value in hundred thousand Haikwan Taels)	
1882–1886	16	2	3	321	66	—	3	35	51	238
1887–1891	14	2	3	293	86	—	11	58	72	335
1892–1896	11	2	4	302	99	—	12	58	96	424
1897–1901	8	2	4	267	120	43	10	77	105	598
1902–1906	7	3	6	263	111	47	14	92	119	747
1907–1911	7	3	6	345	129	54	17	130	169	908
1912–1916	6	3	7	407	136	63	27	144	198	980
1917–1921	2	2	1	174	134	74	30	132	237	1,213
1922–1926	3	3	1	219	150	92	26	188	269	1,743
1927–1931	2	3	3	339	164	107	15	176	269	1,631

[1] Adapted from T. R. Banister, op. cit.
[2] 1 picul = 133⅓ lbs.
[3] The figures for steam filature silk are included in those of the previous column.

5. AVERAGE EQUIVALENT OF THE HAIKWAN TAEL, 1882–1931[1]

Period	U.K. Sterling		U.S.A.
	s.	*d.*	$
1882–1886	5	5	1.32
1887–1891	4	11	1.19
1892–1896	3	7	0.88
1897–1901	3	0	0.72
1902–1906	2	11	0.69
1907–1911	2	9	0.68
1912–1916	2	11	0.71
1917–1921	5	4	1.14
1922–1926	3	6	0.81
1927–1931	2	4	0.57

[1] Adapted from T. R. Banister, *op. cit.*

FOREIGN INVESTMENTS IN CHINA[1]

1. ESTIMATED TOTAL FOREIGN INVESTMENT
(in million U.S. dollars)

Year	Business Investment*	Chinese Government Obligations	Total
1902	503	285	788
1914	1,084	526	1,610
1931	2,532	711	3,243

* i.e. 'direct business investments in the legal possession of foreign business men and corporations, including investments in the "concession" railways'.

2. DISTRIBUTION OF INVESTMENTS BY CREDITOR COUNTRIES
(as percentage of total)

	1902	1914	1931
Great Britain	33·0	37·7	36·7*
Japan	0·1	13·6	35·1*
Russia	31·3	16·7	8·4
United States	2·5	3·1	6·1
France	11·6	10·7	5·9
Germany	20·9	16·4	2·7
Others	0·6	1·8	5·1
	100·0	100·0	100·0

* In 1931 British investments in China represented between 5 and 6 per cent of the total outstanding British overseas investment; over 80 per cent of Japan's foreign investments were in China.

3. DISTRIBUTION OF INVESTMENTS BY PURPOSE OR TYPE OF UNDERTAKING (as percentage of total)

	1914	1931
General Government Purposes	20·5	13·2
Transport	33·0	26·1
Communications and Public Utilities	1·7	4·0
Mining	3·7	4·0
Manufacturing	6·9	11·6
Banking and Finance	0·4	6·6
Real Estate	6·5	10·5
Mercantile Investments (including stocks)	8·8	14·9
Other and Undistributed	18·5	9·1
	100·0	100·0

[1] The figures in these tables have been taken from C. F. Remer, *Foreign Investments in China*. They are intended to cover 'the total of the income-producing holdings in China which are in the hands of foreigners, whether the foreign owners live in China or outside of China'. Hongkong is excluded. See *ibid.*, pp. 62–3.

4. GEOGRAPHICAL DISTRIBUTION OF FOREIGN INVESTMENTS
(as percentage of total)

	1902	1914	1931
Shanghai	14·0	18·1	34·3
Manchuria	27·4	22·4	27·1
Rest of China	22·5	26·9	18·8
Undistributed*	36·1	32·6	19·8
	100·0	100·0	100·0

* Including loans raised for general purposes by the Chinese Government.

5. The Under-Secretary of State for Foreign Affairs, in a written answer to a Parliamentary Question on 24 October 1949, stated: 'The value in 1941 of the direct British business investment in China represented by physical properties, excluding ships, was estimated in 1947 at about £124 million. To this must be added the capital represented by Chinese Government and railway bonds quoted in London. This amounts to £53 million. I would add that unofficial estimates that have been made exceed these figures.'

FOREIGN INVESTMENTS IN JAPAN[1]

(In million yen—at gold parity)

Year end	Govt. Loans Issued Abroad	Govt. Domestic Loans Sold Abroad	Local Govt. Loans Issued Abroad	Debentures Issued Abroad	Foreign Holdings of Domestic Company Issues	Total
1894	2	—	0	0	—	2
1897	0	43	0	0	—	43
1903	98	93	4	0	—	195
1913	1,525	75	177	167	26	1,970
1919	1,311	63	147	165	25	1,711
1923	1,321	7	130	133	22	1,613
1930	1,567	84	245	456	114	2,466
1932	1,398	51	236	468	(114)	2,267

[1] Amount outstanding at year end. These figures exclude foreign-owned liquid balances and direct investments by foreigners in Japan. The value of the latter was estimated at 40 million yen for 1904, 70 million yen for 1913 and 245 million yen for 1929; 245 million yen was also suggested as the value of direct investments for 1932. These estimates for direct investments are subject to a wide margin of error; but the order of magnitude may be taken as correct. The figures make no allowance for the purchase by Japanese nationals of Japanese bonds issued abroad; it is believed that in the early thirties one-third of the total may have been in Japanese ownership. Other estimates give the total British investment in Japan in 1930 at about £63 million and the total American investment at about £92 million; i.e. about 1,500 million yen. At the outbreak of the Second World War, British investments in Japan (other than direct investments) were estimated at about £50 million.

Sources: J. Inouye, *op. cit.*, p. 229; Oriental Economist, *op. cit.*, p. 696; E. B. Schumpeter, *op. cit.*, pp. 918–25; Mitsubishi Economic Research Bureau, *op. cit.*, pp. 82–4; F. V. Field, *Economic Handbook of the Pacific Area*, pp. 358–60; H. G. Moulton, *op. cit.*, pp. 524–5.

OPEN PORTS, FOREIGN SETTLEMENTS AND CONCESSIONS IN CHINA

1. LIST OF TREATY PORTS[1]

Aigun	Kashgar	Shamshui
Amoy	Kiakhta	Sansing
Antung	Kiaochow (Tsingtao)	Shanghai
Canton	Kiayukwan	Shasi
Changsha	Kirin	Soochow
Chefoo	Kiukiang	Suifenho
Changchun	Kiungchow (Hoihow)	Swatow
(Kwangchengtze)	Kongmoon	Szemao
Chinkiang	Kowloon	Taonan
Chuitzuchien	Kuldja	Tarbagatai
Chungking	Lappa	Tatungkow
Dairen	Liaoyang	Tengyueh
Fakumen	Lungchingtsun	Tiehling
Fenghuangcheng	Lungchow	Tientsin
Foochow	Lungkow	Toutaokow
Gartok	Manchouli	Tsitsihar
Gyangtze	Mengtsz	Tungkiangtze
Hailar	Mukden	Urga
Hangchow	Nanking	Urumchi
Hankow	Nanning	Weihaiwei
Harbin	Newchwang	Wenchow
Hsinmintun	Ningpo	Wuchow
Hunchun	Ninguta	Wuhu
Ichang	Pakhoi	Yatung
	Paitsaokow	Yingkow (Port of Newchwang)

2. LIST OF PORTS VOLUNTARILY OPENED BY THE CHINESE GOVERNMENT[1]

Chihfeng	Kalgan	Weihsien
Chinwangtao	Kueihuacheng	Woosung (near Shanghai)
Choutsun	Liaoyuan	Wuchang
Dolonor	Pengpu	Yochow
Haichow	Santuao	Yunnanfu (Kunming)
Hulutao	Tsinanfu	

[1] These lists are based on one supplied by the Foreign Office Research Department and supplemented by reference to the *China Year Book*, 1928, and onwards.

3. LIST OF FOREIGN SETTLEMENTS AND CONCESSIONS IN CHINA
(Existing at various dates between 1843–1943)[1]

(a) THE ORIGINAL FIVE PORTS:

Shanghai   (1) The International Settlement (1843)
The French Settlement (1849)
Woosung (thrown open to foreign trade and residence in 1898, not by treaty with any Power, but by the direct initiative of the Chinese Government).

Amoy   (2) British Concession (1851–2).
Japanese Concession (1900).
American Concession (a continuation of the British Concessions and known by this name until 1899).
Kulangsu International Settlement (proclaimed as an international settlement by the Chinese authorities on 1 May 1902).

Canton   (3) British Concession ⎱ acquired in 1861 and known
French Concession ⎰ locally as 'Shameen'.

Foochow   (4) (Opened in 1842; no defined area.)

Ningpo   (5) ('Campo' location set apart in 1844; no defined area.)

(b) UPPER YANGTSE PORTS:

Hankow   (1) British Concession (1861).
British Concession Extension (1898).
French Concession (1866; extended 1902).
Japanese Concession (1898; extended 1906).

Changsha   (2) General Foreign Settlement (1904).

Chungking   (3) Japanese Settlement (1901).

(c) LOWER YANGTSE PORTS:

Kiukiang   (1) British Concession (1861).

Wuhu   (2) General Foreign Settlement (1904; originally marked out in 1877 for a British Concession but never taken up).

Nanking   (3) General Foreign Settlement.

Chinkiang   (4) British Concession (1861).

(d) NORTHERN PORTS:

Tsinanfu ⎫
Choutsun ⎬ (1) General Foreign Settlements (1916).
Weihsien ⎭

[1] The *China Year Book*, 1928, pp. 1082–3. The dates in parentheses show the years of opening.

Tientsin   (2) British Concession (1861).
               British Concession Extension (1897; extramural area added in 1903).
               French Concession (1861).
               Japanese Concession.
               Belgian Concession.
               Italian Concession.
Newchwang   (3) British Concession (1861).
               Foreign Quarter (1900).
Hangchow   (4) Japanese Concession (1895).
               General Foreign Settlement.
Soochow   (5) Japanese Concession (1895).
               General Foreign Settlement.

4. NOTE ON FOREIGN SETTLEMENTS AND CONCESSIONS IN CHINA

In certain Treaty Ports special districts were set aside for foreign residence. As an extension of extraterritoriality, these districts were administered by the foreign consuls, often with the assistance of a Council representing the foreign ratepayers.

The most important of these districts, the International Settlement at Shanghai, dates as such from 1854. In that year the British, French and American consuls issued regulations for the two settlements—the British and the French—then existing in Shanghai. Later the Americans also obtained a settlement. In 1862 the French Settlement withdrew from the joint arrangement and thereafter remained a separate municipality. The next year the British and American Settlements were brought under a common jurisdiction. In later years other Treaty Powers, especially Japan, participated in the administration of the International Settlement. The executive authority in the Settlement rested with an elected body, the Shanghai Municipal Council. Until 1928 the Council represented only the foreign ratepayers but from that year Chinese also took part.[1]

The terms 'settlement' and 'concession' have at times been taken as synonymous. When used in their strict senses the distinction between the two rests on differences in the registration of land ownership. In settlements properly so called, such as the International Settlement of Shanghai, the land within the delimited area remained on the registers of the Chinese land office. Sales of land by Chinese owners in this area were voluntary. When a foreigner made an agreement with a Chinese owner to buy land in the Settlement, he reported the fact to his consul. The consul then reported it to the Chinese Taotai (Governor) who issued to the foreigner, through the consul, a title of a perpetual lease.

In concessions the area set aside for foreign residence was leased by the Chinese Government to the foreign Power concerned and the consular officials of that Power sub-leased the land to his own or other nationals. Before the Chinese Government leased the concession to the foreign Power,

[1] *Encyclopaedia Britannica*, 11th ed., 1932, vol. 20, p. 458.

267

the land within it was bought, by expropriation if necessary, from the private Chinese owners. (The term 'concession' used in this sense must not be confused with the railway concessions granted by the Chinese Government.)

In ports voluntarily opened for foreign residence by the Chinese Government, foreigners were allowed to obtain leases of land for not longer than thirty years. Foreigners might reside in any part of such ports.[1]

[1] W. Willoughby, *Foreign Rights and Interests in China,* vol. I, pp. 495 *et seq.*

A NOTE ON
TELEGRAPHIC COMMUNICATIONS

Telegraphy on a commercial scale was introduced into China by two companies, one British and the other Danish, which were the predecessors respectively of the Eastern Extension Australasia and China Telegraph Co. Ltd. (now Cable and Wireless Ltd.) and the Great Northern Telegraph Co. Ltd. (of Denmark).[1] The British company approached China from the south, laying a cable between Singapore and Hongkong in 1871. In the same year the Danish concern, which had a line across Siberia, extended it to Nagasaki, and thence to Shanghai and (via Amoy) to Hongkong. In 1883 this company, the Great Northern, duplicated its cables between Vladivostok and Nagasaki and Shanghai, while the Eastern Extension Co. laid a line from Hongkong to Foochow and Shanghai. From the outset the two companies worked closely together. In 1900 they were jointly responsible for laying a cable from Shanghai, via Chefoo, to Taku, near Tientsin; this opened direct telegraphic communication between Peking and Shanghai. The Companies made these lines for the Chinese Government and lent it the necessary funds. By agreement, the two Companies were to work the cables on behalf of the Government until the loans were repaid. Repayment was completed in 1933. In 1906 an American concern, the Commercial Pacific Cable Co., laid a cable between Manila and Shanghai.

The Eastern Extension and the Great Northern had a large part in training Chinese telegraph operators. In 1876 the Chinese authorities established a school of telegraphy at Foochow and staffed it with some of the Great Northern Telegraph Co.'s officers. Operators were also trained within the Companies' own organisation. Most of these remained in the employment of the Companies but some entered the Chinese Telegraphic Administration. The Great Northern Telegraph Company compiled a Chinese dictionary by means of which Chinese characters were expressed in 4-figure groups which could be sent by cable; the addressee re-converted these groups into the corresponding characters.

With the growth of nationalism in China, the Companies had to hand over to the Government the task of dealing directly with the public in accepting and delivering telegraphic messages. The concessions granted by the Chinese Government to the Companies expired in 1944, and were not renewed.[2]

---

[1] The first telegraph in China was laid in 1866 and connected the Shanghai office of Russell & Co., an American firm, with their warehouses on the Bund. *Chinese Customs Report on Trade*, Shanghai, 1866, p. 11.

[2] Information about telegraphic communications is derived from private inquiries.

A NOTE ON FOREIGN RESIDENTS AND EXPERTS IN JAPAN DURING THE EARLY PERIOD OF WESTERNISATION

There are no official statistics of the number of foreigners in Japan during the pre-Meiji era; but from other evidence it appears that in 1862 there were about 200 foreign residents (Westerners) in Nagasaki and about 130 in Yokohama. The British were in the majority; the Americans and Dutch came next in importance. The foreign trade at that time was almost equally divided between those two ports, for Hakodate, in which a number of foreign merchants had settled soon after its opening, had by then been abandoned by the foreigners. After 1862 Yokohama's trade grew rapidly, and its foreign resident population soon outstripped that of Nagasaki. In 1864, when a foreign Chamber of Commerce was established in Yokohama, the number of foreign residents in that port was about 300, while two years later the foreign resident population of Nagasaki was still only about 200. About half of these foreign residents in Japan were British.[1]

After 1872 Japanese official figures are available to show the number of foreigners in the service of the Japanese Government. In that year the Central Government employed 214 foreigners, of whom 119 were British, 50 French and 16 American. The majority of these were employed in connection with railways, lighthouses, telecommunications, shipbuilding and educational services.[2] In addition, foreigners were employed by the prefectures and in various Government arsenals. According to a Japanese authority, the salaries paid to foreigners at this time represented about 5 per cent of the total public expenditure.[3] The numbers employed by Japanese business firms are not known. The following table shows the number of foreigners in the service

Year	Teachers	Technical Advisers	Business and Administration	Skilled Workmen	Others	Total
1872	102	127	43	46	51	369
1873	127	204	72	35	69	507
1874	151	213	68	27	65	524
1875	144	205	69	36	73	527
1876	129	170	60	26	84	469
1877	109	146	55	13	58	381
1878	101	118	51	7	44	321
1879	84	111	35	9	22	261
1880	76	103	40	6	12	237

[1] *The Statesman's Year Book*, 1870, p. 676; and M. Paske-Smith, *Western Barbarians in Japan and Formosa in Tokugawa Days, 1603–1868*, p. 218.
[2] Information supplied by Social Sciences Materials Section, National Diet Library, Tokyo, to which we are indebted for most of the data on which this note is based.
[3] Tokutaro Shigehisa, 'Foreigners in Early Meiji', in *The Japan Advertiser*, 28 October 1939.

of the national and prefectural governments during the eighteen-seventies, classified according to their occupation.[1]

Throughout the decade about half of these employees were British. The other nationalities most strongly represented were French, Americans and Germans in that order of importance. There were also Dutch, Italians, Russians, Belgians, Swiss, Austrians and Chinese.[2] Some additional information is available about the number of foreign technical experts (included in the above table) who were engaged in military and naval establishments. Between 1868 and 1875 the number employed at the naval arsenals of Yokosuka and Yokohama ranged between 25 and 45, and there were a few also in the military arsenals at Tokyo and Maguro.[3]

In 1879 the number of Western residents in Japan was given as 2,475, of whom 1,106 were British, 479 Americans, 300 Germans, 230 French and 209 Russians.[4] By the later years of the Meiji era the number had more than doubled, but from then on it was comparatively stable. In 1935 there were 9,700 resident Westerners in Japan, of whom about 2,700 were British, 2,100 Americans, 1,500 Russians and 1,100 Germans.[5]

[1] *The Fifth Annual Statistics of the Japanese Empire*, 1886 (in Japanese), pp. 939–40.
[2] *ibid.*, pp. 935–7.
[3] H. Koyama, *Outlines of Japanese Military History* (in Japanese), pp. 132–3.
[4] G. Kolb, *The Condition of Nations, Social and Political, with Comparative Tables of Universal Statistics*, p. 858.
[5] *Japan Year Book* (various issues). The citizens of all British countries are included in the figure for 'British'; citizens of the United Kingdom accounted for nearly three-quarters of this total.

BIBLIOGRAPHY

1. CHINA

Anderson, A. M., *Humanity and Labour in China*. London, 1928.

Arnold, J., *China. A Commercial and Industrial Handbook*. Washington, 1926.

Arnold, J., 'The Commercial Problems of China', in *Annals of the American Academy of Political and Social Science*. November 1930.

Bain, H. F., *Ores and Industry in the Far East*. New York, 1933.

Baker, J. E., 'Transportation in China', in *Annals of the American Academy of Political and Social Science*. November 1930.

Banister, T. R., *A History of the External Trade of China, 1834–81*, together with a synopsis of the External Trade of China, 1882–1931. Being an Introduction to the Customs Decennial Reports, 1922–31. Written by order of the Inspector-General of Customs by the Deputy Commissioner of Customs. Shanghai, 1931.

Barnet, R. W., *Economic Shanghai: Hostage to Politics*. New York, 1941.

Baster, A. S. J., 'Origins of British Exchange Banks in China', in *Economic History*. January 1934.

Baster, A. S. J., *History and present position of English Banks operating in foreign countries*. Ph.D. Thesis. London University, 1934.

Bishop, Isabella, *The Yangtse Valley and Beyond*. London, 1899.

Blakiston, T. W., *Five Months on the Yang-tsze*. London, 1862.

Brandt, W., 'Economic and Living Standards: American and Asiatic', in *Pacific Affairs*. June 1941.

British Diplomatic and Consular Reports on Trade. See United Kingdom.

Buchanan, N. S., *International Investment and Domestic Welfare*. New York, 1946.

Cable, Boyd, *A Hundred Years History of the P. and O.* London, 1937.

Chang Kia-Ngau, 'Development of Civil Aviation in China', in *China Quarterly*. Autumn 1939.

Chen, F. S., *Foreign Banking in China*. M.Sc.(Econ.). Thesis. London University, 1937.

Chen Han-Seng, *Industrial Capital and Chinese Peasants*. Shanghai, 1939.

Chen, Ta T., *The Emigrant Communities in South China*. London, 1939.

Cheng Lin, *The Chinese Railways*. Shanghai, 1937.

Cheng Lin-Chuang, 'A Study of the Egg Trade in the Peiping Area', in *Chinese Social and Political Science Review*. October 1937.

Cheng, T. T., *Problems of Monetary Reform in China*. M.Sc.(Econ.). Thesis. London University, 1938.

China Association, *Annual Reports*. Various numbers. London.

China Association, *Minutes of Special General Meeting, 31 July 1905*. London.

China Handbook. Published by the Chinese Ministry of Information. 1937–45.

China Mail. Article on 'The Revision of the British Treaty with China', 5 March 1867.
China Press, Coronation and Sino-British Trade Supplement. 12 May 1937.
China Press, Special Supplement. 10 October 1936.
China Vegetable Oil Corporation, *Trade Report.* 1938.
China Yearbook. Various years, 1912–34. Shanghai.
Chinese Customs, *Decennial Reports.* Shanghai, 1882–1911. *Reports on Trade at the Ports in China.* Shanghai, 1866–81. *Returns of Trade at the Treaty Ports, and Trade Reports.* Shanghai, 1882–1919. *Annual Trade Reports and Returns.* 1921–2. Published with *Quarterly Returns of Trade.* Shanghai. *Annual Trade Reports and Returns.* Shanghai, 1923–8. *Catalogue of Exhibits at Paris.* Shanghai, 1878. *Catalogue of Exhibits at Vienna.* Shanghai, 1873, 1878. *Special Series,* 1880 onwards.
Chinese Government. Memorandum on the Kaiping Mining Case. (Prepared from documents and memoranda in the possession of the Chinese Government.) Peking, 1908.
Chinese Yearbook. Various years, 1935–45. Shanghai.
Cho, T. L., *Joint Stock Banking in China.* M.Sc.(Econ.) Thesis. London University, 1937.
Chu, T. H., *Tea Trade in Central China.* Shanghai, 1936.
Coates, W. H., *The Old Country Trade of the East Indies.* London, 1911.
Colquhoun, A. R., *The Opening of China.* Six letters reprinted from *The Times.* London, August 1884.
Cooke, G. Wingrove, *China: Being 'The Times' Special Correspondence from China in the Years 1857–1858.* London, 1858.
Cooper, T. T., *Travels of a Pioneer of Commerce.* London, 1871.
Crow, C., *Four Hundred Million Customers.* London, 1937.
Dautremer, J., *La Grande Artère de la Chine: le Yangtseu.* Paris, c. 1911.
Dingle, E. J., and Pratt, F. L. (eds.), *Far Eastern Products Manual.* Shanghai, 1921.
Enki, Dai, 'Aviation in China', in *Far Eastern Review.* May 1937.
Far Eastern Products Manual. See E. J. Dingle.
Fauvel, A. A., *Les Séricigènes Sauvages de la Chine.* Paris, 1895.
Feetham, R., *Report to the Shanghai Municipal Council.* Shanghai, 1931.
Fei Hsiao-Tung and Chang Chih-Yi, *Earthbound China.* Chicago, 1947.
Flügge, E., *Rohseide.* Leipzig, 1936.
Fong, H. D., *Tientsin Carpet Industry.* Tientsin, 1929.
Fong, H. D., *Hosiery Knitting in Tientsin.* Tientsin, 1930.
Fong, H. D., *Cotton Industry and Trade in China,* 2 vols. Tientsin, 1932.
Fong, H. D., 'Terminal Marketing of Tientsin Cotton', in *Monthly Bulletin on Economic China.* December 1934.
Fong, H. D., 'China's Silk Reeling Industry', in *Monthly Bulletin on Economic China.* December 1934.
Fong, H. D., and others, *Industrial Capital in China.* Tientsin, 1936.
Fong, H. D., *Industrial Organisation in China.* Tientsin, 1937.
Fong, H. D., and others, 'Principles of Postwar Economic Reconstruction in China', *Institute of Pacific Relations, 8th Conference.* New York, 1942.

Frey, J. W., 'Economic Significance of the Mineral Wealth of China', in *Annals of the American Academy of Political and Social Science.* November 1930.

Friedman, I. S., *British Relations with China, 1931–39.* New York, 1940.

Glass, J. G. H., *Report on the Concession of the Pekin Syndicate Ltd.* London, 1899.

Green, O. M., *The Foreigner in China.* London, 1942.

Greenberg, M., *British Trade and the Opening of China, 1800–1842.* Cambridge, 1951.

Gull, E. M., *British Economic Interests in the Far East.* London, 1943.

Harler, C. R., *The Culture and Marketing of Tea,* London, 1933.

Hewlett, M., *Forty Years in China.* London, 1943.

Ho, F. L., and Fong, H. D., 'Extent and Effects of Industrialisation in China', *Institute of Pacific Relations, 3rd Conference.* New York, 1929.

Ho, F. L., 'Problems of Future Industrial Development in China', in *Problems of the Pacific,* New York, 1931.

Ho Ping-Yin, *The Foreign Trade of China.* Shanghai, 1935.

Hongkong Directory. Hongkong, 1949.

Hosie, A., *Three Years in Western China.* London, 1890.

Hou Shou-Tung, *Currency and Banking Problems of China.* Ph.D. Thesis. Liverpool University, 1935.

Hou Shou-Tung, 'Japanese Bank Notes in Manchuria', in *Yenching Political Science Series,* No. 13. Peking, 1931.

Huang Chin-Tao, 'The Coal Industry in China', in *Chinese Economic Journal.* November 1935.

Hubbard, G. E., *Eastern Industrialization and its Effect on the West* (2nd edition). London, 1938.

Hudson, G. F., *The Far East in World Politics* (2nd edition). London, 1939.

Huebner, S. S., 'Insurance in China', in *Annals of American Academy of Political and Social Science.* 1930.

Hughes, E. R., *The Invasion of China by the West.* London, 1937.

Ishii, Akira, 'China's Radio Communications Problem', in *Institute of Pacific Relations, 2nd Conference.* New York, 1927.

Japan: Manchukuo Year Book. Tokyo, 1934.

Jardine, Matheson & Co. Ltd., *'Jardines' and the Ewo Interests.* New York, 1947.

Jones, F. C., *Shanghai and Tientsin.* New York, 1940.

Jones, F. C., *Manchuria since 1931.* London, 1949.

Kann, E., *The Currencies of China* (2nd edition). Shanghai, 1927.

Kent, P. H. B., *Railway Enterprise in China.* London, 1907.

Kent, P. H. B., *The Twentieth Century in the Far East.* London, 1937.

Koh, T. F., 'Capital Stock in China', in *Institute of Pacific Relations, 8th Conference.* New York, 1942.

Kuang Yung-Pao, 'The Compradore: His Position in the Foreign Trade of China', in *Economic Journal.* December 1911.

Lane-Poole, S., *Sir Harry Parkes in China.* London, 1901.

Lanning, G., and Couling, S., *The History of Shanghai.* Shanghai, 1921.

Lee, Edward Bing-Shuey, *Modern Canton.* Shanghai, 1936.

Lee, B., 'Rehabilitation of China's Cotton Industry', in *Chinese Economic Journal*. December 1933.

Lee, F. E., *Currency, Banking and Finance in China*. Washington, 1926.

Levy, Marion J., & Shih Kuo-Heng, *The Rise of the Modern Chinese Business Class*. New York, 1949.

Lewis, R. S., *Eighty Years of Enterprise, 1869–1949*, being the ultimate story of the Waterside Works of Ransomes and Rapier Ltd. of Ipswich, England. Ipswich (no date).

Lewis, Cleona, *The United States and Foreign Investment Problems*. Washington, 1948.

Lewis, Cleona, *America's Stake in International Investments*. Washington, 1938.

Lieu, D. K., *China's Industries and Finance*. Peking, 1927.

Lieu, D. K., 'China's Industrial Development', in *Institute of Pacific Relations, 2nd Conference*. New York, 1927.

Lieu, D. K., *Growth and Industrialisation of Shanghai*. Shanghai, 1936.

Lieu, O. S., 'Industrial Growth in China', in *Problems of the Pacific*. New York, 1931.

Ling, H. H., 'The Canton–Hankow Railway', in *Far Eastern Review*. October 1935.

Little, Archibald, *Through the Yang-tse Gorges*. London, 1888.

Little, Archibald, *Mount Omi and Beyond*. London, 1901.

Little, Archibald, *Across Yunnan*. London, 1910.

Little, Archibald, *Gleanings from Fifty Years in China*. London, 1910.

Liverpool Chamber of Commerce Reports. 1851–83, 1886–1924. Various years. Liverpool.

Löwenthal, R., 'Public Communications in China before July 1937', in *Chinese Social and Political Science Review*. April 1938.

MacMurray, J. V. A., 'Problems of Foreign Capital in China', in *Foreign Affairs*. April 1925.

MacMurray, J. V. A., *Treaties and Agreements with and concerning China, 1894–1919*, 2 vols. New York, 1921.

Mason, F. R., *The American Silk Industry and the Tariff*. Cambridge, Mass., 1910.

Michie, A., *The Englishman in China—as illustrated in the Career of Sir Rutherford Alcock*, 2 vols. Edinburgh, 1900.

Mission Lyonnaise d'Exploration Commerciale, *Rapports Commerciaux*, 1895–7. Lyon, 1898.

Mitchell, G. E., 'China and Britain: Their Commercial and Industrial Relations', in *Journal of Royal Central Asian Society*. July–October, 1952.

Morrison, G. E., *An Australian in China*. London, 1895.

Morse, H. B., *The Trade and Administration of China*. London, 1908.

Morse, H. B., *International Relations of the Chinese Empire*, 3 vols. London, 1910–18.

Mou Shou-Yu, *History of the Economic Development of the Chinese in the East Indies* (in Chinese). 1947.

Muhse, A. C., 'Trade Organisation and Trade Control in China', in *American Economic Review*. June 1916.

North China Herald, A Retrospect of Political and Commercial Affairs in China 1868–1872. Shanghai.

Nyhus, P. O., 'The Export Peanut Trade of China', in *Chinese Economic Journal.* November 1927.

Orchard, J. E., *Contrasts in the Progress of Industrialisation in China and Japan.* New York, 1937.

Overlach, T. W., *Foreign Financial Control in China.* New York, 1919.

Payne, A. J., 'Aviation Development in China', in *Great Britain and the East.* 7 August 1943.

Pearse, Arno S., *Cotton Industry of Japan and China.* Manchester, 1929.

Pelcovits, N. A., *Old China Hands and the Foreign Office.* New York, 1948.

Plant, Cornell, *Glimpses of the Yangtze Gorges.* Shanghai, 1921.

Rawlley, R. C., *Economics of the Silk Industry.* London, 1919.

Remer, C. F., *Foreign Trade of China.* Shanghai, 1926.

Remer, C. F., *Foreign Investments in China.* New York, 1933.

Remer, C. F., *A Study of Chinese Boycotts.* Baltimore, 1933.

Richthofen, Baron, *Letters 1870–1872* (2nd edition). Shanghai, 1903.

Rondot, N., 'Rapports sur l'Industrie des Soies et Soieries', in *Enquête: Traité de Commerce avec l'Angleterre.* Published by French Ministry of Agriculture, Commerce and Industry. Paris, 1862.

Royal Institute of International Affairs, *Problems of International Investment.* Report by a study group of members. London, 1937.

Sabelberg, F., *Tee: Wandlungen in der Erzeugung und Verwendung des Tees nach dem Weltkrieg.* Leipzig, 1938.

Sargent, A. J., *Anglo-Chinese Commerce and Diplomacy.* Oxford, 1907.

Schooten, J. Ullens De, *Les Chemins de Fer Chinois.* Brussels, 1928.

Smith, Wilfred, *A Geographical Study of Coal and Iron in China.* London, 1926.

Spalding, W. F., *Eastern Exchange, Currency and Finance.* London, 1917.

Spencer, J. E., 'Trade and Trans-shipment in the Yangtze Valley', in *Geographical Review.* January, 1938.

Stein, Gunther, 'American Business with East Asia', in *Institute of Pacific Relations, 10th Conference.* New York, 1947.

Stock Exchange Year Book. Various years. London.

Stringer, H., *The Chinese Railway System.* Shanghai, 1922.

Tamagna, F. M., *Banking and Finance in China.* New York, 1942.

Teichman, E., *Travels of a Consular Officer in North West China.* 1921.

Teichman, E., *Affairs of China.* London, 1938.

Timperly, H. J., and Emerson Sen, Gertrude, 'Wayfoong', in *Asia.* August 1936.

Torgasheff, B. P., *China as a Tea Producer.* Shanghai, 1926.

Torgasheff, B. P., *The Mineral Industry of the Far East.* Shanghai, 1930.

Townley, S., *My Chinese Notebook.* London, 1904.

Toynbee, A. J., *The Situation in China.* London, 1926.

United Kingdom, Board of Trade, Commercial Intelligence Branch, *Report upon the Conditions and Prospects of British Trade in China.* London, 1916.

United Kingdom, Department of Overseas Trade, *Reports on Economic and Commercial Conditions in China.* 1920–1937. London.

United Kingdom, Foreign Office, *Consular Trade Reports. Commercial Reports from Consuls.* 1862–85. London.
United Kingdom, Foreign Office, *Diplomatic and Consular Reports on Trade.* 1886–1915. London.
United Kingdom, Foreign Office, *Diplomatic and Consular Reports on Trade.* Miscellaneous Series: No. 22, *Native Cotton Manufactures of the Ningpo District.* London, 1886. No. 458, *Report of Consul Bourne on the Trade of Central and South China.* London, 1898. No. 665, *Sir A. Hosie's Report on a Visit to the Southern Ports of China.* London, 1907. No. 680, *Memorandum on Chinese Mines by H. H. Fox.* London, 1911.
United Kingdom Paper, No. 1/D, Hongkong, in *Institute of Pacific Relations, 8th Conference.* New York, 1942.
United Kingdom, Trade Mission to China, *Report.* London, 1946.
United States, Department of Commerce, *The Economic Development of Shantung, 1912–1921* (excerpts from Chinese Customs *Decennial Reports*, Tsingtao). Washington, 1922.
Vinacke, H. M., 'Obstacles to Industrial Development in China', in *Annals of the American Academy of Political and Social Science.* November 1930.
Voskuil, W., 'Iron and Steel Industry of China', in *Annals of the American Academy of Political and Social Science.* November 1930.
Wagel, S. R., *Finance in China.* Shanghai, 1914.
Wagel, S. R., *Chinese Currency and Banking.* Shanghai, 1915.
Walton, J., *China and the Present Crisis.* London, 1900.
Ware, E., *Business and Politics in the Far East.* New Haven, 1932.
Weale, B. L. Putnam, *The Coming Struggle in East Asia.* London, 1909.
White, T. H., 'China's Last Lifeline', in *Fortune.* May 1943.
Williams, F. H. B., *The Tea Trade.* M.Sc. Thesis. London University, 1938.
Willoughby, W., *Foreign Rights and Interests in China.* Baltimore, 1927.
Winston, H. P., 'Does Trade Follow the Dollar?' in *American Economic Review.* September 1927.
Worcester, G. R. G., *The Junks and Sampans of the Yangtze.* 2 vols. Shanghai, 1940.
Wright, S. F., *China's Struggle for Tariff Autonomy.* Shanghai, 1938.
Wright, S. F., *Hart and the Chinese Customs.* Belfast, 1950.
Wu Ching-Chao, 'Plan for China's Industrialisation', in *Institute of Pacific Relations, 9th Conference.* New York, 1945.
Wu Ting Chang, 'A Year's Progress in Industrial Reconstruction', in *Chinese Economic Journal.* January 1937.
Young, S. Y. P., 'Chinese Banking Progress in the Past Decade', in *China Quarterly.* September 1935.

American Economic Review. Philadelphia.
Annals of the American Academy of Political and Social Science. Philadelphia.
China Quarterly. Shanghai.
Chinese Economic Journal. Peking.
Chinese Economic Monthly. Peking.
Chinese Repository. Canton.
Chinese Social and Political Science Review. Peking.

Economic History. London.
Economic Journal. London.
Economist. London.
Far Eastern Economic Review. Hongkong.
Far Eastern Review. Shanghai.
Far Eastern Survey. New York.
Financial Times. London.
Foreign Affairs. London.
Geographical Review. New York.
Great Britain and the East. London.
Journal of the Royal Central Asian Society. London
Monthly Bulletin on Economic China. Tientsin.
Nankai Social and Economic Quarterly. Tientsin.
North China Daily News. Shanghai.
North China Herald. Shanghai.
Oriental Affairs. Shanghai.
Pacific Affairs. Camden, N.J.
The Times. London.
Yenching Political Science Series. Peking.

2. JAPAN

The following is a list of publications to which references have been made in the text of Part II. Short bibliographies of works dealing with Japan's modern economic development are given in *Weltwirtschaftliches Archiv*, July 1937, and G. C. Allen, *A Short Economic History of Modern Japan, 1867–1937* (1946).

Asiatic Society of Japan, *Transactions* (various).
The Currency of Japan (a collection of reprints of articles, letters and official reports). Yokohama, 1882.
Federation of British Industries, *Report of Mission to Far East*. London, 1934.
Field, F. V., *Economic Handbook of the Pacific Area*. New York, 1934.
Griffis, W. E., *The Mikado's Empire*, 2 vols. London, 1903.
Hattori, Y., *The Foreign Commerce of Japan since the Restoration*. Baltimore, 1904.
Honjo, E., *The Social and Economic History of Japan*. Kyoto, 1935.
Inouye, J., *Problems of the Japanese Exchange, 1914–1926*. London, 1931.
Japan Chronicle, Jubilee Number. Kobe, 1918.
Japan-Manchukuo Year Book (various years). Tokyo.
The Japan Silk Year Book, 1935–36. Tokyo, 1936.
Japan Year Book (various years). Tokyo.
Japanese Department of Finance, *Financial and Economic Annual of Japan* (various years). Tokyo.
Kinosita, Y., *The Past and Present of Japanese Commerce*. New York, 1902.
Leavens, D. H., *The Gold-Silver Ratio in the Early Foreign Relations of the Far East*. Shanghai, 1928.

Matsukata, M., *Report on the Adoption of the Gold Standard in Japan.* Tokyo, 1899.

Mitsubishi Economic Research Bureau, *Japanese Trade and Industry.* London, 1936.

Mitsubishi Goshi Kaisha, *An Outline of Mitsubishi Enterprises.* Tokyo, 1935.

Mitsui Bank, *A Brief History.* Tokyo, 1926.

Mitsui Gomei Kaisha, *The House of Mitsui.* Tokyo, 1933.

Mori, T., 'Silk Control in Japan', in *Commodity Control in the Pacific Area* (ed. W. L. Holland). New York, 1935.

Moulton, H. G., *Japan: An Economic and Financial Appraisal.* New York, 1931.

Nippon Yusen Kaisha, *Golden Jubilee History.* Tokyo, 1935.

Norman, E. H., *Japan's Emergence as a Modern State.* New York, 1940.

Okuma, S., *Fifty Years of New Japan*, 2 vols. 1909.

Okuma, S., *A General View of Financial Policy during Thirteen Years, 1868–1880.* Tokyo, 1880.

Orchard, J. E., *Japan's Economic Position.* New York, 1930.

Oriental Economist, *The Foreign Trade of Japan.* Tokyo, 1935.

Sansom, G. B., *The Western World and Japan.* London, 1951.

Schumpeter, E. B. (ed.), *The Industrialisation of Japan and Manchukuo, 1930–1940.* New York, 1940.

Smith, N. Skene (ed.), *Tokugawa Japan.* London, 1937.

Takaki, M., *The History of Japanese Paper Currency.* Baltimore, 1903.

Takizawa, M., *The Penetration of Money Economy in Japan.* New York, 1927.

United Kingdom Department of Overseas Trade, *Report on Economic and Commercial Conditions in Japan* (various years).

United States Department of Commerce, *The Currency System of Japan.* 1930. *Japanese Banking.* 1931.

United States National Monetary Commission, *Reports*, vol. XVIII. 1910.

Uyeda, T., *The Small Industries of Japan.* London, 1938.

Uyehara, S., *The Industry and Trade of Japan.* London, 1926.

World Engineering Congress, *Industrial Japan.* Tokyo, 1929.

Yamanaka, T., 'Japanese Small Industries during the Industrial Revolution', in *Annals of the Hitotsubashi Academy.* October 1951.

Yokohama and Tokyo Foreign Board of Trade, *Annual Reports* (various).

MANCHURIA

U. S. S. R.

SAKHALIN

HOKKAIDO

Hakodate

HONSHU

Kamaishi

Sendai

SADO

Niigata

KOREA

Maibashi
Tomioka
TOKYO
Yokohama
Yokosuka
Nagoya
Shizuoka
Shimoda

KYOTO
Kobe
Osaka

Hiroshima

Yawata

SHIKOKU

Nagasaki
(Deshima)

Kagoshima

KYUSHU

MILES
0   50   100   150   200

Key — Railways

JAPAN

MONGOLIA

MANCHURIA

*Harbin

*Kirin
Vladivostock
Hailung

NINGSIA
KANSU

SUIYUAN CHAHAR

JEHOL

Kweihwacheng

Shanhaikwan
Shansi
Newchwang
Fushun
Mukden
Penhsihu
Anshan
Chinwangtao
LIAOTUNG
Dairen (Dalny)
Port Arthur
Unzan
Suiho
KO

PEKING
TIENTSIN
Taku

Tinghsien

Lanchow

TIBET

Chefoo
Weihaiwei
Seoul
Pusan

SHENSI
Hungshan
Tsinan
Fangtze
Tsingtao

Sungpan

SZECHWAN

Chinghua
Taokow
Hoaichow
Hoyang
SHANTUNG

HONAN
KIANGSU
ANHWEI

CHINA

Chengtu
Tachienlu
Wanhsien
Ichang
HUPEH
HANKOW
Hanyang
Wuchang

Fengyang
Pukow
Chinkiang
Nanking
Wuhu
Tatung
Woosung
SHANGHAI
Hangchow
Kiukiang
Kinin
Ningpo

Chungking

Changteh

Tung Ting

Nanchang
CHEKIANG

KWEICHOW

YUNNAN

Changsha

KIANGSI

Wenchow

Tengyueh
Kunming

HUNAN

FUKIEN

Foochow

Mengtsz

KWANGSI

KWANGTUNG

Wuchow
Weihsia
CANTON
Swatow
Amoy

Tamsui
FORMOSA

Nanning

Macao
Kowloon
HONGKONG

Pakhoi

TONGKING

Hoihow
Kiungchow
HAINAN

MILES
0   100   300   500

Key
---- Provincial boundaries
—— Railways

CHINA

INDEX

285

Imports:
  Chinese, Chs. II, V; 22–3, 111, 141, 167, 241 et seq., 257–8
  Japanese, Ch. XII; 215 et seq., 224, 241 et seq.
  See also under various commodities
Indemnities (see also Boxer Indemnity Funds), 21, 24, 26, 114, 118, 233, 244
Indian economic activities in China, 176
  in Japan, 208, 209
Indigo. See Dyestuffs
Indo-China Steam Navigation Company, 35, 128, 132
Industrial Bank of Japan, 214, 234
Industrial labour force, 179, 208
Industry, Chinese. See Chinese industry
Industry, Japanese. See Japanese industry
Innovations, opposition to, 64, 70, 134–5, 149, 151, 153,
Inouye, Marquis, 202
Insurance, 19, 28, 31–5, 119–22, 127, 205, 245
Interest rates, 34, 55, 57, 114–15, 176 197, 214, 234
International Bank(ing) Corporation, 109, 113, 217
International Cotton Manufacturing Company, 175
International Export Company, 78–80
International General Electric Company, 173, 229
International Telephone and Telegraph Company, 96
Investment, Foreign, in China, 15, 262–3
  in Japan, 224, 232–7, 264
Iron and steel industry, 23–4, 157, 162, 165, 180, 189, 190–3, 233
Iron ore and mining, 157, 160–2, 165, 180, 246 n
Ishikawajima, 190
Italian economic activities in China, 63–6, 140, 156
  in Japan, 191, 193, 209, 229, 271
Ito, Prince, 212
Iwasaki, Yataro, 219

Japan Electric Company, 229
Japan Gazette, 197
Japan Nitrate Fertiliser Manufacturing Company, 147
Japan Steel Works, 229
Japanese currency. See Currency, Japanese
Japanese economic activities in China (including Manchuria), 28, 37, 39, 45–6, 49–50, 63, 67, 71–3, 78, 81, 92–3, 98, 109, 116, 124, 126, 131, 137–8, 140, 146–7, 149, 159–62, 167 et seq., 262

Japanese Government:
  economic activities of, 191 et seq., 199, 201, 205–7, 210 et seq., 223 et seq., 242–4, 270
  loans, 192, 217, 221, 224, 233–5, 244, 264
Japanese industry, Ch. XIV; 202–3, 205, 208–9, 243 et seq. See also under various industries and commodities
Japanese merchants, Ch. XII; 187, 211, 226
Japanese-Western enterprises, 217, 228–231, 246
Jardine Matheson and Company, and subsidiaries, 35–6, 54, 61, 65, 79, 94–8, 120, 126 et seq., 134–5, 139, 168, 175, 198, 210, 218
Jardine, William, 35
Jehol, 160
Jui Yung Company, 168

Kagoshima, 191
Kailan Mining Administration, 152 et seq., 169
Kaiping, 152–3
Kaiping Coalmining Company, 135
Kaiso Kaisha, 219
Kamaishi, 191
Kamchatka, 186
Kanchingtze, 147
Kanegafuchi Company, 202
Kang Yu-Wei, 25
Katakura, 227
Kerosene, 23, 46, 100, 258
Kerr, Dick, and Company, 229
Keswick, William, 198
Kiangnan Arsenal, 23
Kiangnan Dock and Engineering Works, 168
Kiangpeiting Coal and Iron Mining Company, 158
Kiangsu, 63, 67, 139, 246 n
Kiaochow, 24, 73
Kimun, 57
Kirin, 147, 169
Kiukiang, 59, 129, 266
Kiungchow, 48
Koban. See Currency, Japanese
Kobe, 190 n, 198, 208–9, 215, 217–18, 221, 231
Kochi, 219
Konoike, 211
Korea, 24, 113, 137, 147, 204, 210, 214, 221, 224 n, 234
Kowloon, 20, 169
Krupps, A. E. G., 97
Kunming, 143, 144
Kwangchow, 25
Kwangsi, 24 n, 103, 113
Kwangtung, 60, 99, 103, 246 n

291